The Psychology of Teaching and Learning Music

The Psychology of Teaching and Learning Music introduces readers to the key theoretical principles, concepts, and research findings about learning and how these concepts and principles can be applied in the music classroom.

Beginning with an overview of the study of teaching and learning, and moving through applying theory to practice, and reflective practice in the process of personal growth, this text focuses on music learning theories, behavioral approaches, cognitive, social-cognitive development, and constructive views of learning. It includes culture and community, learning differences, motivation, effective curricular design, assessment, and how to create learning environments, illustrated by practical case studies, projects, exercises, and photos.

Showing students how to apply the psychology theory and research in practice as music educators, this book provides a valuable resource for undergraduate and graduate music education students and faculty.

Edward R. McClellan is Rita O. Huntsinger Distinguished Professor of Music and Associate Professor of Music at Loyola University of New Orleans.

The Psychology of Teaching and Learning Music

Edward R. McClellan

Routledge
Taylor & Francis Group

NEW YORK AND LONDON

Designed cover image: abstract/Shutterstock.com

First published 2023
by Routledge
605 Third Avenue, New York, NY 10158

and by Routledge
4 Park Square, Milton Park, Abingdon, Oxon, OX14 4RN

Routledge is an imprint of the Taylor & Francis Group, an informa business

© 2023 Taylor & Francis

Library of Congress Cataloging-in-Publication Data
Names: McClellan, Edward R., author.
Title: The psychology of teaching and learning music / Edward R. McClellan.
Description: New York : Routledge, 2023. | Includes bibliographical
    references and index. |
Identifiers: LCCN 2022059127 (print) | LCCN 2022059128 (ebook) | ISBN
    9780367481780 (hardback) | ISBN 9780367481773 (paperback) | ISBN
    9781003038474 (ebook)
Subjects: LCSH: Music--Instruction and study--Psychological aspects.
Classification: LCC MT1.M358 P78 2023 (print) | LCC MT1.M358 (ebook) |
    DDC 780.71--dc23/eng/20221213
LC record available at https://lccn.loc.gov/2022059127
LC ebook record available at https://lccn.loc.gov/2022059128

ISBN: 978-0-367-48178-0 (hbk)
ISBN: 978-0-367-48177-3 (pbk)
ISBN: 978-1-003-03847-4 (ebk)

DOI: 10.4324/9781003038474

Typeset in Sabon
by KnowledgeWorks Global Ltd.

Contents

List of Figures x
List of Tables xi
Preface xii
Acknowledgments xvi

Introduction 1

1 The Study of Teaching and Learning 3

Philosophy of Education 4
Educational Psychology Promotes Teaching and Learning 5
Education Theory and Research 5
Music Education 5
Inquiry-Based Learning 6
Reflective Practice 8
Putting Theory into Practice 8
Questions 9

2 Becoming a Reflective Teacher 13

Reflective Practice 14
The Teacher's Responsibility 14
Your Belief System 15
Acknowledging Anecdotal and Empirical Evidence 15
Cognitive Dissonance 17
Reflective Practice: A Process for Growth and Development 18
Questions 19

PART I
Theories of Learning and Teaching Music 23

3 Behaviorism: Learning Theory and Applications to Teaching 25

Behavioral Learning Theory 25
  Classical Conditioning 26

Operant Conditioning 28

Types of Reinforcement 28

  Positive Reinforcement 29

  Negative Reinforcement 29

  Punishment 29

  Extinction 29

Schedules of Reinforcement 29

  Fixed Interval Schedule 30

  Variable Interval Schedule 30

  Fixed Ratio Schedule 30

  Variable Ratio Schedule 31

Learning Based upon Environmental Control 31

  Teacher Feedback 32

  Student Attentiveness 32

Behavioral Modification 33

Reinforcers in the Classroom 33

Classroom Management Is about Organization 34

  Organize Your Space 34

  Set Clear Expectations 34

  Play More, Talk Less 34

Questions 35

4   Cognitivism: Learning Theory and Applications to Teaching   38

Gestalt Learning Theory 38

Cognitive Learning Theory 40

Basic Principles of Piaget's Theory 41

  Schema 42

  Stages of Cognitive Development 42

Constructivism 43

Constructionism 44

The Difference between Constructivism and Constructionism 44

Constructivism and Discovery Learning (Jerome Bruner) 45

Jerome Bruner's Three Stages of Cognitive Development 45

  *Six Indicators (Benchmarks) Revealing Cognitive
  Development 46*

Information Processing Learning Theory 46

  Sensory Register Memory 46

  Short-Term Memory 47

  Long-Term Memory 47

Cognitivism in Music Teaching 47

Bruner's Conceptual Learning 48

Cognitivist Approaches in the Music Classroom 48

  The Performance-Based Classroom 49

  Information Processing in the Classroom 50

Designing a Unit Lesson: Constructivist and Constructionist
 Instruction 52
 Mr. Wilson's Blues Improvisation Unit Lesson 52
 Mr. Wilson's Constructivist Approach 52
 Mr. Wilson's Constructionist Approach 53
Questions 54

5 Social Learning Theory and Applications to Teaching   57

Bandura's Social Learning Theory 58
 The Modeling Process 59
Vygotsky's Social Constructivism 59
 Zone of Proximal Development (ZPD) 60
 Scaffolding 61
Cognitive Development: Vygotsky versus Piaget 61
Self-Efficacy 62
Self-Efficacy in Teaching and Learning 62
Self-Regulation 63
The Role of Self-Regulation in Self-Efficacy 64
Social Learning Theory in the Music Classroom 64
Applications of Piaget and Vygotsky 64
 Observing and Imitating Others 66
 Self-Efficacy in Music Teaching 66
 Self-Regulation in the Music Classroom 67
Self-Determination Theory 68
 Self-Determination in Music Education 68
 Self-Determination in the Music Classroom 68
Questions 69

6 Humanism: Learning Theory and Applications to Teaching   73

Humanism 74
 Humanistic Psychology 74
 Humanism in Learning 74
Abraham Maslow 74
Carl Rogers 77
 Learner-Centered Teaching 77
Self-Concept 78
Self-Concept in Music Education 79
Humanistic Approaches to Teaching Music 79
Music Class Scenarios 80
 Diversity 80
 Emotional Growth 80
 Learning Styles 80
 Cooperative Learning 81
Questions 81

7   Brain-Based Learning Theory and Applications to Teaching   84
     The Brain 84
     The Amygdala 86
     The Prefrontal Cortex 86
     Plasticity 86
     Pruning 86
     Neural Networks 87
     The Theory of Multiple Intelligences 88
     Brain-Based Learning 88
     Principles of Brain-Based Learning 88
     Teaching Strategies for Brain-Based Teaching and Learning 89
     Music Education and the Brain 91
     Questions 92

PART II
Theory Applied to Practice   97

8   Cognitive Approaches in Teaching and Learning   99
     Implications of Bruner's Theories 99
     Gardner's Multiple Intelligences 100
     Bloom's Taxonomy 100
     Bloom's Taxonomy: Implications for Music Education 103
     Designing Learning Goals 105
     Intelligent Music Teaching 106
     Learning Activities 107

9   Sociocultural Characteristics of Learning in the Music Classroom   111
     Sociological Influences in Music Education 111
        Communities of Practice 112
     Culturally Responsive Teaching 113
     Diversity—Multicultural Education 115
        Authenticity in Student Learning 115
     Social Justice in the Music Classroom 116
     Learning Activities 118

10   School Music Curriculum Design   122
     The Music Curriculum 122
     Levels of Curriculum Development 123
     National Music Standards 124
     Understanding by Design 124
     Bloom's Taxonomy, Backward Design, and Vygotsky ZPD 126
     Music Technology Curriculum 126
     Popular Music Curriculum 127
     Learning Activities 128

PART III
Applications to the Music Classroom   131

11 Effective Instructional Design   133
    Conditions of Learning 133
    The ADDIE Model 134
    Music Class Instruction 136
    Experiential Learning 137
    Sequential Instruction 137
    Differentiated Instruction 139
    Classroom Management 140
    Learning Community as Instructional Model 142
    Learning Activities 142

12 Assessment and Evaluation in the Music Classroom   146
    Types of Assessment 146
    Assessment Tools 148
    Tools in the Music Classroom 148
    Assessment Alignment with Instruction 152
    The Roles of Assessment 153
    Reflective Practice as a Teacher 153
    Learning Activities 155

    Index   159

Figures

3.1	Pavlov's Classical Conditioning	27
4.1	Jean Piaget, Psychologist	41
5.1	Psychologist Albert Bandura, 2005	58
5.2	Zone of Proximal Development (ZPD)	60
6.1	Maslow's Hierarchy of Needs	75
7.1	The Brain Lobes	85
7.2	Areas of the Brain	87
8.1	Bloom's Revised Taxonomy	101
8.2	Krathwohl's Affective Domain	102
8.3	Simpson's Psychomotor Domain	102
8.4	Bloom's Taxonomy Cognitive Verbs	106
10.1	The Backward Design Process	125
11.1	ADDIE Model: Instructional Design	135
12.1	Percussion Hand Position Checklist	149
12.2	Rating Scale: Recorder Solo Assessment	150
12.3	Music Performance Rubric	151
12.4	The Reflective Practice Cycle	154

Tables

7.1	Principles of Brain-Based Learning	89
8.1	The New Bloom's Taxonomy Applied to Select National Standards for Music Education	104
8.2	Sample Music Theory Learning Goals with Clarifying Bloom Verbs	105
10.1	Technology Tools for Music Education	127

Preface

Introduction

This book took shape over the past 15 years as I taught an undergraduate course on the Psychology of Teaching and Learning Music and a graduate course on the Psychology of Music at my university. As I had not found a reliable text on teaching and learning music, the readings in this source come directly from my course, related materials, and the readings that I researched and referenced while designing and refining the course over the years. My own practical knowledge of teaching school music for 20 years, coupled with experience as a masters and doctoral student, and that of a college professor teaching undergraduate and graduate music education for another 15 years, while studying this subject in particular, have set the foundation for this book.

While there have been academic texts published on *Educational Psychology, Developmental Psychology,* and *Psychology Applied to Teaching,* there has not been a book on *The Psychology of Teaching and Learning Music.* As undergraduate and graduate music education courses are taught on this subject throughout the United States and Europe, it is hoped that a text specific to music teaching and learning will not only be a valuable resource to music education professors in the university classroom but also provide preservice music teachers with a useful reference for understanding the principles of teaching and learning in the school music classroom.

Purpose of the Book

This text is to be used to introduce music education students to fundamental learning theories and concepts important to teaching and learning music, their applications in the music classroom, and principles of the psychology of teaching and learning music. Though general psychology, child psychology, and the pedagogical psychology may be taught in the college of education, many music educators advocate for teaching the psychology of teaching and learning, specific to music, in the university college or school of music. As there is currently no viable text for such course, this text *The Psychology of Teaching and Learning Music* fills a niche in the music education degree program curricula.

Approach

In this book, I have opted to provide a general introduction to a variety of related topics. In doing so, I worked hard to balance breadth with depth. As this is always a tough call, some of you may wish for more or less coverage on certain topics while others may wish certain topics had been included or deleted. I have done my best to strike a happy medium—broad coverage with sufficient depth to capture the essence of the topic.

Organization

The Psychology of Teaching and Learning Music introduces readers to the key theoretical principles, concepts, and research findings about teaching and learning and how these precepts apply in the music classroom. The opening chapters present an overview of the study of teaching and learning music, philosophical and psychological precursors that help to establish the foundation for putting theory into practice, and reflective practice as a process for growth and development as a music teacher. The ensuing chapters are comprised of three parts, Theories of Learning and Teaching Music, Theory Applied to Practice, and Applications to the Music Classroom. After the introduction (Chapters 1–2), the text is organized into three parts (i.e., Chapters 3–7, 8–10, and 11–12).

Chapters 3–7 (i.e., Part I) introduce the reader to prominent learning theories (e.g., behaviorism, cognitivism, social learning, humanism, brain-based learning) that are important in the music classroom. After description of each theory, introduction of notable theorists who have influenced teaching and learning, and applications of the theory in the music classroom, specific examples are presented in a variety of class settings (e.g., general music, band, chorus, orchestra, music theory, and music appreciation). These illustrations are enhanced with discussion questions to be considered among students and professors.

Chapters 8–10 (i.e., Part II) will broaden the scope of theory applied to practice. This section will introduce the significant work of researchers and scholars such as Bruner, Bloom, Gardner, Gagne, Duke, Lind and McKoy, Abril, and Hess to provide reference for the conditions of music learning, principles of learning in the context of teaching music, and understanding the nature of music learning, musicianship, and music performance in cognitive and sociocultural contexts. Chapter 8 presents recent research on the cognitive approaches to instruction, cognitive, psychomotor, and affective domains of learning, instructional design, and music teaching that are enhanced with the social conditions of learning, learning communities of practice, and social culture of the music classroom. Sociological influences in music education bring attention to culturally responsive teaching, diversity, and social justice in the music classroom (Chapter 9). Chapter 10 examines principles of music curriculum design; music content as knowledge, skill, and musical expression relevant to the national music standards; and models of music curricula used in the backward design process. Each chapter includes learning activities to initiate student reflection, collaboration, and implementation of conceptual frameworks among students and professors.

Chapters 11 and 12 (i.e., Part III) examine principles of effective instructional design and assessment in the music classroom. Chapter 11 introduces the reader to models of creating instruction plans, learning experiences, assessment tasks, and the materials used in the acquisition of knowledge, skills, and feelings or emotions and the principles of learner-centered instruction, experiential learning, sequential instruction, differentiated instruction, classroom management, and the learning community as an instructional model. Chapter 12 presents the definition and types of assessment, assessment tools used in the music classroom, the alignment of assessment with instruction, and the roles of assessment in the music program. The chapter closes with a description of the process of the teacher's own self-assessment, self-improvement, and professional development, bringing conclusion to the subject of reflective practice first introduced at the beginning of the text. Learning activities in each chapter equip the reader with strategies for effective instructional design and assessment in the music classroom and continued reflective practice for professional growth as a music educator. The professor can engage students in pairs or groups to collaboratively develop plans of action or design for each scenario or context.

To the Teacher

How you use the book will depend significantly on the level and background of your students. With younger or less experienced students, you may wish to focus more literally on the text. With more advanced students, you may wish to assign outside readings that provide additional details and more in-depth discussions on specific topics.

In a similar manner, there are numerous instances throughout a semester where you and your students can investigate different ideas beyond the text. For example, there are numerous cases where the teacher can direct students to observe the applications of any of the learning theories, introduced in Chapters 3–7, in local school music classrooms. The professor can create particular criteria for the students to implement in fieldwork and clinical experiences to document the utilization of specific behavioral, cognitive, or social approaches in practice in the local school classroom.

Regarding Chapter 9, a qualified faculty member in the sociology department could lecture on the sociological influences on education, diversity in the classroom, or social justice in educational programs in the university or school program. An ensemble director can discuss programming literature that facilitates the study of music from diverse cultures and implements the multicultural education of students in the music program. An enthnomusicology professor could lecture on world music and/or the inclusion of music from world cultures in the program's curriculum.

In regard to Chapter 8, the teacher can guide students in the analysis of how the cognitive, psychomotor, and affective domains are integrated into a school music class lesson. How did the music teacher design class learning goals in the classroom? How were the learning goals tied to instructional activities and assessment in the lesson? How did the teacher implement the backward design process to integrate instruction, assessment, and the learning activities of the lesson?

The teacher can further advise students in examining the integration of technology along with lesson design in the overall curricular plan for a school music class throughout the term or semester (Chapter 10). Deeper discussions on the elements of instructional design (Chapter 11) and types of assessment implemented in the observed music classroom (Chapter 12) can engage students in the application of these principles in real-life school settings.

Although our understanding of some of the topics may not change too much from year to year, most of the psychology of teaching and learning music is quite fluid with rapid and frequent changes in what we know about a given subject. With that in mind, you will want to guide students in finding connections between their own personal experiences as students and their developing social identities and pedagogical contexts as music teachers.

To the Student

Perhaps the most important suggestion I can give is to encourage you to explore and discover with enthusiasm and to be open to new ideas, research, and understandings. While we often use previous teachers as our role models for our preconceptions as a new music teacher, it is important to consider the research, studies, and examples throughout the text in stretching your own approach to teaching in today's music classroom; participate in classroom discussions, and reflect on class learning activities that engage you and your peers; and follow through with projects by taking it upon yourself to investigate supplemental readings as assigned throughout the semester. The psychology of teaching and learning music is all around you, in your college music classes and the local school music programs. I hope you will take advantage of these resources in exploring the fascinating and meaningful world of music teaching and learning that surrounds you.

Acknowledgments

In producing *The Psychology of Teaching and Learning Music*, I had the assistance of wonderful colleagues, friends, and students. Thanks go to Dr. Lorie Enloe, retired professor of music education for her review, feedback, and encouragement for writing this book. Thank you to Cali Traina Blume for designing figures for this book. I am grateful to my university students for their review and very helpful feedback during the process of taking my Psychology of Teaching and Learning Music course. I am also appreciative for the efforts of several anonymous reviewers who reviewed select chapters through the writing process.

Introduction

Chapter 1

The Study of Teaching and Learning

Teaching can be defined as engagement with learners to enable their understanding and application of knowledge, concepts, and processes. It includes design, content selection, delivery, assessment, and reflection. To teach is to engage students in learning; thus, teaching consists of getting students involved in the active construction of knowledge. A teacher requires not only knowledge of the subject matter but also knowledge of how students learn and how to transform them into active learners. Teaching is fundamentally about creating the pedagogical, social, and ethical conditions under which students agree to take charge of their own learning, individually and collectively.[1]

Learning can be defined as the activity or process of acquiring new understanding, knowledge, skills, values, or attitudes by studying, practicing, being taught, or experiencing something.[2] Learning is about what students do, not about what we as teachers do. *Students learn in different ways* as identified in various "learning styles."[3] Learning can be shallow or deep.[4] If knowledge is only memorized, it is soon forgotten; however, if the learner connects the new knowledge to the concepts s/he already understands, it is much more likely to be remembered and used. Some are motivated to learn because they want to do a better job or that they will be rewarded for their achievement.[5] Learning may be formal: we attend a course that is planned in a structured way in a school or college. We also learn informally from what we experience day by day: things that happen to us make us change the way we think and act. Of course, Learning continues throughout one's lifetime—at least informally.[6]

The academic study or scholarship of teaching and learning (SOTL) is often defined as systematic inquiry into student learning that advances the practice of teaching by making inquiry findings public.[7] SOTL necessarily builds on many past traditions including classroom and program assessment, action research,[8] reflective practice, peer review of teaching, traditional educational research, and faculty development efforts to enhance teaching and learning.

Learning Objectives

1 What elements of a philosophy of education and philosophy of music education impact teaching and learning music?
2 In what ways have psychology influenced the field of education and music education?
3 What are the principles, components, and aspects of music education in the 20th and 21st centuries?
4 What are the benefits of implementing systematic inquiry and putting theory into practice in teaching and learning music?

DOI: 10.4324/9781003038474-2

Philosophy of Education

The *philosophy of education* is the study of the purpose, process, nature, and ideals of education. This can be within the context of education as a social institution or more broadly as the process of human existential growth, that is, how it is that our understanding of the world is continually transformed (be it from facts, social customs, experiences, or even our own emotions).[9]

Fundamental purposes that have been proposed for institutional education include

1 The enterprise of civil society depends on educating young people to become responsible, thoughtful, and enterprising citizens.
2 Progress in every practical field depends upon having capacities that schooling can educate; fostering the individual's, society's, and even humanity's future development and prosperity.
3 One's individual development and the capacity to fulfill one's own purposes can depend upon an adequate preparation in childhood. Therefore, Education can attempt to give a firm foundation for the achievement of personal fulfillment.[9]

A philosophy of music education refers to the value of music, the value of teaching music, and how to practically utilize those values in the music classroom.[10] Bennet Reimer, a renowned music education philosopher, wrote the following, regarding the value of studying the philosophy of music education: "To the degree we can present a convincing explanation of the nature of the art of music and the value of music in the lives of people, to that degree we can present a convincing picture of the nature of music education and its value for human life."[11]

Paul Lehman (2002), former President of the *Music Education National Conference*, conveyed that music education is important not only for the marketable skills it teaches such as creativity, discipline, flexibility, and the ability to cooperatively work with others but also because it simply makes life more enjoyable. Music education is very important because it is a great way to engage diverse learners. Ultimately, the role of the music educator is to facilitate learning and discourse, and prepare students to be productive members of society. Through music, the music teacher will engage students in activities that require them to be creative, disciplined, flexible, and work cooperatively with others. S/He must also help them explore the emotions that various types of music bring them and help them learn to articulate what they feel and why. Lastly, s/he must educate students about other cultures so that they learn to see the world through another's eyes and can appreciate other ways of thinking and living.[12]

Philosophical inquiry has developed throughout history in regards to the fundamental issues of music education, music teachers' decisions and actions in teaching and learning music, their comprehensive, systematic, and consistent understanding of these decisions and actions, and the nature of the world in which we live. Such viewpoints have grown from different premises and approaches such as rationalism, empiricism, naturalism, and pragmatist belief systems.[13] Rationalist theories, often referred to as idealism, maintain logic as the basis for understanding our world. Empiricist theories are arrived at through observation. An important variant of the empirical philosophic viewpoint is called Naturalism, the belief in the reality of the natural world. The Pragmatist determines the meaning of any idea by putting it into practice in the objective world. Whatever the consequences of this circumstance prove it to be, lies the meaning of the idea.

Educational Psychology Promotes Teaching and Learning

Psychologists working in the field of education study how people learn and retain knowledge.[14] They study learners and learning contexts—both within and beyond traditional classrooms—and evaluate ways in which factors such as age, culture, gender, and physical and social environments influence human learning. They leverage educational theory and practice based on the latest research related to human development to understand the emotional, cognitive, and social aspects of human learning.[15] They apply psychological science to improve the learning process and promote educational success for all students.

Educational psychology can influence programs, curricula, and lesson development, as well as classroom management approaches. Although the discipline of educational psychology includes numerous theories, many experts identify five main schools of thought: behaviorism, cognitivism, constructivism, experientialism, and social learning theories.[15] Educational psychologists apply theories of human development to understand individual learning and inform the instructional process. Psychologists working in this subfield examine how people learn in a variety of settings to identify approaches and strategies to make learning more effective.[14]

Education Theory and Research

Education theory seeks to know, understand, and prescribe education practices. Education theory includes many areas of concentration such as pedagogy, curriculum, teaching strategies, learning, and education policy, organization, and leadership. Educational thought is informed by many disciplines, such as history, philosophy, sociology, and psychology. Educational thought is concerned with the "reflective examination of educational issues and problems from the perspective of diverse disciplines."[16] Educational philosophies or theories of education may make use of the results of philosophical thought and of factual inquiries about human beings and the psychology of learning, but in any case, they put forward views about what education should be, what dispositions it should cultivate, why it ought to cultivate them, how and in whom it should do so, and what forms it should take.[17]

A psychologist or educational researcher who starts with the insight that humans are an integral part of the animal kingdom may try to explain human learning in the same way that animal learning is explained. Different theories of learning have resulted from various investigators approaching the phenomenon of learning from different directions with different hunches. As a result, there are many more varieties of learning theories than the types of learning. Theorists do not all agree about what learning is or how it happens. While they may differ on concept, model, or hypothesis on the circumstances of learning, they generally have some good ideas that will help you think about learning. Ultimately, it is you who will have to make the best sense of how to foster human learning in order to become an effective music educator.

Music Education

Music education is a field of study that focuses on the teaching and application of music in the classroom.[18] Music education touches on all learning domains, including the psychomotor domain (the development of skills), the cognitive domain (the acquisition of knowledge), and, in particular, the affective domain (the learner's willingness to receive, internalize, and share what is learned), including music appreciation and sensitivity.

Music training from preschool through postsecondary education is common because involvement with music is considered a fundamental component of human behavior and culture. Cultures from around the world have different approaches to music education, largely due to their varying histories and politics. The creative capability so inherent in music is a unique human trait.[19]

Music is implemented as an academic subject in schools around the world, in places such as Greece, Germany, Slovenia, Spain,[20] India, and Africa. This is not a comprehensive list, as music is considered a cultural necessity in many countries worldwide. Although the *National Association for Music Education* (NAfME) in the United States addresses the plan for implementation of music and arts as core subjects at the national level, the fulfillment of the revision of the "Every Child Achieves Act" varies from state to state. As of 2014, 41 states currently have an arts education requirement at all levels. Twenty-seven of the 50 United States consider the arts a core subject.[21]

Music educators are trained for careers as elementary or secondary music teachers, and school ensemble directors. In the United States, teaching colleges with four-year degree programs developed from the Normal Schools (first founded in 1839) and included music.[22] After 1865, pragmatism and the scientific aspects of sequential skill building, accurate evaluations, examinations, systematic teaching methods, and scientific methods were popular in education. Music educators' responses showed that music could be studied scientifically through the use of different methodologies, systematic textbooks and graded music series, and instructional material for teachers. The scientific and more pragmatic goals of education in the 19th century had a profound effect on the development of music education in the schools.[23]

Music education is a research area in which scholars do original research on ways of teaching and learning music. Music education scholars publish their findings in peer-reviewed journals and teach undergraduate and graduate music education students at university education or music schools, who are receiving training to become music teachers. Music education departments in North American and European universities also support interdisciplinary research in such areas as music psychology, music education historiography, educational ethnomusicology, sociology of music education, and philosophy of music education.[24]

In the late 20th and early 21st centuries, social aspects of teaching and learning music came to the fore.[24] This emerged as paraxial music education,[25] critical theory,[26] and feminist theory.[27] With a new focus on social aspects of music education, scholars have analyzed critical aspects such as music and race,[28] gender,[29] class,[30] institutional belonging,[31] and sustainability.[32]

Inquiry-Based Learning

Increasing evidence, both in general education and music education, points to the significance of inquiry as a part of teacher preparation.[33] Preservice teachers, like the general population, form their views of teaching largely through an "apprenticeship of observation" (Lortie, 1975).[34] Many undergraduate music education students embark on their teacher education journey with a model of good teaching in mind; an image informed by their former high school band, choir, or orchestra teacher-conductor (Dolloff, 1999; Teachout, 1997).[35]

Given the complexities, dynamics, and array of tasks that comprise the work of the music teacher, the need for inquiry-based study as part of teacher preparation can aid the development of a broader view of teaching, foster a disposition toward research mindedness, and influence the ways preservice teachers construct their identity and imagine their work (Kruse & Taylor, 2012; Price, 2001).[36] Such activity also addresses a need for providing preservice teachers with opportunities to reflect on and assess their beliefs as they move through their teacher education program and form their distinct ideas of what comprises good teaching (Schmidt, 1998; Zeichner, 1999).[37] The literature supports the practice of inquiry-based study at the undergraduate level and as a novice music teacher develops a knowledge base that includes subject matter, pedagogy, disposition, and knowledge of self (Grossman et al., 2000)[38] toward more sophisticated thinking about teaching (Hammerness, Darling-Hammond, & Shulman, 2002).[39]

Linking theory to practice has been a primary method of teacher educators to help students relate principles of teaching and learning with real-life whereby they can apply and integrate knowledge, skills, theories, and experience.[40] Shulman (1992) stresses that teacher education programs should link theoretical concepts with practical, "real-world" teaching settings.[41] Heitzman (2008) says it's a pedagogy that offers many strategies and opportunities for prospective teachers to gain insight into events that occur within the school and classroom. It enables preservice teachers to analyze and think critically so that they can make decisions to solve potential problems faced in the classroom.[42]

Ching (2014) found in the analysis of classroom activities that preservice teachers are able to use psychological, behavioral, pedagogical, and classroom management theories and models in solving issues in classroom case studies.[43] The significance of the analysis shows that preservice teachers are able to apply theories in solving behavioral problems in the classroom and thus helping and training them to make decisions on their own when they encounter problems in the classroom. Preservice teachers report that "[In-class] assignments help to strengthen our mind while we have to face these kinds of students in our future days. At least we have a little concept about them. We won't be nervous in facing them."[43]

While assessing preservice teacher attitudes toward classroom and behavior management, a participant responded

> I learnt the proper ways to solve classroom discipline and problems. Before, I wasn't confident while handling a class. I didn't set rules and procedures while entering the class and being too nice to them and the class ended up uncontrolled. I was quite disappointed with myself because I found that it's not so easy to handle a class as what others think. From analysis of [principles of] classroom behavior management, I learnt that we as teachers, need to be assertive while facing the students at the beginning. I realized the importance of enforcing rules and procedures with the students and of course to reach agreement with them.[43]

Through the inquiry-based process of linking theory to practice, pre- and in-service teachers can develop a better understanding of important elements of conceptual complexity, use acquired concepts for reasoning and inference and flexibly apply conceptual knowledge to new situations. It helps preservice teachers to think about educational dilemmas, gather information, applying the information or theories, and construct imaginative solutions for action.[44]

Educators in professional or service-related fields desire their students not only to learn theory and understand why theories are important but also to learn how to apply the theoretical frameworks in practice. Too often we hear anecdotal accounts of students in internships who are unable to make this transition from theory to practice with confidence and effectiveness. Perhaps the difficulty in making the transition from theory to practice arises, at least in part, from a failure of the teacher to integrate both theory and practice into the same course in the curriculum in ways that are relevant and meaningful to the student. Such integration helps students to more closely associate the practical value of learning theoretical concepts.[45]

It is imperative that students in professional programs be able to put into practice what they have learned in the classroom. As Hutchings (1990) wrote, "What's at stake is the capacity to perform, to put what one knows into practice (p. 1)."[46]

Reflective Practice

Reflective practice is initially conceptualized and revisited in conclusion to the examination of the psychology of teaching and learning music as a continual process for growth and development as a music teacher. While reading each chapter, it is important for you to reflect on readings, find additional information based on your own research, create your own questions, and obtain supporting evidence to answer these questions through explanation with the evidence you've collected.

Your learning involves making observations, developing your own methods of experimentation and investigation, and connecting your explanation of knowledge attained through critical thought and analysis.[47] Your study of teaching and learning music should include fieldwork, case studies, investigations, individual and group projects, research projects, and encourage you to demonstrate your learning using a range of media.[48] Through class discussions, collaborative work with peers, and active observation in other college classes and school clinical experiences, you may gain insights of teaching and learning music in real-world contexts.

Putting Theory into Practice

We should embrace learning as the intertwining of theory and practice (McLean, 2021). Theory can be of practical use because naming concepts enables contemplation, discussion, and memory of specific aspects of experiences (Vygotsky, 1978).[49] As music educators, it is fundamental that we relate concepts or theories to the practical and meaningful. We can establish or[50] demonstrate a connection between the theory and something we were previously taught or experienced. By forming a relationship with the content or principles of the theory, our learning can become more meaningful.[51]

It is important to understand that there is a balance between theory and practice. You cannot have theory without practice and you cannot have practice without theory. There are several definitions for theory based on this context but the best definition can be found in the Merriam-Webster dictionary. This definition states that a theory is "a belief, policy or procedure proposed or followed as the basis of action."[52] Therefore, if you do not put into practice the belief, policy, or procedure you learn, the theory becomes meaningless.[52]

Throughout your use of this text, you need to use what you learn as a guide. When you put theories, concepts, principles, and procedures into practice, you develop your reasoning ability, and become a better decision-maker and analytical thinker as a music teacher. When you are able to put this level of value on what you are learning, it is more likely that you will ensure the effort that it is learned.[52]

We are always learning, even in informal ways. Our ability to understand and apply what we read, observe, hear, and do into practice helps us grow as individuals and hone new skills. To make the best use of this knowledge, skills, and sensitivity, we need to put these theories and concepts into practice.

Questions

1 Describe teaching and learning. What are the characteristics, principles, and systems of teaching and learning music?
2 In a one-page essay, describe your own philosophy of education. In another one-page essay, describe your philosophy of music education.
3 In what ways do psychology, research, and education theory influence music education? Describe the influences that each has had on the music education field.
4 Describe the various elements, aspects, and principles of music education that influence teaching and learning music in today's society. Discuss ways that music education is an academic subject that is important in the school curriculum.
5 Describe music education. Discuss the learning domains included in this field of study, how it is conceptualized in different countries, and the role music teachers play in the music education profession.
6 Discuss the importance of inquiry-based learning in your own training as a music teacher as you prepare to teach in today's music classroom. Share examples of inquiry-based learning from this and other classes that may contribute to your preparation as a music educator.
7 Discuss the importance of the process of linking theory to practice in your own training as a music teacher as you prepare to teach in the music classroom. How can discovering these connections support your own understanding of the learning activities that take place in today's music classroom?
8 How can the inquiry-based process of linking theory to practice empower preservice teachers in their preparation for teaching in the music classroom? What methods and strategies does this process engage to prepare future music educators?
9 Describe reflective practice in the context of teaching and learning music. What are specific methods or strategies of reflective practice that you can engage in while reading this book?
10 Describe specific strategies, methods, and techniques you can engage to augment your own professional growth in your study of teaching and learning music. Discuss how particular class activities may benefit your own understanding of music pedagogy and instruction.

Notes

1 Christensen, C. R., Garvin, D. A., & Sweet, A. (Eds.). (1991). *Education for judgment: The artistry of discussion leadership*. Cambridge, MA: Harvard Business School.
   Stellenbosch University. (2021). *Teaching, learning, assessment, curriculum and pedagogy*. Stellenbosch University Center for Teaching and Learning (South Africa). Retrieved July 27, 2021, from http://www.sun.ac.za/english/learning-teaching/ctl/t-l-resources/curriculum-t-l-assessment
2 Merriam-Webster. (2021). *Learning*. Retrieved July 27, 2021, from https://www.merriam-webster.com/dictionary/learning
   Gross, R. (2012). *Psychology: The science of mind and behaviour* (6th ed.), Hachette, England: Hodder Education.
3 Harris, D., & Bell, C. (1986). *Evaluating and assessing for learning* (pp. 118–126). London, England: Kogan Page.
4 Pedler, M. (1974). Learning in management education. *Journal of European Training, 3*(3), 182–195.
5 Handy, C. B. (1976). *Understanding organizations* (pp. 31–47). Harmondsworth, England: Penguin.
6 Prozesky, D. (2000). Teaching and learning. *Community Eye Health, 13*(34), 30–31. Retrieved July 27, 2021, from https://www.ncbi.nlm.nih.gov/pmc/articles/PMC1764819/

7 Hutchings, P., & Shulman, L. (1999). The scholarship of teaching: New elaborations, new developments. *Change: The Magazine of Higher Learning, 31*(5), 10–15.

8 Sappington, N., Baker, P., Gardner, D., & Pacha, J. (2010). A signature pedagogy for leadership education: Preparing principals through participatory action research. *Planning and Changing, 41*(3/4), 249–273.
Zambo, D. (2010). Action research as signature pedagogy in an education doctorate program: The reality and hope. *Innovative Higher Education, 36*(4), 261–271.
Jacobsen, D., Eaton, S., Brown, B., Simmons, M., & McDermott, M. (2018). Action research for graduate program improvements: A response to curriculum mapping and review. *Canadian Journal of Higher Education, 48*(1), 82–98. Retrieved July 27, 2021, from https://journals.sfu.ca/cjhe/index.php/cjhe/article/view/188048

9 Psychology Wikia. (2021). *Philosophy of education.* Retrieved July 28, 2021, from https://psychology.wikia.org/wiki/Philosophy_of_education

10 Barba, M. E. (2017). *Philosophy of Music Education.* Honors Theses and Capstones. 322. Retrieved from https://scholars.unh.edu/cgi/viewcontent.cgi?article=1326&context=honors

11 Reimer, B. (1970). *A philosophy of music education* (p. 1). Englewood Cliffs, NJ: Prentice-Hall.

12 Lehman, P. (2002). A personal perspective. *Music Educators Journal, 88*(5), 47–51.

13 Abeles, H., Hoffer, C., & Klotman, R. (1984). Philosophical foundations of music education. In *Foundations of music education* (pp. 41–60). New York, NY: Schirmer Books.

14 American Psychological Association. (2017). *Educational psychology promotes teaching and learning.* Retrieved July 28, 2021, from https://www.apa.org/education-career/guide/subfields/teaching-learning

15 Psychology.org. (2021). *Introduction to educational psychology theory.* Retrieved July 28, 2021, from https://www.psychology.org/resources/educational-psychology-theories/

16 *Journal of Thought.* Retrieved on July 22, 2014, from http://journalofthought.com

17 Frankena, W. K., Raybeck, N., & Burbules, N. (2002). Philosophy of education. In J. W. Guthrie (Ed.), *Encyclopedia of education* (2nd ed.), New York, NY: Macmillan Reference. ISBN 0-02-865594-X.

18 Wikipedia. (2021). *Music education and programs within the United States.* Retrieved July 29, 2021, from https://en.wikipedia.org/wiki/Music_education_and_programs_within_the_United_States

19 Schulkin, J., & Raglan, G. (2014). The evolution of music and social capability. *Frontiers in Neuroscience, 8*(292), 1–13, p. 10. doi: 10.3389/fnins.2014.00292.

20 Rodriguez-Quiles y Garcia, J., & Dogani, K. (2011). Music in schools across Europe: Analysis, interpretation and guidelines in music education in the framework of the European Union. In L. Airi & M. Marit (Eds.), Music Inside and Outside the School, Series: Baltische Studien zur Erziehungs- und Sozialwissenschaft (pp. 1–24). Frankfurt am Main Publisher: Peter Lang.

21 Ujifusa, A. Roughly half of states consider arts a "Core" subject, new report finds. Education Week—State EdWatch. Retrieved July 29, 2021, from https://www.edweek.org/policy-politics/roughly-half-of-states-consider-arts-a-core-subject-new-report-finds/2014/03?cmp=SOC-SHR-FB

22 Wikipedia. (2021). *Music education.* Retrieved July 29, 2021, from https://en.wikipedia.org/wiki/Music_education

23 Wikipedia. (2021). The scientific method and how it affected music. In Music education and programs within the United States. Retrieved from https://en.wikipedia.org/wiki/Music_education_and_programs_within_the_United_States

24 Wikipedia. (2021). Overview. In Music Education. Retrieved from https://en.wikipedia.org/wiki/Music_education

25 Elliott, D. (2005). *Praxial music education: Reflections and dialogues.* New York: Oxford University Press.

26 Regelski, T. (2005) Critical theory as a foundation for critical thinking in music education. *Visions of research in music education* (p. 6). Retrieved July 29, 2021, from http://users.rider.edu/~vrme/v6n1/visions/Regelski%20Critical%20Theory%20as%20a%20Foundation.pdf

27 Gould, E. (2007). Feminist theory in music education research: Grrlilla games as nomadic practice (or how music education fell from grace). *Music Education Research, 6*(1), 67–79. Doi: 10.1080/14613800032000182849.

28 Bradley, D. (2006). Music education, multiculturalism, and anti-racism – can we talk? *Action, Criticism & Theory in Music Education, 5*(2), 2–30. Retrieved from http://act.maydaygroup.org/articles/Bradley5_2.pdf

29 Lamb, R. (2004). Talkin' musical identities blues. *Action, Criticism & Theory in Music Education, 3*(1), 2–27. Retrieved from http://act.maydaygroup.org/articles/Lamb3_1.pdf

30 Bates, V. C. (2012). Social class and school music. *Music Educators Journal, 98*(4), 33–37. Doi: 10.1177/0027432112442944.

31 Froehlich, H. (2007). Institutional belonging, pedagogic discourse and music teacher education: The paradox of routinization. *Action, Criticism, and Theory for Music Education, 6*(3), 7–21. Retrieved from http://act.maydaygroup.org/articles/Froehlich6_3.pdf

32 Bates, V. (2011). Sustainable school music for poor, white, rural students. *Action, Criticism, and Theory for Music Education, 10*(2), 100–127. Retrieved from http://act.maydaygroup.org/articles/Bates10_2.pdf

33 Sindberg, L. (2016). Learning how to be a research-minded teacher: Four instrumental music education students investigate good music teaching through case study methodology. *Journal of Music Teacher Education, 25*(2), 50–65.

34 Lortie, D. (1975). *Schoolteacher: A sociological study.* Chicago, IL: University of Chicago Press.

35 Dolloff, L. (1999). Imagining ourselves as teachers: The development of teacher identity in music teacher education. *Music Education Research, 1,* 191–207.
Teachout, D. J. (1997). Preservice and experienced teachers' opinions of skills and behaviors important to successful music teaching. *Journal of Research in Music Education, 45,* 41–50.

36 Kruse, N., & Taylor, D. (2012). Preservice music teachers' perceptions of a mentored research experience: A study within a study. *Journal of Music Teacher Education, 22*(1), 35–49.
Price, J. (2001). Action research, pedagogy and change: The transformative potential of action research in pre-service teacher education. *Journal of Curriculum Studies, 33,* 43–74.

37 Schmidt, M. (1998). Defining "good" music teaching: Four student teachers' beliefs and practices. *Bulletin of the Council for Research in Music Education, 138*(Fall), 19–46.
Zeichner, K. (1999). The new scholarship in teacher education. *Educational Researcher, 28*(9), 4–15.

38 Grossman, P. L., Valencia, S. W., Evans, K., Thompson, C., Martin, S., & Place, N. (2000). Transitions into teaching: Learning to teach writing in teacher education and beyond. *Journal of Literacy Research, 32,* 631–662.

39 Hammerness, K., Darling-Hammond, L., & Shulman, L. (2002). Toward expert thinking: How curriculum case writing prompts the development of theory-based professional knowledge in student teachers. *Teaching Education, 13,* 219–243.

40 Ching, C. P. (2014). Linking theory to practice: A case-based approach in teacher education. *Procedia—Social and Behavioral Sciences, 123,* 280–288. Retrieved from https://www.sciencedirect.com/science/article/pii/S1877042814014633

41 Shulman, J. H. (1992). *Case methods in teacher education.* New York: Teachers College Press.

42 Heitzmann, R. (2008). Case study instruction in teacher education: Opportunity to develop students/critical thinking, school making. *Education, 128*(4), 523–541.

43 Ching, C. P. (2014). Linking theory to practice: A case-based approach in teacher education. *Procedia—Social and Behavioral Sciences, 123,* 285.

44 Ching, C. P. (2014). Linking theory to practice: A case-based approach in teacher education. *Procedia—Social and Behavioral Sciences, 123,* 286.

45 Wrenn, J., & Wrenn, B. (2009). Enhancing learning by integrating theory and practice. *International Journal of Teaching and Learning in Higher Education, 21*(2), 258–265.

46 Hutchings, P. (1990, June). Assessment and the way it works: Closing plenary address. *Association of Higher Education Conference on Assessment* (p. 1). Washington, DC. Retrieved July 29, 2021, from https://files.eric.ed.gov/fulltext/EJ899313.pdf

47 National Institute for Health. (2005). *Doing science: The process of science inquiry.* Retrieved July 30, 2021, from https://science.education.nih.gov/supplements/nih6/inquiry/guide/info_process-a.htm
InquirED. (2021). *Inquiry-based learning: A student-centered learning process.* Retrieved July 30, 2021, from https://www.inquired.org/what-is-inquiry

48 Ontario Ministry of Education. (2021). *Inquiry-based learning.* Retrieved July 30, 2021, from http://www.edu.gov.on.ca/eng/literacynumeracy/inspire/research/CBS_InquiryBased.pdf

49 Vygotsky, L. S. (1978). *Mind in society: The development of higher psychological processes.* Edited by M. Cole, V. John-Steiner, S. Scribner, & E. Souberman. Translated by A. R. Luria, M. Lopez-Morillas, M. Cole, & J. Wertsch. Cambridge, MA: Cambridge University Press.

50 McLean, C. (2021). PICTURE. *Theory vs. Practice.* Retrieved July 30, 2021, from https://christinemclean10.wordpress.com/2013/08/25/putting-theory-into-practice/

51 McLean, C. (2021). *Putting theory into practice.* Retrieved July 30, 2021, from https://christinemclean10.wordpress.com/2013/08/25/putting-theory-into-practice/

52 Merriam-Webster. (2021). *Definition of theory.* Retrieved July 30, 2021, from https://www.merriam-webster.com/dictionary/theory

Chapter 2

Becoming a Reflective Teacher

The music teacher employing reflective practices studies his/her own teaching methods to determine what works best for his/her students in the music rehearsal or classroom.[1] As teaching and learning are very complex processes, there is not one right approach in a given setting. Reflecting on different versions of teaching and reshaping past and current experiences will lead to improvement in teaching practice.[2] Schön's reflection-in-action assists teachers in making the professional knowledge that they will gain from their experience in the classroom is an explicit part of their decision-making.[3]

Learning Objectives

1 What is Reflective Practice?
2 What factors influence the development of your belief system?
3 How can anecdotal and empirical evidence help you to be an effective music teacher?
4 In what ways does reflective practice enhance your growth and development as a music teacher?

Though the marching band director had devoted a great deal of thought in preparing to teach the opening drill designs to this season's fall marching show, it was obvious in today's marching rehearsal that his students were not executing the required maneuvers to accomplish his goal of getting the first five designs on the marching field with marching and playing the show opener. That evening, the director gave considerable thought to what instructional methods he had been using, the environment on the rehearsal field and ensuing heat during rehearsal, the response of his students to his instruction during rehearsal, the instructional methods used and the pros and cons of these strategies in rehearsal. The director even called up his friend and colleague at a neighboring school to pick her brain about the challenges he had in the day's rehearsal. She was very helpful in sharing what she had learned at a summer workshop on marching design and instruction, and also explaining a fundamental theory of music learning that she found very useful in a similar situation. After his own personal reflection and dialogue with a colleague about these issues of concern, the director devised a new plan for tomorrow's rehearsal which assimilated some new strategies among the one's already implemented in today's rehearsal.

DOI: 10.4324/9781003038474-3

Reflective Practice

Reflective practice is the ability to reflect on one's actions so as to engage in a process of continuous learning.[4] According to one definition it involves "paying critical attention to the practical values and theories which inform everyday actions, by examining practice reflectively, that lead to developmental insight."[5] A key rationale for reflective practice is that experience alone does not necessarily lead to learning; deliberate reflection on experience is essential.[6]

Central to the development of reflective theory was interest in the integration of theory and practice, the cyclic pattern of experience, and the conscious application of lessons learned from experience. Since the 1970s, there has been a growing literature and focus around experiential learning, learning through reflection on doing,[7] and the development and application of reflective practice.

The concept of reflective practice is now widely employed in the field of teacher education and teacher professional development and many programs of initial teacher education claim to espouse it.[6] Without reflection, teachers are not able to look objectively at their actions or take into account the emotions, experience, or consequences of actions to improve their practice. It is argued that, through the process of reflection, teachers are held accountable to the standards of practice for teaching, such as commitment to students and student learning, professional knowledge, professional practice, leadership in learning communities, and ongoing professional learning.[8]

The Teacher's Responsibility

The Merriam-Webster Dictionary defines philosophy as the study of ideas about knowledge, truth, and the nature and meaning of life.[9] It is the study of basic concepts, underlying principles, or belief systems through time and all cultures, in all times, have had their own unique schools of philosophy.

In a very real sense, music teachers define their own philosophy of teaching and learning when they make decisions and take actions in the music classroom. The decisions music teachers make as to 'what to do,' 'what to say,' 'how to react,' or 'where to go next,' affect not only themselves but also many students under their care. Their decisions and the associated actions are made under broad authorization from society in the form of tax funds for education and compulsory laws. Their comprehensive philosophy of music education guides what the music teacher is trying to do and serves as a guide for action. These formative beliefs and principles will also guide the music teacher through tough situations in teaching and throughout his/her teaching career. A solid philosophy gives the music teacher a sense of direction and perspective, helps in overcoming problems and disappointment, and sense of purposes as a music educator. Music teachers with a sense of purpose are consistent in their decisions, follow-through in their actions, and lead productive achievement in the music classroom.

The music teacher's responsibility includes promoting learning in the classroom, motivating students in learning, and achieving musical objectives in the classroom. S/he needs to be aware of the different learning styles of students and accommodate these differences through the methods of instruction used in the music class. Music instruction also requires understanding of varied learning rates of the students in the classroom. The music teacher must comprehend the cognitive, physical, and emotional development of his/her students to provide diverse levels of instruction that engage all students. As a result, the music teacher is constantly making judgment calls regarding student learning.

Your Belief System

As the music teacher's actions in the classroom are based on his/her own underlying convictions, beliefs, and theories of learning, it is very difficult to get teachers to change.[10] As a preservice music teacher, you have already learned from experience without instruction, study, or practice. You have observed, participated in, and experienced teaching in many diverse forms as a student in elementary and secondary school. You have developed your own personal beliefs about what you think is good teaching and what you think is poor teaching through your experiences with numerous teachers throughout your career as a student, both in school and in college.

As a result of your love of music and music making, you have been in contact with a variety of music teachers, from private instructors to classroom teachers, to directors of performing ensembles such as band, chorus, and orchestra. In these circumstances, you have developed long-term relationships with these teachers while participating in afterschool rehearsals, music camps, spring trips, and other musical activities outside the regular school day and regular school year. In many cases, these individuals not only know you but also have longstanding relationships with your parents and even siblings who have participated in the music program as part of their education. Research shows that high school band, choral, and orchestra directors have a major influence on students' choice to major in music and music education in college.[11] Beyond this influence, this individual also has a strong impact on college students' belief system about what may be appropriate or correct rehearsal methods and music teaching.

While beliefs guide our thinking and our actions, successful experienced music teachers are continually examining, questioning, and probing to find different ways of doing things in the music classroom. Agne, Greenwood, and Miller (1994) found marked differences between the belief systems of novice teachers and those of expert teachers (i.e., Teacher of the Year).[12] Expert teachers tended to be more student oriented (i.e., Humanistic) in their approaches to classroom management while novice teachers were stricter and more detached from their students. Conclusions from this research indicate that the beliefs of expert teachers may have changed from the time that they were novices.

Acknowledging Anecdotal and Empirical Evidence

As music teachers form such an extended community with their students and other teachers, much of what is shared regarding music making, musical rehearsal, and music instruction is passed down from mentor teacher to student. These personal accounts, stories, and anecdotes of musical experience are shared during musical rehearsal, in the music classroom, and between experienced teachers and beginning music teachers to illustrate specific points. They are shared at professional conferences, after music rehearsals, and through mentoring as preservice college students and beginning music teachers seek to become enculturated in the music education profession.

While a personal account or anecdote of successful musical method may demonstrate a worthy approach to music teaching, it is a single report of how the individual uses the technique in the classroom. As the particular pedagogy may work for the individual, it may or may not have effect on another person in similar situation. Such reference has limited and narrow claim that may or may not apply in general terms. While the testimony of a credible music teacher presents strong argument for a particular methodology, the beginning music educator should consider the reasoning of the narrative. Whereas the novice teacher appreciates the account, it is of particular value that s/he experiments with its application in his/her own classroom setting. The beginning teacher may try the application in a variety of settings in order to learn from the advisor, reshape or reapply the technique to learn for one's own personal teaching experience, or include the method as experiential knowledge that is added to one's personal experience in music teaching.

Empirical evidence is a source of knowledge acquired through observation or experimentation.[13] In the empiricist view, one can claim knowledge only when one has justified a belief in the truth or falsity of a claim.[14] Empirical evidence is usually considered the outcome of an experiment that confirms a theory or hypothesis. This scientific testing proves or disproves a premise and gains acceptance in a community. Typically, the scientific method of hypothesis, experimental design with experimental controls, statistical testing and/or critical peer review, and publication of findings and conclusions of the experiment achieve this proof or validation.

The research and study of education trace its roots back to the late 1830s and early 1840s with the revival of the common school and it is the first time that both school supervision and planning were influenced by systematic data collection.[15] Horace Mann and Henry Barnard were early pioneers in educational data collection and in the production and dissemination of educational literature during the mid- to late-19th century. Additionally, they held prominent educational leadership positions by being the first secretaries of educational boards of Massachusetts (Horace Mann) and of Connecticut (Henry Barnard).[16] In 1954, the United States Congress passed the Cooperative Research Act as a means for the federal government to take a more active role in advancing and funding research on education in academia.

Today, university professors, researchers, and scholars are dedicated to research such issues as general education, teaching and learning, education and training of teachers, pedagogy, and professional development. In the music education field, music educators continue to examine such subjects as the philosophy of music education, psychological issues of the music classroom, sociology of music education, socialization and identity construction of preservice music teachers, effective music instruction, classroom management, assessment, teacher evaluation, and policy regarding music education in the school program. Some of the research journals that publish such research include the *International Journal of Music Education, Research in Music Education, Bulletin for the Council of Research on Music Education, Contributions to Music Education, Music Perception, Research and Issues in Music Education,* and *Journal of Music Teacher Education.* Music education researchers are also active in such organizations as the International Society of Music Education, National Association for Music Education, Society of Music Teacher Education, and MayDay Group.

Some of the reasons university music education professors, researchers, and scholars participate in research and research activities are to solve issues and problems in music education, discover new more effective ways to teach music, improve music education in the classroom and performance hall, and advance music teacher education, training, and professional development. The purpose of this book is to introduce you to research-based information that has and continues to impact music teaching, instruction, assessment, and general music education of today's students. The theories of learning presented in this text, originally proven through scientific experimentation, continue to form the basis for teaching and learning used by teachers in today's music classroom and provide empirical evidence upon which to build your education and training as a future music educator.

Different theories of learning have resulted from various investigators approaching the occurrence of "learning" from different viewpoints and equipped with different initial intuitive premonitions about it. These initial ideas or hypotheses formed by the investigator may influence his/her later conclusions. As a result, particular theorists differ from others in theory, which provides different perspectives for examining music teaching and learning in the classroom. While the novice music teacher should heed the evidence in each of the theories of music teaching and learning, it is of particular value that s/he experiments with its application in the music classroom setting.

Music teachers also differ a great deal in the fundamental impression they have of the nature of their students. Some regard all members of their school classes as generally being the same in ability to learn, while other music teachers consider their students as integrally quite different. Whatever your viewpoint on these matters, as a professional charged with cultivating the intellectual and musical development of your students, you should be acquainted with the variety of theories that have been set forth. As a beginning music teacher, you may try to apply the theory in a setting similar to those illustrated in this text to get first-hand experience applying the theory in authentic "real-life" settings, apply the theory in a variety of new settings in order to learn from one's own personal teaching experience, and become familiar with the theory and resultant methodology as experiential knowledge that is added to your own personal experience in music teaching.

Cognitive Dissonance

Cognitive dissonance is the discomfort experienced by an individual who holds two or more contradictory beliefs, ideas, or values at the same time or is confronted by new information that conflicts with existing beliefs, ideas, or values.[17] This extreme discomfort may occur within the individual who holds a belief and performs an action inconsistent with this belief.[18] Cognitive dissonance theory is founded on the assumption that individuals seek consistency between their expectations and their reality.[17]

Cognitive dissonance occurs when there is need to accommodate new ideas with existing beliefs. In such instances, it is necessary for the individual to be open and accepting of these new ideas. If someone is called upon to learn something that contradicts what they already think they know or committed to their knowledge or belief system through prior personal experience, they may be likely to resist the new learning. If learning something has been difficult or uncomfortable, the individual may be less likely to accept the new information. To release the discomfort or tension, the individual can change his/her behavior, justify his/her behavior by changing the conflicting belief or mental action, or justify his/her behavior by accommodating new knowledge and understanding with prior information.

While you have a defined musical and music teaching belief system based on your many years of experience as a student in the school and college classroom, it is important to continue to question, examine, and explore new ways of learning and teaching music. Within this text, there are theories of learning that may be new or different from your experience in the classroom or vary from anecdotes you have heard from mentors or former teachers. In some cases, you may find a theory or practice that contradicts what you had thought was the best and/or only strategy to teach or learn in a particular circumstance. In such situations, even though it may cause anxiety or cognitive discomfort, it is important that you find connections between new or unfamiliar information and previous knowledge or experience.

Cognitive dissonance emerges in almost all evaluations and decisions and is the principal means by which we experience new differences in the world. As a professional music teacher, it is essential that you direct your attention toward understanding new and/or different concepts, methods, strategies, and techniques of music teaching and learning.

Just as particular theorists or teachers may differ from others in theory or practice, there are often many different methods of teaching the same concept or technique. The greater your understanding of diverse applications of theory and practice, the broader your knowledge and expertise to be effective in any given setting as a music teacher.

Reflective Practice: A Process for Growth and Development

The major theoretical roots of reflection can be found in John Dewey among others. John Dewey declared that we do not learn from experience; we learn from reflecting on experience.[19] Reflection is thinking for an extended period by linking recent experiences to earlier ones in order to promote a more complex and interrelated mental schema. The thinking involves looking for commonalities, differences, and interrelations beyond their superficial elements. The goal is to develop higher order thinking skills.[20]

Reflection is a form of mental processing (i.e., thinking) that we use to fulfill a purpose or to achieve some anticipated outcome. It is applied to relatively complicated or unstructured ideas for which there is not an obvious solution and is largely based on the further processing of knowledge and understanding and possibly emotions that we already possess.[21] Given the complexities and dilemmas that characterize today's classrooms, effective teachers need to engage in both critical inquiry and thoughtful reflection, the hallmarks of reflective practitioners.[22] Many view the development of reflective practice as the foundation for the highest professional competence (Cole & Knowles, 2000; Jay, 2003; Larrivee, 2000; Osterman & Kottkamp, 2004; Valli, 1997; Zeichner & Liston, 1996).[23]

An essential approach of reflective practice is being open to other points of view, appreciating that there are many ways to view a particular situation or event, and staying open to changing your own viewpoint. Part of open-mindedness is also letting go of needing to be right or wanting to win.[24] Another important attribute of the reflective practitioner is responsibility. Responsibility refers to a music teacher's willingness to examine all decisions (e.g., regarding curriculum, instruction, organization, administration, evaluation, and management) from a comprehensive philosophical basis for music teaching and learning.[24] For Dewey, reflective thinking leads to responsible action. Therefore, the explicit goal of reflective practice is to create deeper understanding and insight, forming the basis for not only considering alternatives but also for taking action to continually improve practice throughout one's music teaching career.[25]

The reflective music teacher is constantly engaged in thoughtful observation and examination of his/her actions in the music classroom before, during, and after interactions with his/her students. Prior to instruction, reflective music teachers may think about the knowledge, skills, and musical encounters students need to experience to learn, the kind of classroom or rehearsal atmosphere and teaching techniques that will produce this learning, and the kinds of assessments that will provide clear evidence that these goals are being completed.

An open-minded music teacher is continually seeking new information that might challenge his/her notions about teaching. The reflective music educator wants to have a broad range of potential solutions to any situation or set of conditions to meet the needs of his/her students in music learning. As they interact with students, reflective music teachers are highly conscious of how students are responding to what they are doing and are prepared to make small yet important adjustments in their lesson to focus attentiveness toward their predetermined goal. In situations that cannot be managed on the spot, the reflective teacher devotes time outside of school for reflection, analysis, assessment, and formulating a plan for dealing with the dilemma.

To become a reflective music teacher, it is essential that you are open-minded yet inquisitive about educational theories and practices of music teaching and learning, develop an introspective outlook on your own role and behavior in regard, and take responsibility for your decisions and actions in the music classroom. You also need to be willing to view situations from the perspectives of others such as students, parents, administrators, and other teachers, discover information that allows for alternative explanations and more effective instructional methods in particular events in the music classroom, and employ convincing evidence in support of your decision (Eby & Hicks, 2002; Ross, Bondy, & Kyle, 1993).[26] While reflection many times involves solitary consideration and contemplation, it is necessary for you to challenge your assumptions about music teaching and learning, and discuss your apprehensions with colleagues, friends, students, and parents to gain distinct perspectives on music teaching and learning. By reflecting on the content in this text, you will increase your command of knowledge about the nature of students, the process of music learning, and the music instruction process. Through mastery of this information in a reflective context, you broaden your range of understanding, which contributes to your effectiveness in the rehearsal and music classroom.

Questions

1 Describe reflective practice in the daily preparation for instruction in one of the common performance-based music classes (e.g., band, choir, orchestra, general music). What methods might the music teacher use as a reflective practitioner in preparing on a daily basis for this music class or rehearsal?
2 Describe the various responsibilities of the music teacher in the school music program.
3 What influence do the teacher's philosophy and belief system have in the daily instruction, policies, and procedures of the music program?
4 As a beginning music teacher, how can anecdotal evidence help you to be an effective teacher? What advantages are there to considering empirical evidence in your own teaching? How may anecdotal evidence hinder your effectiveness? How may empirical evidence impede your effect?
5 What role does research play in music teaching and learning? Why do music educators, researchers, and scholars do research on music teaching and learning? What issues do they currently research? What are the reasons for their research? Name five music education journals.
6 Describe the concept of theory of learning. What is the process that a theory of learning is proposed and justified? What relevance do theories of learning have to teaching and learning music? The music classroom? Your students? The music curriculum?
7 Define Cognitive Dissonance. Describe how cognitive dissonance may influence a music teacher's growth, understanding, and development as a teacher. Are there ways for the music teacher to manage cognitive dissonance?
8 Describe John Dewey's premise regarding reflection. What are the major theoretical roots of his definition?
9 Describe reflection and reflective practice. What is an essential approach to reflective practice?
10 What are some of the best ways for you to be a reflective practitioner or reflective music teacher? What are some ways the reflective music teacher may prepare for instruction? How might the reflective teacher gain insight from the perspectives of others in the instructional environment?

Notes

1 Larrivee, B. (2000). Transforming teaching practice: Becoming the critically reflective teacher. *Reflective Practice, (1)*3, 293–307. Doi: 10.1080/713693162.

2 Leitch, R., & Day, C. (2000). Action research and reflective practice: Towards a holistic view. *Educational Action Research, (8)*1, 179–193. Doi: 10.1080/09650790000200108.

3 Fien, J., & Rawling, R. (1996). Reflective practice: A case study of professional development for environmental education. *The Journal of Environmental Education, (27)*3, 11–20. Doi: 10.1080/00958964.1996.9941462.

4 Schön, D. A. (1983). *The reflective practitioner: How professionals think in action.* New York: Basic Books.

5 Bolton, G. (2010). *Reflective practice: Writing and professional development* (3rd ed.), Los Angeles, CA: Sage Publications, xix. (Original work published 2001).

6 Loughran, J. (2002). Effective reflective practice: In search of meaning in learning about teaching. *Journal of Teacher Education, 53*(1), 33–43.
Cochran-Smith, M., & Lytle, S. S. (1999). Relationships of knowledge and practice: Teacher learning in communities. *Review of Research in Education, 24*(1), 249–305.

7 Felicia, P. (2011). *Handbook of research on improving learning and motivation* (p. 1003). Information Science Reference: IGI Global Publishing.

8 Standards of practice. *Ontario College of Teachers.* Retrieved May 24, 2021, from https://www.oct.ca/public/professional-standards/standards-of-practice

9 Merriam-Webster. (2014). *Philosophy.* Retrieved July 22, 2014, from http://www.merriam-webster.com/dictionary/philosophy

10 Smith, K. E. (1997). Student teachers' beliefs about developmentally appropriate practice: Pattern, stability, and the influence of locus of control. *Early Childhood Research Quarterly, 12,* 221–243.

11 Bergee, M. (2001). *Influences on collegiate students' decision to become a music educator.* Reston, VA: Music Educators National Conference.

12 Agne, K. J., Greenwood G. E., & Miller, L. D. (1994). Relationships between teacher belief systems and teacher effectiveness. *Journal of Research and Development in Music Education, 27,* 141–152.

13 Pickett, J. P. (Ed.). (2011). Empirical. *The American Heritage Dictionary of the English Language* (5th ed.), Houghton Mifflin. ISBN 978-0-547-04101-8.

14 Feldman, R. (2001). Evidence. In R. Audi (Ed.), *The Cambridge Dictionary of Philosophy* (2nd ed.) (pp. 293–294), Cambridge, England: Cambridge University Press ISBN 978-0521637220.

15 Travers, R. (1983). *How research has changed American schools: A history from 1840 to the present* (p. 7). Kalamazoo, MI: Mythos Press.

16 Bowen, J. (1981). *A history of western education; Volume III: The modern west* (p. 360). London: Methuen.

17 Festinger, L. (1957). *A theory of cognitive dissonance.* Redwood, CA: Stanford University Press.

18 Festinger, L. (1962). Cognitive dissonance. *Scientific American, 207*(4), 93–107.

19 Dewey, J. (1933). *How we think: A restatement of the relation of reflective thinking to the educative process.* Boston, MA: D.C. Heath.

20 Clark, D. (2014). Learning through reflection. Big Dog, Little Dog and Knowledge Jump Production. Retrieved July 12, 2014, from http://www.nwlink.com/~donclark/hrd/development/reflection.html

21 Moon, J. (1999). *Reflection in learning and professional development.* London, England: Kogan Page.

22 Larrivee, B., & Cooper, J. (2006). *An educator's guide to teacher reflection* (p. 1). Boston, MA: Cengage Learning.

23 Cole, A. L., & Knowles, J. G. (2000). *Researching teaching: Exploring teacher development through reflective inquiry.* Boston, MA: Allyn and Bacon.
Jay, J. K., & Johnson, K. L. (2002). Capturing complexity: A typology of reflective practice for teacher education. *Teaching and Teacher Education, 18,* 73–85.
Larrivee, B. (2000). Transforming teaching practice: Becoming the critically reflective teacher. *Reflective Practice, 1*(3), 293–307.

Osterman, K. P., & Kottkamp, R. B. (1993/2004). *Reflective practice for educators: Improving schooling through professional development.* Thousand Oaks, CA: Corwin Press.

Valli, L. (1997). Listening to other voices: A description of teacher reflection in the United States. *Peabody Journal of Education, 72*(1), 67–88.

York-Barr, J., Sommers, W. A., Ghere, G. S., & Montie, J. (2001). *Reflective practice to improve schools.* Thousand Oaks, CA: Corwin Press.

Zeichner, K. M., & Liston, D. P. (1996). *Reflective teaching: An introduction.* Mahwah, NJ: Lawrence Erlbaum.

24 Larrivee, B. & Cooper, J. (2006). *An educator's guide to teacher reflection* (p. 7.). Boston, MA: Cengage Learning.

25 Larrivee, B. & Cooper, J. (2006). *An educator's guide to teacher reflection* (p. 2). Boston, MA: Cengage Learning.

26 Eby, J. W., & Hicks, J. L. (2002). *Reflective planning, teaching, and evaluations: K-12.* Upper Saddle River, NJ: Merrill Prentice Hall.

Ross, D. D., Bondy, E., & Kyle, D. W. (1993). *Reflective teaching for student empowerment.* New York: Macmillan.

Part I

Theories of Learning and Teaching Music

Behaviorism

Learning Theory and Applications to Teaching

Behaviorism examines relationships between the environment and the individual. Behaviorists view the learning process as a change in behavior and arrange the environment to elicit desired responses and advocate a system of rewards and targets in education. Theories by researchers such as Ivan Pavlov who introduced classical conditioning, and B. F. Skinner (operant conditioning) looked at how environmental stimulation could impact learning. The research of Clifford Madsen and others builds on the operant conditioning model focusing on guiding "good" or "successful" teaching by analyzing the role of appropriate reinforcement such as praise and feedback on musical discrimination, attitude, and performance in music learning.

Learning Objectives

1 What is Behavioral Learning Theory?
2 What are the key principles of Classical Conditioning and Operant Conditioning?
3 How are reinforcements effectively applied in music learning?
4 How are principles of behavioral learning applied to management of the music classroom?

Music teachers employing behavioral applications in the classroom use reinforcers[1] in a variety of ways to bring about desirable behaviors and sometimes eliminate those that are less desirable.

By setting up chairs, stands, and equipment for rehearsal, the music teacher structures a physical environment that is conducive to learning. Setting behavioral objectives for the students to enter the room, get their instruments and music, and are seated in preparation for rehearsal; the class setting creates stimuli for proper response. The music teacher gives praise or admonishes students, uses a smile or frown, and other nonverbal indicators of approval or disapproval to give instant feedback regarding their behavior in the classroom.

Behavioral Learning Theory

Learning can be defined as the process leading to relatively permanent behavioral change or potential behavioral change. As we learn, we alter the way we perceive our environment, the way we interpret the incoming stimuli, and therefore the way we interact, or behave.[2] Evidence of learning is found not only in actual but also in potential changes in behavior, because not all changes involved in learning are obvious and observable.

DOI: 10.4324/9781003038474-5

There may also be other important changes that are not apparent but still a fundamental part of learning.[3]

Behaviorism is an approach to psychology that combines elements of philosophy, methodology, and theory.[4] It emerged in the early 20th century as a reaction to "mentalistic" psychology, which often had difficulty making predictions that could be tested using rigorous experimental methods.

Behavioral psychology is one of the first scientific approaches to understanding learning. *Behaviorism* begins by trying to explain simple behaviors—observable and predictable responses. Accordingly, it is mainly concerned with conditions (called *stimuli*) that affect organisms and that may lead to behavior and with simple behaviors themselves (called *responses*). Behavior-oriented researchers try to discover the rules that govern the formation of relationships between stimuli and responses (which are the rules of *conditioning*). Thus, *Behaviorism deals with associative learning—a largely unconscious process by which associations form between stimuli, responses, and response consequences.*

Behavioral Psychology basically examines how our behavior results from the stimuli both in the environment and within ourselves. Behavioral Psychologists study, in minute detail, the behaviors we exhibit while controlling for as many other variables as possible. Often a grueling process, but results have helped us learn a great deal about our behaviors, the effect our environment has on us, how we learn new behaviors, and what motivates us to change or remain the same.

Behaviorists define learning in terms of changes in behavior and look to the environment for explanations of these changes. Their theories are associative; they deal with connections or associations that are formed among stimuli and responses. These behaviorist theories make use of one or both of two principal classes of explanations for learning; those based on *contiguity* (i.e., simultaneity of stimulus and response events) and those based on the *effects of behavior* (i.e., reinforcement and punishment). Contiguity theorists John Watson and Ivan Pavlov use "contiguity" to frequently explain the occurrence of *Classical Conditioning* and refer to the occurrence of things both simultaneously and in the same space. Reinforcement theorists E. L. Thorndike and B. F. Skinner assign an important role of reinforcement in bringing about learning in their definition of *Operant Conditioning*.

Classical Conditioning

John B. Watson (1878–1958) was the first to study how the process of learning affects our behavior, and he formed the school of thought known as *Behaviorism*. Watson is considered the father of behaviorism due to his opposition to the mainstream psychological view of the unconscious and psychoanalytic thought. His resistance split the field of psychology into two distinct and almost always oppositional schools of thought. The central idea behind behaviorism was that only observable behaviors are worthy of research since other abstractions such as a person's mood or thoughts are too subjective. This belief was dominant in psychological research in the United States for a good 50 years.

Classical Conditioning was discovered accidentally by Russian physiologist Ivan Pavlov (1849–1936) while doing research on the digestive patterns in dogs. Pavlov determined that we make associations so as to cause us to generalize our response to one stimulus onto a neutral stimulus with which it is paired. *Classical Conditioning* is a type of associative learning involving the repeated pairing of a previously neutral *conditioned stimulus* (CS) with an effective *unconditioned stimulus* (US) so that the CS eventually brings about a *conditioned response* (CR) similar to that brought about by the US.

Pavlov presented dogs with a ringing bell (CS) followed by food (US). The food elicited salivation (unconditioned response, UR), and after repeated bell-food pairings the bell also caused the dogs to salivate. In this experiment, the US is the dog food as it produces a UR, saliva. The CS is the ringing bell and it produces a CR of the dogs' producing saliva.[5]

These findings support the idea that we develop responses to certain stimuli that are not naturally occurring. An example of this principle is evident when we try to pet an overly aggressive dog. If the dog tries to bite our hand, our reflex pulls our hand back. It does this instinctually, with no learning involved. It is merely a survival instinct. But why do some people, after this experience, avoid petting and physical contact even with an obedient and docile dog? Pavlov discovered that we make associations that cause us to generalize our response to one stimulus onto a neutral stimulus it is paired with. Thus, if

Unconditioned Response
(Salivation)

Unconditioned Stimulus
(Food)

No Response

Neutral Stimulus
(Bell Ringing)

Unconditioned Response
(Salivation)

Neutral Stimulus
(Bell Ringing)

Unconditioned Stimulus
(Food)

Conditioned Response
(Salivation)

Conditioned Stimulus
(Bell Ringing)

Figure 3.1 Pavlov's Classical Conditioning.

Salehi.s, CC BY-SA 4.0 <https://creativecommons.org/licenses/by-sa/4.0>, via Wikimedia Commons.

we associate being bitten and pain from the dog, we relate the dog with pain. We generalize our response to one stimulus onto a neutral stimulus to which it is paired.

Operant Conditioning

Operant Conditioning Theory is based on the work of E. L. Thorndike and B. F. Skinner. Thorndike's research focused on learning (called instrumental learning) developed from an organism doing something.[6] Thorndike's experiments centered around placing a cat inside the wooden box to observe methods the cat used to get out of the box. By hitting a lever quickly, the cat successfully escaped.

Thorndike's theory assigns an important role of reinforcement in bringing about learning. His *Law of Effect* (1898) states that the effect of a response leads to its being learned or not learned.[7] Further, in the absence of previous learning, behavior will take the form of trial and error with attempted responses affected by position, identical elements in stimulus situations, or classical conditioning. Thorndike's *Law of Effect* simply stated is

Learning = behavior + consequences

Behavioral learning theories culminated with the work of B. F. Skinner. Skinner followed much of Watson's research and findings, however, believed that internal states could influence behavior just as external stimuli. He made important changes to Thorndike's theory to combine many different ideas that serve as the basis for a variety of applications to human behavior. Skinner's theory, *Operant Conditioning*, takes as its starting point the fact that many of the voluntary responses of animals and humans are strengthened when they are reinforced (followed by a desirable consequence) and weakened when they are either ignored or punished.[8]

Skinner invented the operant conditioning chamber, also known as the Skinner Box, as a variation of the *Puzzle Box* originally created by Thorndike.[9] An operant conditioning chamber permits experimenters to study behavior conditioning (training) by teaching a subject to perform certain actions (like pressing a lever) in response to specific stimuli (like a light or sound signal). When the subject correctly performs the behavior, the chamber mechanism delivers food or another reward. In some cases, the mechanism delivers a punishment for incorrect or missing responses. These types of apparatuses allow experimenters to perform studies in conditioning and training through reward/punishment mechanisms. Skinner's operant chamber allowed him to explore the rate of response as a dependent variable, as well as develop his theory of schedules of reinforcement.

While *Classical Conditioning* deals with *respondents* that are elicited by stimuli and appear involuntary, *Operant Conditioning* recognizes a much larger and more important class of behaviors that are not elicited by any known stimuli. These *operants* are voluntarily emitted responses in which the organism acts upon the environment. Whereas sneezing, blinking, and being excited are respondents, singing, reading a book, or driving a car are generally operant and subject to operant conditioning. *Operant Conditioning* is a type of learning that involves an increase in the probability that a response will occur as a function of reinforcement.

Types of Reinforcement

The *Skinner Box* contained food, water, an exercise wheel as well as a lever that a rat could press repeatedly for more food. Through experimentation, Skinner discovered four types of reinforcement: positive, negative, punishment, and extinction that followed a behavior. These reinforcements or consequences were either desirable or aversive to the rat. Depending on the conditions, consequences either increased or decreased the likelihood that the preceding behavior recurs under the same or similar circumstances.

Positive Reinforcement

Skinner used the term *positive* to refer to the act of "adding" stimulus. When an organism performs the desired behavior and gets a desirable reward, as demonstrated by a rat pressing a lever and being rewarded with a food pellet in the Skinner Box. In the classroom, the teacher rewards a student for correctly clapping a rhythm on the Smartboard with a piece of candy. Positive reinforcement is the most powerful of all reinforcers.

Negative Reinforcement

Negative reinforcement occurs when an unpleasant stimulus is removed as a result of operant behavior and the rate of the behavior increases.[10] An undesirable event occurs until the organism performs the desired behavior. The floor of the Skinner Box is electrified until the rat presses a lever to turn off the electricity. Imagine a teenager who is nagged by his mother to take out the garbage week after week. After complaining about the nagging, he finally performs the task and to his amazement, the nagging stops.

Punishment

Punishment is a term used to refer to any change that occurs after a behavior that reduces the likelihood that behavior will occur again. While positive and negative reinforcement are used to *increase* behaviors, punishment is focused on reducing or eliminating unwanted behaviors.[11]

Punishment is often mistakenly confused with negative reinforcement. Remember, reinforcement always increases the chances that a behavior will occur and punishment always decreases the chances that a behavior will occur. The organism performs an undesirable behavior and gets an aversive consequence or punishment. A student continuously misbehaves in music class and receives after-school detention. The punishment is not liked and therefore to avoid it, s/he will stop behaving in that manner. Interestingly, punishment can also invoke other negative responses such as anger and resentment.

Extinction

Extinction also weakens undesired behavior. When you remove something in order to decrease a behavior, this is called *Extinction*. You are taking something away so that a response is decreased and eventually ceases to exist. When a mother ignores a crying child, who wants to stay up and not go to bed at his regular bedtime, the child will eventually stop crying, if the mother continues to ignore his crying. A student continuously speaks out during class and is ignored by the general music teacher and other students. Eventually, the student's behavior will cease.

Schedules of Reinforcement

During his research and experiments, Skinner also discovered *Schedules of Reinforcement*. Applying one of the four types of reinforcement every time the behavior occurs is called a *Continuous Schedule*. While this is the best approach when using punishment, we are not always present when a behavior occurs or may not be able to apply the punishment. Inconsistencies in the punishment of children often result in confusion and resentment. Rather than giving a reinforcement (i.e., a food pellet) after every response (i.e., pressing the lever), Skinner adjusted the operant conditioning chamber to give reinforcements on a noncontinuous or intermittent basis to continue the behavior. He tested four basic intermittent reinforcement schedules: *Fixed Interval*, *Variable Interval*, *Fixed Ratio*, and *Variable Ratio*. Each schedule produces a different pattern of behavior.

Fixed Interval Schedule

In this schedule, reinforcement is applied for the desired response that occurs after a predetermined amount of time has passed. Once the response has occurred and been reinforced, the next interval begins. Any desired behaviors that are made during an interval are ignored. The reinforced behavior occurs at a lower level during the early part of the interval and gradually increases as the time for reinforcement draws close. A major problem with this schedule is that people tend to improve their performance right before the time period expires so as to "look good" when the review comes around.

Fixed Interval Schedules of reinforcement occur in the music classroom when the music teacher schedules tests at regular intervals. While the test grade or score is intended to be a reinforcement, students may practice or study considerably less during the early part of the interval. Though the marching band may have a performance at a football game every Friday for the community to view, evaluate, and provide reinforcement, students may be less attentive and focused in marching band rehearsal on Monday or Tuesday than on Thursday afternoon as they prepare for a Friday game that has received much publicity throughout the week from the school community, local newspapers, and home and neighboring communities.

Variable Interval Schedule

To observe a more consistent pattern of behavior, reinforcement is applied for the desired response that occurs after random amounts of time have passed. Successive reinforcements may occur after five days, three days, seven days, two days, ten days, etc. Music teachers who give surprise tests or call on students to perform an excerpt on every third day, from the music literature rehearsed, are invoking a variable interval schedule. If you have a school principal who checks your class periodically, you understand the power of this schedule. Because you don't know when the next 'check' might come, you have to be engaging your students at all times. In this sense, the variable interval schedules are more powerful and result in behaviors that are more consistent. This may not be as true for punishment since consistency in the application is so important, but for all other types of reinforcement, they tend to result in stronger responses.

Fixed Ratio Schedule

In this schedule, reinforcement is applied after a specific number of responses. A rat in the Skinner box may be reinforced with a food pellet after pressing a lever for the fourth time. A parent grounding a child after asking him three times to clean his room is an example of a fixed ratio schedule. The problem is that the child will begin to realize that he can get away with two requests before he has to act. Therefore, the behavior does not tend to change until right before the preset number. A music teacher may reinforce a student with praise on every fourth time for correctly executing a technical musical phrase in an ensemble class rehearsal. Fixed ratio schedules tend to produce high-response rates because the more rapidly the student responds meeting the standard of execution, the earlier the reinforcement is given.

Variable Ratio Schedule

Variable Ratio Schedules have been found to work best under many circumstances because the reinforcement is applied after a variable number of responses from one time to the next occasion. If you used a variable ratio schedule, you may reinforce a response after the eleventh, sixth, sixteenth, ninth, twentieth, third, eighth, and nineteenth corresponding occurrence of the behavior. As the occurrence of reinforcement is so unpredictable, learners tend to respond fairly rapidly for long periods of time.

Imagine walking into a casino and heading for the slot machines. After the third coin you put into the machine, you get two back. Two more coins and you get three back. Another five coins and you receive two more back. How difficult is it to stop playing?

In a marching band rehearsal, the band director awards students a piece of candy for successfully executing seven consecutive marching fundamentals verbally commanded during a block band marching contest (i.e., march-off). Unsuccessful students are dismissed from the formation to the sideline. Continuing the competition, the director awards remaining students a slice of free pizza at lunchtime for correctly executing thirteen successive marching maneuvers quickly commanded to the block band. As this sequence eliminates all but three students, the music teacher continues the rivalry by rapidly calling a series of nine commands for a variety of intricate, simple, and moderately complex marching moves for student execution. With two students dismissed for imprecise performance, the director rewards the lone-standing student with two complimentary tickets to a local movie theatre and the esteemed honor of being "Champion Marcher" for the day. The director reminds all students that the band will have a similar "march-off" at an undetermined time later in the week.

Learning Based upon Environmental Control

Since 1950, behavioral psychologists have produced a vast amount of research mostly directed at understanding how behavior is developed and maintained.[12] The research of Clifford Madsen, Robert Duke, Harry Price, and Cornelia Yarbrough builds on the operant conditioning model focusing on guiding "good" or "successful" teaching. Here, the role of appropriate and inappropriate reinforcement is integral to understanding learning behaviors. In this regard, researchers in music education (e.g., Duke & Henninger, 1998; Madsen & Duke, 1985) have looked at a wide variety of issues regarding the effect of reinforcement (praise) and feedback (verbal corrections) on music discrimination, attitude, and performance. In addition, the use of music itself serving as a mechanism of reinforcement has been studied, among others, by Greer (1981) and Madsen (1981).[13]

Madsen began investigating behavioral modification approaches to learning based upon environmental control of behavior in the music classroom. According to Madsen, behavior is modified by explicitly arranging the consequences of responses based upon reinforcement principles.[14] As students' successes and failures can be directly attributed to teacher effectiveness, the ability to understand how each student learns will often determine the overall effectiveness of the teacher. Since a teacher will only be effective if s/he is able to get the desired responses from students, successfully interacting with students must be developed in order to become a good teacher (Madsen & Yarbrough, 1985). A positive student/teacher interaction should be a goal for all music educators (Madsen & Yarbrough, 1985).[15]

Teacher Feedback

Teacher approval may be the most important aspect of teacher/student interaction (Madsen, 1982; Madsen & Duke, 1987; Marlow, Madsen, Bowen, Reardon, & Louge, 1978)[16] and perhaps accounts for differences in the teaching effectiveness of music educators (Madsen & Madsen, 1998).[17] Feedback from the teacher has been considered a critical component of effective teaching. A person's ability to give and receive appropriate feedback from other individuals appears to be a basic and requisite skill for effective human interaction ... of great importance to a teacher in order to further a student's academic grasp of the subject matter as well as in shaping socially acceptable behavior (Madsen & Duke, 1985, p. 119).[18]

The effects of praise may be bolstered when the praise describes a specific desired behavior and is combined with other strategies. Providing contingent praise along with either established classroom rules (Becker, Madsen, & Arnold, 1967)[19] or classroom rules while ignoring inappropriate behavior (Yawkey, 1971)[20] increases appropriate classroom behavior. Generally, desired academic and social behavior can be increased by providing specific and contingent praise, and establishing classroom expectations.

Student Attentiveness

Student attentiveness or student on-/off-task behavior has been researched extensively.

If student on-task behavior is a measurement of the teacher's effectiveness, the most effective teachers maintain high levels of student attentiveness in the classroom to achieve optimal learning outcomes. Research in the field of music has provided evidence that student learning suffers when off-task behavior exceeds 20% (Madsen, Becker, & Thomas, 1968).[21] It has also been suggested that student off-task behavior decreases when teacher approval is high (Dorow, 1977; Forsythe, 1975; Hall, Lund, & Jackson, 1968; Kuhn, 1975)[22] and that students are more on-task when they are engaging in performance versus nonperformance activities (Brendell, 1996; Madsen & Geringer, 1983; Murray, 1975; Spradling, 1985; Yarbrough & Price, 1981), suggesting that music may be intrinsically reinforcing.[23] Likewise, Forsythe (1975) and Kuhn (1975) concluded that approving reinforcement for social and academic behaviors increases the amount of on-task student behavior.[24]

Research studies have revealed that teachers who maintain a higher rate of approval within the classroom in turn maintain a higher rate of student attentiveness (Hall, et al., 1968; Madsen, Becker, & Thomas, 1968).[25] Within the music classroom, many types of activities are accomplished; some are high activity and some are more passive or transitional. While music education students can identify the need for approving feedback (Madsen & Duke, 1985a), specific training on behavioral feedback appears to increase the effectiveness of approval statements (Madsen & Duke, 1985b).[26] As it appears that training and experience also affects teachers' abilities to identify and offer appropriate feedback,[27] behavioral training can increase specific and verbal approval feedback (Madsen & Duke, 1987).[28]

Behavioral Modification

Behavior modification refers to the use of operant conditioning techniques to modify behavior. The first use of the term behavior modification appears to have been by Edward Thorndike in 1911.[29] After Skinner and others examined methods of operant conditioning in modifying the behavior of animals, they concluded that similar techniques could be used with humans. Behavioral change techniques such as altering an individual's behavior and reaction to stimuli through positive and negative reinforcement to increase the frequency of behavior and/or through punishment or extinction to reduce behaviors were used to modify human behavior. Most attempts at shaping important classroom behavior should include at least the following steps:[30]

1 Select a target behavior.
2 Determine how often the target behavior occurs (i.e., collect data to record a reliable baseline).
3 Select potential reinforcers.
4 Reinforce successive approximation of the target behavior each time it occurs.
5 Reinforce the newly established target behavior each time it occurs.
6 Reinforce the target behavior on a variable reinforcement schedule.

Reinforcers in the Classroom

In the music classroom, there are many types of reinforcers. Elementary music teachers may use a smile, verbal praise, classroom privileges, or token rewards such as a piece of candy or musical sticker to shape student behavior. Middle and high school music teachers can use verbal responses, numerical or letter grades, public praise, and private reprimand to bring about desirable behaviors and sometimes eliminate those that are less desirable.

Within the performance-based music classroom, the music director typically provides individual students, groups of students (i.e., sections of the ensemble), and the full ensemble a large number of reinforcers, in the form of verbal and nonverbal feedback, throughout the class rehearsal. The director can give a thumbs up or an exasperated look at a section providing instant feedback to the students about their performance of an excerpt in the musical selection. The music teacher may also provide praise or admonish the students by using a smile or frown, and other nonverbal indicators of approval or disapproval to provide instant feedback regarding typical students' behavior in any music classroom (e.g., talking, posture, participation, disruption, etc.).

A good rule of practice is to set four to five clear behavioral objectives that have specific consequence for the class to elicit appropriate behaviors from the students. Being consistent and immediate with reinforcers will aid in shaping student behavior. Over time, variable ratio schedules of reinforcement may be appropriate in keeping desired student behavior in check.

Generally, behaviors such as remaining attentive and engaged that receive a "Thank you for being so attentive!" will be learned; those behaviors that receive a "Those who keep talking will not be dismissed early today," or maybe briefly ignored, will not be learned. If certain negative behaviors persist, the director would conference with a student outside of class should punishment (e.g., detention) be needed as a reinforcer to deter the unacceptable behavior.

Classroom Management Is about Organization

Classroom management is not about discipline. It is about organization and consistency. Effective teachers have a classroom management plan consisting of a series of practices and procedures that are used to maintain an environment in which instruction and learning can take place. They prevent problems with a plan that keeps their students focused and on task from the moment the opening bell sounds until the end of each day. This is done with procedures, which simplify the tasks students must accomplish to increase learning and achievement. Once taught, procedures become the responsibility of the students to carry out at the appropriate times. A well-managed classroom is safe, predictable, nurturing, and focus-driven.[31]

Organize Your Space

Organize your room with the correct number of chairs and stands. It is important to set up the room with aisles for you to be able to get off the podium and move about the room during the class. Your proximity among students monitors student behavior and sees the rehearsal from the students' perspective.

Keep your room clean and organized. Have a place for everything including tuners, metronome, music, and everything needed for music instruction. Put the class objective and agenda on the board so students know what to set up for when they enter the room. Students crave and need structure to be productive during class. They like the safe feeling of knowing what to expect and how they are expected to conduct themselves during musical rehearsal and activities.

Set Clear Expectations

When introducing expectations to students, explain and show them how you expect them to complete each task, including entering the room, where to build instruments, where to store cases, how to set up music stands, and the routine of musical warm-up and rehearsal. Consistently require that routines are properly completed each time to become habits for you and your students.

Make clear rules and enforce them consistently. Discuss your rules and expectations with students. Let them know the consequences for breaking each rule or unmet expectation. Follow through with the consequences you establish and acknowledge when students follow the rules. Here are examples of expectations in the music classroom.

1 Come prepared for class (with music, instrument, and home practice).
2 Be seated with music, instrument, etc. to begin class promptly after the bell.
3 Raise your hand for comments and questions.
4 Treat others the way you want to be treated.
5 Show respect for music, materials, and instruments.

Play More, Talk Less

Students are in music to make music. The more they sing or play, the more they will like it. When stopping, make corrections using three short statements addressing who, where, and what. For example, altos, measure 15, raise your soft palate to improve the resonance of the phrase. After making brief corrections, get students re-engaged in making music. It is also very effective to model the correction by singing or playing on your instrument. Every stop should be 20 seconds at most.

Questions

1 Describe how Behaviorism was different from previous approaches or philosophical movements.
2 Define learning in behavioral terms.
3 Describe Classical Conditioning and Operant Conditioning. What are the principal differences between Classical and Operant Conditioning?
4 Describe the underlying principle of Thorndike's *Law of Effect*.
5 How was B. F. Skinner's *Operant Conditioning* different from other behavioral theories?
6 Define each type of behavioral reinforcement. Describe applications of each reinforcement in the music classroom.
7 Define each schedule of reinforcement. Describe applications of schedules of reinforcement in the music classroom.
8 What relevance does Behavioral Modification have to the music classroom? Describe a hypothetical situation in which a behavioral modification plan may be implemented with an individual student or in the music classroom setting. Remember to include the target behavior to be shaped, potential reinforcers, and standards of accountability in your example.
9 List five behavioral objectives you may use in your (future) music classroom. Include your plan of consequence accountability in your expectations.
10 Explain the statement, "Classroom Management is about Organization."

Notes

1 MSN Encarta. (2011, June 6). Retrieved from http://encarta.msn.com/encnet/features/dictionary/DictionaryResults.aspx?lextype=3&search=reinforcer
2 All PsychONLINE: The Virtual Psychology Classroom. (2011, June 6). Psychology 101. Retrieved from http://allpsych.com/psychology101/learning.html
3 LeFrancois, G. A. (2000). *Psychology for teaching*. Belmont, CA: Wadsworth/Thomson Learning.
4 Graham, G. (2013). Behaviorism. In E. N. Zalta (ed.), *The Stanford Encyclopedia of Philosophy* (Fall 2010 ed.), Retrieved from http://plato.stanford.edu/archives/fall2010/entries/behaviorism/
5 Pavlov, I. P. (1927/1960). *Conditional reflexes*. New York: Dover Publications (the 1960 edition is not an unaltered republication of the 1927 translation by Oxford University Press). Retrieved from http://psychclassics.yorku.ca/Pavlov/
6 Thomson, G. (1949). Professor Edward L. Thorndike. *Nature, 164*, 474. Doi: 10.1038/164474a0.
7 Thorndike, E. L. (1898). Animal intelligence: An experimental study of the associative processes in animals. *Psychological Monographs: General and Applied, 2*(4), i–109.
8 Snowman, J., McCown, R., & Biehler, R. (2009). *Applying psychology to teaching* (p. 221). Boston, MA: Houghton Mifflin Company.
9 Schacter, D. L., Gilbert, D. T., & Wegner, D. M. (2011). *Psychology* (2 ed.), New York: Worth Publishers.
10 Flora, S. (2004). *The power of reinforcement*. Albany, GA: State University of New Press.
11 Skinner, B. F. (1974). *About Behaviorism*. New York: Knopf.
   Cherry, K. (2013). *What is punishment?* About.com-Psychology. Retrieved July 18, 2013, from http://psychology.about.com/od/operantconditioning/f/punishment.htm

12 Madsen, C. K. (1968). A behavioral approach to music therapy. *Journal of Music Therapy, 5*(3), 15–23.

13 Duke, R. A., & Henninger, J. (1998). Effects of verbal corrections on student attitude and performance. *Journal of Research in Music Education, 46*(4), 482–495.

    Madsen, C. K., & Duke, R. A. (1985). Perception of approval/disapproval in music education. *Bulletin of the Council for Research in Music Education, 85*, 119–130.

    Greer, R. D. (1981). An operant approach to motivation and affect: Ten years of research in music learning. In J. A. Mason (Ed.), *Documentary report of the Ann Arbor Symposium.* Reston, VA: Music Educators National Conference.

    Madsen, C. K. (1981). Music lessons and books as reinforcement alternatives for an academic task. *Journal of Research in Music Education, 29*(2), 103–110.

    Colwell, R., & Richardson, C. (2002). *The new handbook of research in music teaching and learning. A project of the music educators national conference* (p. 281). New York: Oxford University Press.

14 Madsen, C. K. (1971). Music and behavior: How reinforcement techniques work. *Music Educator Journal, 57*(8), 38–41.

15 Madsen, C. K., & Yarbrough, C. (1985). *Competency-based music education.* Raleigh, NC: Contemporary Publishing.

16 Madsen, C. K. (1982). The effect of contingent teacher approval and withholding performance on improved attentiveness. *Psychology of Music, Special Issue,* 76–81.

    Madsen, C. K., & Duke, R. A. (1987). The effect of teacher training on the ability to recognize need for giving approval for appropriate student behavior. *Bulletin of the Council for Research in Music Education,* 91, 103–109.

    Marlow, R. H., Madsen, Jr., C. H., Bowen, C. E., Reardon, R. C., & Louge, P. E. (1978). Sever classroom problems: Teachers as counselors. *Journal of Applied Behavioral Analysis,* 11, 53–66.

17 Madsen, Jr., C. H., & Madsen, C. K. (1998). *Teaching discipline: A positive approach for educational development* (4th ed.), Raleigh, NC: Contemporary Publishing.

18 Madsen, C. K., & Duke, R. A. (1985). Perception of approval/disapproval in music education. *Bulletin of the Council for Research in Music Education, 85*, 119–129.

19 Becker, W. C., Madsen, C. H., & Arnold, C. (1967). The contingent use of teacher attention and praise in reducing classroom behavior problems. *Journal of Special Education, 1*(3), 287–307.

20 Yawkey, T. (1971). Conditioning independent work behavior in reading with seven-year-old children in a regular early childhood classroom. *Child Study Journal, 2*(1), 23–34.

21 Madsen, Jr., C. H., Becker, W. C., & Thomas, D. R. (1968). Rules, praise, and ignoring: Elements of elementary classroom control. *Journal of Applied Behavior Analysis, 1*(2), 139–150.

22 Dorow, L. (1977). The effect of teacher approval disapproval ratios on student music selection and concert attentiveness. *Journal of Research in Music Education, 25*(1), 32–40.

    Hall, R. V., Lund, D., & Jackson, D. (1968). Effects of teacher attention on study behavior. *Journal of Applied Behavior Analysis, 1*, 1–12.

    Forsythe, J. L. (1975). The effect of teacher approval, disapproval, and errors on student attentiveness: Music versus classroom teachers. In C. K. Madsen, R. D. Greer, & C. H. Madsen, Jr. (Eds.), *Research in music behavior: Modifying music behavior in the classroom.* New York: College Teaching Press.

    Kuhn, T. L. (1975). The effect of teacher approval and disapproval on attentiveness, musical achievement, and attitude of fifth grade students. In C. K. Madsen, R. D. Greer, & C. H. Madsen, Jr. (Eds.), *Research in music behavior: Modifying music behavior in the classroom.* New York: College Teaching Press.

23 Brendell, J. K. (1996). Time use, rehearsal activity, and student off-task behavior during initial minutes of high school choral rehearsals. *Journal of Research in Music Education, 44*(1), 6–14.

    Madsen, C. K., & Geringer, J. M. (1983). Attending behavior as a function of in-class activity in university music classes. *Journal of Music Therapy, 20*(1), 30–38.

    Murray, K. (1975). The effect of teacher/approval on the performance level, attentiveness, and attitude of high school choruses. In C. K. Madsen, R. D. Greer, & C. H. Madsen. Jr. (Eds.), *Research in music behavior* (pp. 165–180). New York: College Teachers Press.

Spradling, R. A. (1985). The effect of timeout from performance on attentiveness and attitude of university band students. *Journal of Research in Music Education, 32*(2), 123–137.

Yarbrough, C., & Price, H. E. (1981). Prediction of performer attentiveness based on rehearsal activity and teacher behavior. *Journal of Research in Music Education, 29,* 209–217.

24 Forsythe, J. L. (1975). The effect of teacher approval, disapproval, and errors on student attentiveness: Music versus classroom teachers. In C. K. Madsen, R. D. Greer, & C. H. Madsen, Jr. (Eds.), *Research in music behavior: Modifying music behavior in the classroom.* New York: College Teaching Press.

Kuhn, T. L. (1975). The effect of teacher approval and disapproval on attentiveness, musical achievement, and attitude of fifth grade students. In C. K. Madsen, R. D. Greer, & C. H. Madsen, Jr. (Eds.), *Research in music behavior: Modifying music behavior in the classroom.* New York: College Teaching Press.

25 Hall, R. V., Lund, D., & Jackson, D. (1968). Effects of teacher attention on study behavior. *Journal of Applied Behavior Analysis, 1,* 1–12.

Madsen, Jr., C. H., Becker, W. C., & Thomas, D. R. (1968). Rules, praise, and ignoring: Elements of elementary classroom control. *Journal of Applied Behavior Analysis, 1*(2), 139–150.

26 Madsen, C. K., & Duke, R. A. (1985a). Perception of approval/disapproval in music education. *Bulletin of the Council for Research in Music Education, 85,* 119–129.

Madsen, C. K., & Duke, R. A. (1985b). Observation of approval/disapproval in music: Perception versus actual classroom events. *Journal of Research in Music Education, 33,* 205–214.

27 Juchniewicz, J. (2008). The influence of social intelligence on effective music teaching. Doctoral Dissertation, Florida State University. Tallahassee, Florida.

28 Madsen, C. K., & Duke, R. A. (1987). The effect of teacher training on the ability to recognize need for giving approval for appropriate student behavior. *Bulletin of the Council for Research in Music Education, 91,* 103–109.

29 Thorndike, E. L. (1911). Provisional laws of acquired behavior or learning. *Animal Intelligence.* New York: The McMillian Company. Retrieved July 27, 2013, from http://archive. org/stream/animalintelligen00thor/animalintelligen00thor_djvu.txt

30 Miltenberger, R. G. (2004). *Behavior modification: Principles and procedures.* Belmont, CA: Wadsworth/Thompson Learning.

Walker, J. E., Shea, T. M., & Bauer, A. M. (2007). *Behavior management: A practical approach for educators* (9th ed.), Upper Saddle River, NJ: Pearson/Merrell Prentice Hall.

31 Scholastic. (2020). *Classroom Management 1 From Day One.* Retrieved June 6, 2020, from https://www.scholastic.com/teachers/articles/teaching-content/classroom-management-day-one/

Chapter 4

Cognitivism

Learning Theory and Applications to Teaching

Cognitive theories grew out of Gestalt psychology. Gestalt psychologists believed that learning takes place by making sense of the relationship between what is new and what is known. Cognitivism is a theoretical framework for understanding the mind. Cognitive theory focuses on conceptualizing the student's learning process: how information is received, how information is processed and organized, and how information is retrieved upon recall. Learning is not about the mechanics of what a learner does, but rather a process depending on what the learner already knows (existing information) and their method of acquiring new knowledge. Constructivism emphasizes the importance of the active involvement of learners in constructing knowledge for themselves. The learning theories of John Dewey, Maria Montessori, Jerome Bruner, and others serve as the foundation of the application of constructivist learning theory in the classroom.

Learning Objectives

1 What are the key principles of Gestalt Learning Theory?
2 What are the components of Cognitive Theory? What are the Stages of Piaget's Theory?
3 What are the differences between Constructivism and Constructionism?
4 What are the fundamental tenets of Bruner's Stages of Cognitive Development and Discovery Learning?

Music teachers employing cognitive applications in the classroom focus on the intellectual or mental aspects of learning. Cognition is a faculty for the processing of information, applying knowledge, and changing preferences.[1] Cognitive approaches deal mainly with cognition or knowing.

> The choral director clearly states goals at the beginning of the chorus class, reviewing information covered from the previous day's class. She then presents a series of short, detailed, and explicit steps to introduce new material that includes systematic feedback to students, and ample time for individual and group practice during the class period. The director may begin with review of the d minor tonality by leading the class through a variety of solfeggio hand sign and vocalize exercises and then lead the choir through select passages in d minor in the composition in which the ensemble is currently working.

Gestalt Learning Theory

Early cognitive views placed emphasis not on the acquisition of a new behavior (Behaviorism) but on the perception and understanding of relationships within an

DOI: 10.4324/9781003038474-6

organized whole. Wolfgang Köhler, Kurt Koffka, and Max Wertheimer were among the principal advocates of Gestalt theory that emphasized higher-order cognitive processes in the midst of behaviorism.[2]

Gestalt theorists believed that for learning to occur, prior knowledge must exist on the topic. When the learner applies their prior knowledge to the advanced topic, the learner can understand the meaning of the advanced topic, and learning can occur. Learning was considered to be a product of perception and what was learned was determined by the hypothesized laws of perceptual organization. Learning depended on the learner doing or achieving something.

Gestalt means "whole" and refers to an organized configuration or pattern, the parts of which are subordinate to the existence of the whole and which are perceived in relation to the whole. Kurt Koffka's most notable contribution appears in his text Principles of Gestalt Psychology (1935).[3] Koffka's *Law of Prägnanz* states that an individual always seeks to organize incoming sensory information in the simplest and best manner possible according to a set of subsidiary principles such proximity, similarity, common direction, simplicity, and closure.

> *The Law of Proximity* asserts that sensory phenomena are grouped according to their nearness to one another. The *Gigue* from *J. S. Bach's Suite no. 2 for Unaccompanied Cello* is a clear musical example of *proximity* in that the closeness of the notes creates the illusion that multiple parts are present simultaneously.
> *The Law of Similarity* maintains that phenomena that are similar in color, shape, texture, form, and the like will be grouped together. The sounds of the brass section, as other sections, share similar timbral qualities and are often grouped on the basis of similarity.
> *The Law of Common Direction* asserts that people tend to group phenomena on the basis of direction that they perceive the phenomena to lead. A descending melodic passage performed by the principal clarinet, tenor sax, horn, and trombone would be grouped together according to this principle.
> *The Law of Simplicity* affirms that people organize phenomena into simple figures according to symmetry, regularity, and smoothness. The performance of a lyrical quarter-note melody by the low brass section would be grouped by simplicity when orchestrated over the complex 16th-note passages of the accompanying woodwinds and high brass.
> *The Law of Closure* refers to perceptual restructuring that leads to a moment when all the pieces come together and the light goes on. (!) The Aha! Moment. Perhaps the most obvious example of musical closure is the cadence (e.g., V–I), which brings a musical idea to completion.

According to the Gestalt viewpoint, "learning is the organization and re-organization of behavior which arises from the interaction of a maturing organism and its environment."[4] Gestalt theory of learning essentially consists in problem-solving by understanding the relative position of the elements in the entire perspective or situation.

Wolfgang Köhler designed a series of problem situations for chimpanzees in which every one of the elements that were needed for a solution was clearly visible to the animals. In one famous experiment with a chimp named Sultan, Köhler placed bananas some distance outside the bars of the large chimp's enclosure. But lying nearby inside the cage were two bamboo poles, each itself too small to reach the bananas. Sultan first tried to reach the bananas through the bars using one stick, then the other. He tried to push a nearby box through the bars but quickly got it out of the way as useless.

After an hour Köhler abandoned the test and left Sultan to play. Only hours later did a keeper watch Sultan pick up the two sticks, eventually placing the thinner stick lengthwise into the opening of the other thicker stick. Joining both sticks together, Sultan used the fused bamboo poles to draw the bananas toward him.[5]

From this and similar experiments, Köhler drew the conclusion that learning takes place through an act of insight. The learner must be familiar with the elements that make up the problem and its solution. The learner seems to mentally manage the meaningful elements until suddenly a "mental connection" is made, the solution is seen, and the learner can be put into action.[6] The individual does not perform random activities, but perceives the situation as a whole, and intuitively reaches the goal. Insight is often called as the 'Aha' experience, the flash of understanding that comes to us all of a sudden.[4]

Cognitive Learning Theory

The word "cognition" was used to define "thinking and awareness" as early as the 15th century.[7] Aristotle was the first to devote attention to the cognitive process, focusing on cognitive areas pertaining to memory, perception, and mental imagery. The Greek philosopher found great importance in ensuring that his studies were based on scientific information gathered through thorough observation and scientific experimentation.[8]

Cognition involves the acquisition, storage, retrieval, and use of knowledge obtained through the sensory and perceptual systems. From an information processing perspective, there are three main stages in the formation and retrieval of memory:

- *Encoding* or registration (processing and combining of received information).
- *Storage* (creation of a permanent record of the encoded information).
- *Retrieval* or *recall* (calling back the stored information in response to some cue for use in a process or activity).

Parallels can be drawn between these human cognitive processes and the functions of a computer in processing information. When you type on the computer keyboard to enter information, the computer encodes the received information. Saving the information on the computer desktop or in a folder on the hard drive, creating a permanent record of the encoded information. When you return to the file on a later date, you can retrieve the information for use in infinite ways from changing the information to cutting and pasting it into another document to adding additional information that has much deeper, complex meaning.

Human memories give a person the capability to learn and adapt from previous experiences as well as build relationships. From birth and leading into elementary school, the child assimilates and interprets new musical ideas based on his/her musical experiences with parents, family members, and music teachers. Through the lullabies of parents, the early childhood songs of family, and the other musical experiences of his/her preschool environment, the child develops musical knowledge. In the course of the musical experiences, the child is an active participant, constantly generating expectations based on past experience and interpreting auditory information on the basis of immediately preceding sounds (Hodges, 1996).[9]

Cognition-oriented researchers attempt to understand the nature of information. They are interested in how learners acquire information and how learners organize the information. How learners recall, modify, apply, and analyze this information have importance in determining how learners understand, evaluate, and control the activities involved in cognition. *Cognitive theorists* are concerned with how we develop our fund of knowledge and how we eventually arrive at notions of ourselves as learners, rememberers, and problem-solvers. Their attention is focused on the strategies children can use to acquire and process information and ability to evaluate their own cognitive activities in this process. In general terms, these theories have found that learners who recognize that they do not know something and are aware that they remember things better when they write them down or have decided that a particular other method of study works for them are demonstrating *Metacognitive Behavior.*

Basic Principles of Piaget's Theory

Jean Piaget[10] (1896–1980), shown in Figure 4.1, was a Swiss biologist, philosopher, and psychologist best known for his work in the area of developmental psychology. His particular focus was on the intellectual or cognitive development of children and on the way in which their minds processed and progressed in knowledge. Piaget's extensive work with children revealed many insights about what happens as children move through these stages of development.

Figure 4.1 Jean Piaget, Psychologist.

CC BY-SA 4.0 <https://creativecommons.org/licenses/by-sa/4.0>, via Wikimedia Commons.

Piaget believed that intellectual development was a process of adapting rather than a level of ability, and was based on two ongoing biological processes found in all organisms, assimilation, and accommodation. *Assimilation* is the tendency of individuals to integrate experiences into an existing coherent system or schema. *Accommodation* is the tendency to interact with the environment through curious investigative activity and adaptation by the child in order to modify existing schema with the new object or event. When a child interacts with the environment, s/he either assimilates the experience with previous learning or s/he adapts to accommodate the new experience.

Piaget developed the concept of *Equilibrium* to represent a state of balance between a child's mental schemata or coherent systems, and his/her environment. Such balance occurs when one's expectations, based on prior knowledge, fit with new knowledge. He described equilibration as an ongoing process intended to refine and transform mental structures, which is the basis for cognitive development.

Whenever a child's experience (i.e., interaction with the environment) aligns with previous coherent systems of knowledge, she can easily assimilate the experience and is in equilibrium. However, when the child's interaction with the environment results in a new and unexpected experience, she is in disequilibrium. The child is confused and frustrated in not making sense of the experience. Eventually, she will adapt or change her cognitive structures to accommodate or account for the new experience and move back into equilibrium. Individuals naturally seek equilibrium because disequilibrium is inherently dissatisfying.

Schema

Piaget defined a schema as the mental representation of an associated set of perceptions, ideas, and/or actions. Piaget considered schemata to be the basic building blocks of thinking (Woolfolk, 1987).[11] In Piaget's view, a schema includes both a category of knowledge and the process of obtaining that knowledge. A schema describes both the mental and physical actions involved in understanding and knowing. Schemata are categories of knowledge that help us to interpret and understand the world. As experiences happen, this new information is used to modify, add to, or change previously existing schemas.

A schema may be as specific as recognizing a type of instrument such as a trumpet, or as elaborate as categorizing different types of instruments. If a child's sole experience has been with trumpets, he might believe that all instruments are small, metal, and have three valves. Suppose then that the child encounters a bassoon. The child will take in this new information, modifying the previously existing schema to include this new information. As cognitive development proceeds, new schemata are developed, and existing schemata are more efficiently organized to adapt to the environment.

Stages of Cognitive Development

Jean Piaget's extensive work with children revealed many insights regarding human children as they move through certain stages in cognitive development. After studying his own and many other children, Piaget postulated a series of stages of intellectual development beginning at birth and progressing through adolescence. Development through these stages was considered *invariant*, that is, progress at a higher level is difficult without first achieving the desired level of development at a lower level. These stages correspond roughly to various age periods of the child. Piaget generalized these stages as:

- The *Sensorimotor Stage* (birth-age 2) in which learning is acquired through motor activities and manipulation of objects. The child interacts with environment through physical actions (e.g., sucking, pushing, grabbing, shaking, etc.).
- The *Preoperational Stage* (ages 2–7) involves language acquisition and developing the ability to distinguish actual objects or events from symbols used to represent objects or events. The child is not yet able to form abstract conceptions, must have hands-on experiences and visual representations in order to form basic conclusions.
- The *Concrete Operational Stage* (ages 7–11) is characterized by increasing ability to classify objects and events and the relationships existing therein. The child begins to draw on a knowledge base from physical experiences to make more sophisticated explanations and predictions. There is growth in the child's language skills, quantitative ability, some abstract problem-solving, and the use of *conservation* are evident.

  - *Conservation* refers to the child's ability to recognize that objects originally perceived as wholes remain essentially unaltered in spite of the fact that the shape of the whole or parts of the whole may be rearranged.

- The *Formal Operations Stage* is characterized by those thought processes typical of the adult. The child's knowledge base and cognitive structures are much more similar to those of an adult. The child's ability for abstract thought increases markedly.

During the 1970s and 1980s, Piaget's works inspired the transformation of European and American education, including both theory and practice, leading to a more 'child-centered' approach. Piaget defined knowledge as the ability to modify, transform, and "operate on" an object or idea, such that it is understood by the operator through the process of transformation. In Piaget's view, learning takes place as a result of our experience, both physical and logical, with the objects themselves and how we interact with them.[12]

Constructivism

Constructivism is a theory of knowledge that argues that humans generate knowledge and meaning from an interaction between their experiences and their ideas.[13] The theory of constructivism suggests that learners construct knowledge out of their experiences. Whether the learner uses his/her experience to understand a lecture or follow the instructions for singing a melody using solfeggio syllables, *Constructivism* describes how learning occurs in individuals.

Piaget's theory about how young learners construct their knowledge structures inspired the *Constructivist Movement*. He articulated mechanisms by which knowledge is internalized by learners and called these systems of knowledge *schemata*. Piaget suggested that through processes of *accommodation* and *assimilation*, individuals construct new knowledge from their experiences. Constructivism is often associated with pedagogic approaches that promote active learning or learning by doing. Piaget's theory of constructivist learning has had wide-ranging impact on learning theories and teaching methods in education.

Writers who influenced constructivism include:

- John Dewey (1859–1952)
- Maria Montessori (1870–1952)

- Lev Vygotsky (1896–1934)
- Heinz von Foerster (1911–2002)
- George Kelly (1905–1967)
- Jerome Bruner (1915–2016)
- Herbert Simon (1916–2001)
- Paul Watzlawick (1921–2007)
- Ernst von Glasersfeld (1917–2010)

Constructionism

Seymour Aubrey Papert (1928–), an MIT mathematician, computer scientist, and educator, developed a theory of learning called *Constructionism*. Papert had worked with Jean Piaget at the University of Geneva from 1958 to 1963[14] and is widely considered the most brilliant and successful of Piaget's protégés. Papert based his learning theory of *Constructionism* upon the work of Piaget in Constructivism theory in which learners construct mental models to understand the world. However, *Constructionism* is connected to *Experiential Learning* and contends that learning can happen most effectively when people are also active in making tangible objects in the real world.[15] *Experiential learning* is the process of making meaning from direct experience (i.e., learning through reflection on doing; learning from experience).[16]

From constructivist theories, Seymour Papert defined Constructionism learning as a reconstruction rather than a transmission of knowledge. "Then we extend the idea of manipulative materials to the idea that learning is most effective when part of an activity the learner experiences as constructing is a meaningful product."[17] While constructionism has been primarily used in science and mathematics teaching, it has also been developed in a different form in the field of media studies in which students often engage with media theory and practice simultaneously, in a complementary praxis.

The Difference between Constructivism and Constructionism

Piaget's Constructivism offers a window into what children are interested in, and able to achieve, at different stages of their development. The theory describes how children's ways of doing and thinking evolve over time, and under which circumstances children are more likely to let go of—or hold onto—their currently held views.

> Constructivist teaching is based on the belief that learning occurs as learners are actively involved in a process of meaning and knowledge construction as opposed to passively receiving information. Learners are the makers of meaning and knowledge. Constructivist teaching fosters critical thinking and creates motivated and independent learners.

Papert's Constructionism, in contrast, stems from the constructivist model, adds that students learn best when they are able to "construct" a tangible product in which they can share with others. Constructionism focuses more on the "art of learning," or "learning to learn," and on the significance of making things in learning. Papert stresses the importance of tools, media, and the processes by which individuals come to make sense of their experience, gradually optimizing their interactions with the world. Students learn from creating and constructing concepts into objects or products that are relevant to their lives (Orey, 2001).[18]

Constructivism and Discovery Learning (Jerome Bruner)

Jerome Bruner (1915–2016), a Harvard-educated psychologist who has been very influential among educators in the 1960s, was influenced by Piaget's ideas about cognitive development in children. During the 1940s, his early work focused on the impact of needs, motivations, and expectations, and their influence on perception. He presented the point of view that children are active problem-solvers and capable of exploring difficult subjects.

Bruner's theoretical framework proposes that learners construct new ideas or concepts based upon existing knowledge. He views people as being active in the process of learning, continually structuring and restructuring their environment. Bruner believes that people selectively perceive certain aspects of their environment, represent those perceptions internally, and then act on those internal representations. Learning is an active process. Facets of the process include selection and transformation of information, decision-making, generating hypotheses, and making meaning from information and experiences.

Bruner has been a prime proponent of the *Discovery Learning* approach. *Discovery learning* provides the opportunity for students to construct their own meaning rather than simply memorizing the meaning someone else has assigned to something. *Discovery learning* has students as active, engaged participants in the process, which also enhances their intrinsic motivation for learning. In this approach, students may be presented with a problem and some evidence: they must seek to reconcile that information and "discover" the solution to the problem. *Discovery learning* is also more resistant to forgetting. When students are actively engaged in *discovery learning*, there are also much less likely to be disruptive or "problem students" in the classroom.

Jerome Bruner's Three Stages of Cognitive Development

In his research on the cognitive development of children, Bruner proposed a course of cognitive development in which a child progressively develops three modes of representation.[19] Modes of representation are the way in which information or knowledge are stored and encoded in memory. Rather than age-related stages, as Piaget, the modes of representation are integrated and loosely sequential as they transform into each other. The mode of instruction should match the mode that the learner is using in order to be successful.

Enactive Stage (from birth to about age 3).
Children perceive the environment solely through actions that they initiate. They describe and explain objects solely in terms of what a child can do with them. The child cannot tell how a clarinet works but can show what to do with it. Showing and modeling have more learning value than telling for children at this stage.
Iconic Stage (from about age 3 to about age 7).
Children can remember and use information through imagery such as mental pictures or icons. Visual memory increases and children can imagine or think about actions without actually experiencing them. Decisions are still made on the basis of perceptions, rather than language.
Symbolic Stage (from about age 7).
Children begin to use symbols such as words or draw pictures to represent people, activities, and things. They have the ability to think and talk about things in abstract terms. They can also use and understand what Gagné[20] would call "defined

concepts." For example, they can discuss the concept of drums and identify various kinds of drums, rather than defining them only in terms of drums they have seen or handled. They can better understand mathematical principles and use symbolic idioms such as "Don't cry over spilt milk."

Six Indicators (Benchmarks) Revealing Cognitive Development

Bruner identified six indicators or benchmarks that revealed cognitive growth or development:

1 Responding to situations in varied ways, rather than always in the same way.
2 Internalizing events into a "storage system" that corresponds to the environment.
3 Having increased capacity for language.
4 Systematically interaction with a tutor (e.g., parent, teacher, or other role models).
5 Using language as an instrument for ordering the environment.
6 Increasing capacity to deal with multiple demands.

Information Processing Learning Theory

Information processing theory seeks to explain how the mind functions.[21] Broadbent and others in the 1950s adopted a model of the brain as a limited capacity information processing system, through which external input is transmitted.[22] Information processing theory is based on the principle that humans process information they receive, rather than responding to stimuli. According to the standard information-processing model for mental development, the human's mental structure includes attention capacity for bringing information in, working memory for actively manipulating information, and Long-Term Memory for passively holding information so that it can be used in the future.[23]

Information processing theory accounts for mental development in terms of maturation changes in basic parts of the mind. This theory addresses how as children grow, their brains likewise mature, leading to advances in their ability to process and respond to the information received through their senses. This cognitive processing theory emphasizes a continuous pattern of development; in contrast to Jean Piaget's cognitive stage development theory that proposes that thought development occurs in stages.

At the center of Information Processing Theory is its proposed memory system. As mentioned, this theory uses the computer metaphor to represent human mental processes. The cognitive information-processing model has three components: *Sensory Register Memory, Short-Term Memory* (working memory), and *Long-Term Memory.*

Sensory Register Memory

Sensory register memory processes incoming information associated with the senses (e.g., vision, hearing) just long enough for the information to be processed further. The main purpose of sensory register memory is to screen incoming stimuli and process only those stimuli that are most relevant. Information processing usually occurs too quickly (½ to 3 seconds) for people to consciously control to what they attend. Rather, attention allocation and sensory processing are fast and unconscious. Information that is relevant to the task at hand and information that is familiar are the most likely types of information to be processed and forwarded to the Short-Term Memory.

Short-Term Memory

After stimuli enter sensory memory, they are either forwarded to working Short-Term Memory or fade away from cognitive awareness. Short-Term Memory is created by our paying attention to an eternal stimulus, an internal thought, or both. Stimuli that are perceived and given attention are then actively processed, based on information stored in Long-Term Memory. Short-Term Memory is limited to five to nine items. It will initially last somewhere around 15–20 seconds unless it is repeated at which point it may be available for up to 20 minutes. Interference to one's thinking is the principal cause of forgetting. Repetition or rote rehearsal is a technique used to "learn" something, committing it to Long-Term Memory.

Long-Term Memory

Long-Term Memory is the stored representation of everything a person knows and knows how to do. Unlike sensory and working memory, Long-Term Memory is not constrained by capacity or duration of attention limitations. Most researchers believe that Long-Term Memory is capable of holding millions of pieces of information for very long periods of time (Anderson, 2000).[24]

Long-Term Memory can be categorized as Declarative, Procedural or Episodic. *Declarative* knowledge generally refers to information we can talk about. It is the factual information stored in memory that describes how things are. Things, events, processes, their attributes, and the relations between them describe the declarative knowledge domain. *Procedural* knowledge is the information on how to perform, or how to operate. Procedural knowledge is often more difficult to verbalize and articulate than declarative knowledge; however, one becomes more skilled in problem-solving when s/he relies more on procedural knowledge than declarative knowledge. *Episodic* or anecdotal knowledge is memory for specific events in one's life. The personal stories in one's life comprise episodic memory. These memories can include your high school graduation or audition for college.

Long-Term Memory consists of *explicit* and *implicit* Long-Term Memory systems. *Explicit knowledge* is that which can be put into words. For example, it is possible to tell someone that the key of "g" minor has two flats (i.e., Bb, Eb). However, it is quite difficult to discuss the subject of "musical expression" that consists of *Implicit Knowledge* (i.e., nonverbal procedures). In music instruction, the student who is trying to produce a characteristic tone on clarinet may encounter some challenges in understanding what is a characteristic clarinet sound? The music teacher will often demonstrate or model the characteristic sound by playing recordings or using other sources to transform this implicit knowledge into explicit knowledge from which the student can "make sense" through the musical experience. Beginning in early infancy, children exhibit implicit Long-Term Memory. These procedural memories affect the child's behavior but with which we are able to report.

Cognitivism in Music Teaching

Cognitivists maintain that the learner actively constructs his/her own understandings of reality through interaction with objects, events, and people in the environment, and reflecting on these interactions. According to Piaget, the learner organizes his or her understandings in organized structures (i.e., schemas). When something new is presented, the learner must modify these structures through assimilation or accommodation in order to deal with the new information. From infancy through adolescence, the child goes through four distinct stages or levels in his/her understandings of the world.

In the Piagetian constructivist classroom, the teacher provides a variety of activities to challenge students to accept individual differences, increase their readiness to learn, discover new ideas, and construct their own knowledge. Familiar with the four stages of cognitive development, the teacher creates an environment conducive to cognitive phase. In the elementary classroom, the teacher creates concrete learning experiences, such as the physical enactment and/or creation of models of concepts, field trips that involve hands-on opportunities to see, hear, touch, taste, and smell. These early activities and the use of tangible manipulative and visual aids serve as building blocks for more sophisticated tasks. At the secondary school levels, the teacher builds on the child's knowledge base through verbal description of concepts, written and verbal exercises, logical questioning, and problem-solving. The teacher may provide more sophisticated explanations and use deductive reasoning in explaining concepts and facilitating abstract thought on the part of the adolescent.

Bruner's Conceptual Learning

Bruner's constructivist theory proposes that effective learners of all ages follow a progression from enactive (action-based) to iconic (image-based) to symbolic (language-based) representation when faced with new material. His work also suggests that a learner is capable of learning any material so long as the instruction is organized appropriately. This principle holds true of very young learners and is in sharp contrast to the beliefs of Piaget and other stage theorists.

According to Bruner, "the role of the teacher should not be to teach information by rote learning, but instead to facilitate the learning process. A good teacher will design lessons that help students discover the relationship between bits of information. To do this a teacher must give students the information they need, but without organizing for them."[25]

In Bruner's constructivist classroom, the teacher actively engages the students in an active, involved "process" of learning. In this Discovery Learning approach, the teacher presents students with a problem and some related information. The students must bring together these bits of evidence to "discover" the solution to the problem.

Bruner's writings declare that when "structure of knowledge" is emphasized, the learners will be more able to improve their ability to go beyond the information they are given to find meaning and solve problems. This "Intuitive Thinking" involves the use of hunches or guesses that extend beyond that which is known. Bruner considered this to be the essence of creativity. Bruner believes that when the basic structure of a subject, consisting of the ideas, concepts, principles, and their relationships, is emphasized, the learners will be more able to improve their intuitive thinking.[26]

Cognitivist Approaches in the Music Classroom

Familiarity with Piaget's stages of cognitive development is important to understanding how to teach students of various ages. Applying Bruner's conceptual approach to learning, the music director would teach concepts of tone production, tonality, and musical interpretation differently to elementary students than to high school students.

At the elementary school level, the band director would use action-based activities such as having brass students buzz their lips to emulate the physical actions necessary to create a fundamental tone on their brass instruments. S/he could lead the class through breathing and mouthpiece buzzing exercises necessary to tone production and demonstrate or model these techniques on a brass instrument so that students can get a visual image of the appropriate embouchure and air capacity needed to support a quality tone on the brass instrument.

In the high school band, the director continues to facilitate students' physical actions and visual imagery to create characteristic tone quality on their brass instruments. However, the music teacher uses verbal metaphorical narratives to create symbolic representations of quality tone production in the musical context of the musical literature performed in the classroom. At students' stage of cognitive development, deeper and more complex understanding of tone production, and more advanced development as a musician, the director may talk in more abstract terms regarding the quality of tone—in regards to the musical phrasing, interpretation, and characteristic musical style of the musical selection being rehearsed. S/he may ask questions regarding tone production, musical technique, and musicianship with the related information necessary for students to solve musical problems in their own performance, in order that each student finds meaning in their own cognitive/musical development as a musician in the ensemble.

The music director who understands these theories emphasizes that meaningful learning and development result from a highly active process in which his/her students construct knowledge. In addition, the director familiar with these theories provides experiences that are familiar enough that his/her students can understand or assimilate them and also be challenged so they will be forced to construct or accommodate new understanding on the back of old learning thus bringing equilibrium to students cognitive understanding.

This Constructivist approach is apparent in discovery learning and cooperative approaches to teaching. Bruner's approach to instruction through which students interact with their environment, exploring and manipulating objects, wrestling with questions and controversies, or performing experiments leads to discovery learning. The use of structure, readiness to learn, intuitive and analytical thinking, and desire to learn[27] are important components of the music classroom.

The Performance-Based Classroom

In a performance-based classroom, the orchestra director using a cognitive approach begins rehearsal by stating goals clearly for the rehearsal at the beginning of class, followed by a brief review of information, objectives, and achievements from the previous day's class. The music teacher then presents new information in small, detailed, and explicit steps to the students. S/he shares systematic feedback to students while discussing concepts, questioning them to discern understanding of new material, and rehearsing novel techniques and musical interpretations. The director may provide ample time for individual and group practice of musical techniques, etudes, and musical and technical phrases in order that each student constructs personal meaning, and solves musical problems through the discovery learning process.

The director may begin class with the review of the b minor tonality by having the ensemble play the concert b minor scale in a variety of rhythmic patterns learned as part of yesterday's class rehearsal. After diligent practice of these exercises, s/he conducts the ensemble in a slow, lyrical chorale while instructing students to listen carefully and devote their attention to the tonality in harmonic progression. The director then introduces a new challenging technical passage in concert b minor in a musical work recently distributed to the ensemble. S/he first conducts the ensemble in sight-reading the section before questioning the students about the relationship between the technical passage and the opening exercises of the day's rehearsal. The director describes, plays musical recordings, and models the intricate patterns of the various parts for the students so that they gain aural, visual, and symbolic reference to the musical work they rehearse.

A variety of rehearsal methods may be engaged in which the director repeatedly conducts the ensemble through the musical passage while verbally directing student attention toward specific elements of musical execution such as tone, rhythmic accuracy, tempo, articulation, and interpretation. The orchestra teacher may give specific detailed attention to a particular pattern of the section or give the ensemble members 30 seconds to work out the passage before resuming as a full ensemble. S/he may have individual students who would benefit from additional practice go to practice rooms in order to work out the passage(s) before returning to resume with the full ensemble. When confronted with sections or passages that require extended or exhaustive individual rehearsal, the orchestra director may have the students break into musical sectionals, led by student leaders, to practice, work out musical problems, and master the musical passage(s). Throughout the entire process, the director would give verbal and nonverbal feedback to individuals, sections, and the full ensemble, as the students gradually become familiar with and develop their own understanding of the musical work.

Information Processing in the Classroom

According to information processing theory, humans have the attention capacity to act on information in working memory in ways that improve understanding. In working memory, humans integrate new information with existing knowledge retrieved from Long-Term Memory. As shown in the previous examples, the orchestra director enhances student learning by making material relevant and meaningful to the students. When students realize that learning and remembering how to finger a concert b minor scale used in a warm-up exercise is valuable in playing a technical sixteenth note passage in an orchestra selection, the students are more likely to store such information in Long-Term Memory. Consequently, the orchestra director may use *Transfer of Learning*[28] to relate this new material (the sixteenth-note passage) to previous learning of the old material (the b minor scale) and emphasize similarities and differences to enhance student learning.

Information processing theory also endorses processes that help to transfer information from memory stage to memory stage. These processes include attention, rehearsal, encoding, retrieval, and chunking.

Selective attention refers to the learner's ability to select and process certain information while simultaneously ignoring other information. When we are selectively attending to one activity, we tend to ignore other stimulation, although our attention can be distracted by something else, like the telephone ringing or someone using our name. It is important for educators to understand what makes children attend to one thing rather than another; why children sometimes switch their attention to something that was previously unattended, and how many things they can attend to at the same time. With this knowledge, music teachers can better design instruction and manage student behavior in the classroom.

Rehearsal means the repetition of information in order to maintain it in Short-Term Memory. Music teachers are familiar with the term "rehearsal" as a common language describing what is done in the typical performance-based classroom. Therefore, music teachers are already familiar with methods such as repeating and drilling technical and musical passages as part of instruction in the classroom. In this context, this not only helps students in cementing information into Long-Term Memory but also repetitive physical movements of posture, breathing, embouchure, hands, fingers, and establish more unified muscle memory into students' Long-Term Memory processes. As musicians and music teachers know through their own experience, it is important to review these physical movements and mental structures correctly in the beginning in order to establish productive learning of new material in these rehearsal settings.

Encoding is the process of relating incoming information and material already in memory in such a way that the new information is more memorable. As illustrated in the performance-based classroom example earlier, the orchestra director encodes the b minor tonality by beginning with teaching students the fundamental concert b minor scale and then progressing to having students practice the scale in a variety of rhythmic patterns and lyric choral passages that then lead to performance in more technically challenging passages within a particular musical work. In this context, the music teacher relates new incoming material with information already in the students' cognitive and physical motor memory.

The process of *Retrieval* or *recall* from Long-Term Memory involves bringing to mind previously learned information for either understanding or to make a response. The orchestra teacher's sequential design just described aids students' understanding by retrieving these fingering patterns from long-term muscle memory so that they may then be able to execute related patterns in a new musical context. For learning and instruction to be meaningful and relevant, they must build upon the learner's prior knowledge and help the learner to make connections relevant between what they already know and what they are about to learn.

Chunking is a process by which a person organizes information into meaningful groups. While Short-Term Memory has a limited capacity of seven (7 ± 2) bits of information for a great variety of materials, working memory capacity may be increased through *Chunking* that creates larger bits of information. A common example to illustrate the way one retains a long number such as a telephone number is to chunk the digits into three groups, the area code then the first three-digit chunk, followed by the last four-digit chunk. This method of remembering phone numbers is far more effective than attempting the 10-digit code.

In the music classroom, the teacher can use chunking in teaching complex and detailed concepts. While teaching the Circle of Fifths as a representation of all the major and minor keys, the relationships of their key signatures, and the overall overview of Western Art music, the music teacher would do best by first introducing the structure of a major scale, then building on this information by teaching students how to use this structure to build all major scales around the circle. More specifically, the teacher breaking down the structure of the scale into small bits of information—such as whole-step, whole-step, half-step (i.e., the first tetrachord of the scale), and another whole-step, whole-step, half-step (i.e., the second tetrachord of the scale), connected by a whole-step—breaks the scale structure into small chunks of information that students can organize into meaningful groups.

Major Scale Structure

Step Size:	Whole – Whole – Half – (Whole) – Whole – Whole – Half

Note Name:	C	D	E	F	G	A	B	C

The music teacher can use chunking in the performance-based ensemble by breaking down complex and/or technical musical passages into smaller grouping of notes and rhythms that can be repeated until engrained into long-term cognitive and muscle (motor) memory. As these smaller chunks are learned, the teacher can direct students to combine chunks into larger and more multifaceted sections of music. Correspondingly, as students develop understanding and technical proficiency of these larger meaningful groups, the music teacher can use verbal description, aural models such as musical recordings, and visual images such as pictures and personal drawings to facilitate individual student's personal understanding of musical phrasing, interpretation, and relationships of parts they are performing to the overall context of the musical work. These examples illustrate how the music teacher uses chunking in music instruction and musical rehearsal. It is an integral part of music teaching and learning.

Designing a Unit Lesson: Constructivist and Constructionist Instruction

Mr. Wilson's Blues Improvisation Unit Lesson

While there are overlapping similarities between constructivism and constructionism, it is hoped that you will see the subtle differences between these approaches in the music classroom.

Mr. Wilson set a long-term (i.e., 6-week unit) objective for his high school jazz ensemble members to demonstrate understanding, musical technique, and proficiency to improvise to a standard Blues Progression as part of his biweekly jazz band class rehearsal. As he believes in constructivist and constructionist approaches in his classroom, he engages several principles of each method in his teaching.

Mr. Wilson's Constructivist Approach

As a Constructivist, Mr. Wilson placed photos of well-known Blues Artists Billie Holiday, Bessie Smith, Shirley Horn, Diane Schuur, Etta Jones, Art Tatum, Thelonious Monk, Charles Mingus, Art Blakey, Dizzy Gillespie, Max Roach, John Coltrane, Count Basie, Coleman Hawkins, Benny Goodman, Miles Davis, Charlie Parker, Duke Ellington, and Louis Armstrong on walls all around his rehearsal hall. He also made a huge chart that he posted on the rehearsal hall bulletin board that displayed a common 12-bar blues progression:

C7 C7 C7 C7 F7 F7 C7 C7 G7 G7 C7 C7

Wilson also posted another chart with Functional Notation of the Blues Progression:

T T T T S S T T D D T T
(T = Tonic; S = Subdominant; D = Dominant)

Mr. Wilson regularly played recordings of these artists before and after jazz ensemble classes, during lunch when many students hung-out in the rehearsal hall, and selected blues recordings during jazz ensemble rehearsal. Wilson also shared iTunes tracks and website links such as JazzStandards.com (http://www.jazzstandards.com/index.html)[29] and the Smithsonian Jazz Education Resources website (https://americanhistory.si.edu/smithsonian-jazz/education)[30] with students to listen to inside and outside of school. Many times, during jazz ensemble rehearsals, Mr. Wilson would encourage students to talk with their peers and him about what they heard in these recordings. He also encouraged them to hold listening parties and gatherings to just hang out and listen to the music, feel the groove, and pay attention to the patterns, licks, and melodies that the Artists used to express themselves in the tune.

Using his music budget, Mr. Wilson purchased and issued the Book/CD Set of Jamey Aebersold's VOLUME 2 - NOTHIN' BUT BLUES[31] to all of his students in the jazz ensemble. This volume contains blues at the beginning/intermediate level. As the blues have contained the very essence of the jazz sound since the 1920s, the volume contains 11 different blues melodies presented in a variety of moods from slow to rock. Tempos are not fast. Chords and scales are written in the staff for each track. Each track has piano, bass, and drum set accompaniment over which students can play scales, chordal and digital patterns, and creative melodies as they develop their improvisational skills. Mr. Wilson requested that his students spend at least 15 minutes each evening playing along with one of the tracks during his/her practice regiment. He explained that he wanted the students to use the scales, chords, and digital patterns in the book and supplementary materials to experiment and be creative with the various blues styles on the CD tracks. Each jazz ensemble class rehearsal, he would select one of the tracks over which students would volunteer to play. During these tracks, he would always facilitate student individuality in performance and model fundamental musical technique, phrasing, and musicality when he occasionally improvised himself over the changes.

Mr. Wilson's Constructionist Approach

Mr. Wilson's Constructionist Approach included suggesting to his students that they get together with one to three other students during select times of the jazz ensemble class and outside of school to "Jam" to the tracks with their peers in order to polish their improvisational skills. He encouraged students to "constructively critique" (i.e., informally evaluate) each other's performances and exchange ideas about methods that could be used to be more expressive in their performances. Mr. Wilson suggested that the students emulate musical licks, melodies, and musical phrases they heard on the Blues Artists' recordings in their own performances. He explained that students should discuss the melodies and musical phrases they admired in these artists' recordings with their peers and to support each other in learning these musical melodies in the appropriate contexts on the Jamey Aebersold tracks.

By the end of the third week, Mr. Wilson's students began gaining confidence and proficiency with the Jamey Aebersold Book and CD. With student competence, he observed that students were becoming more and more engaged in the "experience" of making music. Students were gradually losing themselves in the moment and becoming quite creative and expressive in each solo.

So, at the beginning of the fourth week of Mr. Wilson's Jazz Improvisation Unit, he instructed the jazz ensemble that he would like to hear their progress (i.e., their musical outcomes; musical product) in performing a standard Duke Ellington Blues Chart, "C Jam Blues." He explained that the jazz ensemble would perform the selection at a school assembly in three weeks. The ensemble would be playing music as the school student population entered the school auditorium for the assembly. He had great confidence that the entire ensemble could play "C Jam Blues" with each member of the group playing at least one 12-bar blues solo.

In preparation, Mr. Wilson, shared an online version of Duke Ellington's "C Jam Blues" (https://youtu.be/gOlpcJhNyDI)[32] with the ensemble. He instructed the students that there were also numerous recordings on the Internet, iTunes, and other sources to which they could watch and listen. He suggested that just as students collaborate, critique, and model each other with the Jamey Aebersold tracks, they should also model and critique recordings of Artist performances of the Ellington standard they find through other sources. As Mr. Wilson wanted students as well as himself to get some measure of their final product(s), he directed all students to practice along with "C Jam Blues" on the music department's subscribed SmartMusic[33] program. He sets up a quiz on SmartMusic for the students to play along on one chorus and then improvise on one chorus of the tune to assess their progress with this tune.

In addition, Mr. Wilson incorporated "C Jam Blues" into the opening warm-up portion of each jazz ensemble class. He believed it important to create a warm, open, environment during these sessions in order for students to feel relaxed, uninhibited, and comfortable to be creative, and experience the "groove" or "feel" of the music. As Mr. Wilson provided guidance and feedback to each performer about his/her improvisation, he also encouraged the students to be expressive and listen to each other. He instructed students to reassure, inspire, and promote each other while emulating the style, interpretation, and musical artistry that they heard on the Duke Ellington and other recordings of this jazz standard. In the actual school assembly performance, the jazz ensemble very much enjoyed the experience of making music, both as individuals and as an ensemble, while demonstrating great poise during the school assembly. In jazz ensemble class the following day, the members had much pride as they listened to the fruits of their labor in this final product—the "C Jam Blues" school assembly jam session.

Questions

1 Define Cognition and provide an overview of human cognitive processes.
2 Describe Piaget's principles of intellectual development. Include definitions for assimilation, accommodation, equilibrium, and schema.
3 Describe Piaget's Cognitive Development Theory. Include descriptions of the stages of cognitive development.
4 Define/describe Cognitivism. Describe Constructionism. How is Constructionism different from Cognitivism?
5 Describe Bruner's Discovery Learning approach. Describe and give examples of each mode of representation in Bruner's cognitive development framework.
6 Outline the principles of the Information Processing Learning Theory.
7 Describe Sensory Register, Short-Term, and Long-Term Memory.
8 Define and give examples for Information Processing terms Attention, Rehearsal, Encoding, Retrieval, and Chunking.
9 What value do Cognitive Learning Theory approaches have to teach in the music classroom? Describe in detail the principles of Cognitive Theory that result in effective instruction and student learning in the music classroom. Reference the information presented in this chapter to justify how these principles may be applied to instruction in the music classroom.
10 Design an effective single-class lesson on a select musical objective in your area of concentration (e.g., band, chorus, general music, orchestra) that incorporates principles of Cognitivism outlined in this chapter. Use a lesson plan format that indicates the Objective(s), Standard(s) of Learning, Materials, Activities, Assessments, and Evaluation(s) in your design.

Notes

1 Boundless. (2013). *Anatomy and physiology* (p. 975). Boundless Learning Incorporated.

2 InstructionalDesign.org. (2020). Gestalt theory (Wertheimer). Retrieved June 15, 2020, from https://www.instructionaldesign.org/theories/gestalt/

3 Koffka, K. (1935). Principles of Gestalt psychology. New York, NY: Harcourt, Brace.

4 Psychology.net. (2020). *Gestalt theory of learning.* Retrieved June 15, 2020, from https://www.psychologydiscussion.net/learning/learning-theory/gestalt-theory-of-learning-with-objections-psychology/13473

5 Phillips, D. C., & Soltis, J. (2009). *Perspectives on learning* (pp. 36–37). New York: Teachers College Columbia University.

6 Phillips, D. C., & Soltis, J. (2009). *Perspectives on learning* (p. 37). New York: Teachers College Columbia University.

7 Revlin, R. (2012). *Cognition: Theory and practice.* New York: Worth Publishers.

8 Matlin, M. (2009). *Cognition* (p. 4). Hoboken, NJ: John Wiley & Sons, Inc.

9 Hodges, D. (1996). Neuromusical research supports the concept of music as intelligence. In V. Brummett (Ed.), *Music as intelligence: A sourcebook* (pp. 45–64). Ithaca, NY: Ithaca College.

10 Biography. (2020). PICTURE, Jean Piaget. Retrieved June 14, 2020, from https://www.biography.com/scientist/jean-piaget

11 Woolfolk, A.E. (1987). *Educational psychology* (3rd ed.), Englewood Cliffs, NJ: Prentice-Hall.

12 Piaget, J. (1964). Development and learning. In R. E. Ripple & V. N. Rockcastle (Eds.), *Piaget rediscovered: A report on the conference of cognitive studies and curriculum development* (pp. 7–20). Ithaca, NY: Cornell University.

13 Piaget, J. (1967/1971). *Biology and knowledge.* Chicago, IL: University of Chicago Press.

14 MIT Media. (2014). Seymour Papert. Retrieved from MIT Media Webpage on June 14, 2014, from http://web.media.mit.edu/~papert/

15 Cakir, M. (2008). Constructivist approaches to learning in science and their implications for science pedagogy: A literature review. *International Journal of Environmental & Science Education, 3*(4), 193–206. Retrieved from EBSCOhost.

16 Itin, C. M. (1999). Reasserting the philosophy of experiential education as a vehicle for Change in the 21st century. *The Journal of Experiential Education, 22*(2), 91–98.

17 Sabelli, N. (2008). *Constructionism: A new opportunity for elementary science education.* DRL Division of Research on Learning in Formal and Informal Settings (pp. 193–206). Retrieved June 14, 2014, from http://nsf.gov/awardsearch/showAward.do?AwardNumber=8751190

18 Orey, M. (Ed.). (2001). *Emerging perspectives on learning, teaching, and technology.* Retrieved June 8, 2020, from http://epltt.coe.uga.edu/

19 Bruner, J. S. (1966). *Toward a theory of instruction.* Cambridge, MA: Belkapp Press.

20 Gagné, R. (1916–2002) was an American educational psychologist who developed a series of studies and works that simplified and explained "good instruction." He was also involved in applying concepts of instructional theory to the design of computer-based training and multimedia-based learning.

21 Ashcraft, M. H. (1994). *Human memory and cognition* (2nd ed.), New York: Harper Collins.
   Brown, H. D. (1987). *Principles of language teaching and learning* (2nd ed.), Englewood Cliffs, NY: Prentice-Hall.

22 Broadbent, D. (1958). *Perception and communication.* London, England: Pergamon Press.

23 Gray, P. O. (2011). *Psychology* (6th ed.), New York: Worth Publishers: A Macmillan Higher Education Imprint.

24 Anderson, J. R. (2000). *Cognitive psychology and its implication* (5th ed.), New York: Worth Publishing.

25 McLeod, S. (2008/2012). *Bruner. Simply psychology.* Retrieved June 24, 2014, from http://www.simplypsychology.org/bruner.html

26 Learning Theory Fundamentals. (2014). *Jerome Bruner's theory.* Retrieved June 24, 2014, from http://www.theoryfundamentals.com/bruner.htm

27 Bruner organized key themes of the role of structure, readiness to learn, intuitive and analytical thinking, and motives for learning in his *Process of Education.*
   Bruner, J. S. (1977). *The process of education.* London: Harvard University Press. (Original work published 1960).

28   Ellis, H. C. (1965). *The transfer of learning.* New York: The Macmillan Company.
Thorndike, E. L., & Woodworth, R. S. (1901). The influence of improvement in one mental function upon the efficiency of other functions. *Psychological Review, 8*(1), 247–261.

29   Jazz Standards.com. (2020). Watch, listen, learn and the tunes just keep getting better. Retrieved June 14, 2020, from http://www.jazzstandards.com/index.html

30   Smithsonian National Museum of American History. (2020). Smithsonian Jazz Education Resources. Retrieved June 14, 2020, from https://americanhistory.si.edu/smithsonian-jazz/education

31   Jamey Aebersold Jazz. (2020). Volume 2 – Nothin' but Blues, JazzBooks.com. Retrieved June 14, 2020, from http://jazzbooks.com/jazz/product/V02DS

32   YouTube. (2020). Duke Ellington – C Jam Blues (1942). Retrieved June 14, 2020, from https://www.youtube.com/watch?v=gOlpcJhNyDI

33   Smartmusic.com. (2020). Music practice transformed. Retrieved June 14, 2020, from https://www.smartmusic.com/

Chapter 5

Social Learning Theory and Applications to Teaching

Social Learning Theory expands on behavioral theories by placing emphasis on the important roles of various internal processes in the learner.[1] Recall that behavioral theory is governed exclusively by different reinforcements. Social Learning Theory emphasizes that behavior, personal factors, and environmental factors are all equal, interlocking determinants of each other.[2] Bandura's Social Cognitive Theory holds that an individual's knowledge acquisition can be directly related to observing others within the context of social interactions, experiences, and outside media influences. Vygotsky Sociocultural Theory suggests that changes in children's thought and behavior depends on their interaction with people and the tools that the culture provides to help form their own view of the world. Social Learning Theory includes the study of children's abilities to self-regulate and self-reflect, and a child's perception and beliefs about his/her ability to produce effects, or influence events that concern their lives known as self-efficacy.

Learning Objectives

1 What are the connections among Behavioral, Cognitive, and Social Learning Theories?
2 What are the key components of Bandura's Social Learning Theory?
3 What is Vygotsky's Sociocultural Development Theory?
4 What are the comparisons between Piaget and Vygotsky's views of Cognitive Development?
5 What are Self-Efficacy, Self-Regulation, and Self-Determination?

Music teachers employ social learning through direct instruction or observation and do not need direct reinforcement or motor reproduction to take place.[3] Learning may occur through the observation of behavior and/or vicarious reinforcement (i.e., the learner's observation of rewards and punishments).

On the first day of freshmen marching band camp, the band director instructs the band section leaders to take their sections to various parts of the marching field to teach their freshmen how to "forward march." As the band director previously taught the section leaders the appropriate sequence and methodology for such instruction at their leadership camp, each section leader lines their section on their respective field yard line. Each leader continues by first demonstrating forward march, breaking down the maneuver by individual steps to model technique to their section. The officers then sequentially lead their students through the physical steps of marching forward on the marching field. While each section leader provides constructive feedback on their section's performance, the band director moves from section to section,

DOI: 10.4324/9781003038474-7

observing the activity and intervening where necessary, to clarify instruction by the section leader or solidify understanding by freshmen marchers. While at first, the novice marchers can only understand and accomplish the maneuver with the help of their more competent peers, the freshmen marchers can eventually effectively accomplish the move independently and alone.

Bandura's Social Learning Theory[4]

Social Learning Theory proposes that learning is a cognitive process that takes place in a social context. Published theories of learning were heavily influenced by theories of classical conditioning, operant conditioning, and the psychoanalytic concept of drives prior to 1960.[5] Unlike Skinner, Albert Bandura (1977b)[6] (Figure 5.1) believed that humans are active information processors and think about the relationship between their behavior and its consequences. Observational learning could not occur unless cognitive processes were at work.

Social Learning Theory integrated behavioral and cognitive theories of learning in order to provide a comprehensive model that could account for the wide range of learning experiences that occur in the real world. Bandura and Walters (1963)[3] outlined key tenets of Social Learning Theory with further detail in 1977.[6] The main principles of Social Learning Theory are:

1 Learning is not purely behavioral. Rather, learning is a cognitive process that occurs in a social context.
2 Learning can occur by observing a behavior "and" by observing the consequences of the behavior (i.e., vicarious reinforcement).

Figure 5.1 Psychologist Albert Bandura, 2005.

CC BY-SA 4.0 <https://creativecommons.org/licenses/by-sa/4.0>, via Wikimedia Commons.

3 Learning involves observation, extraction of information from these observations, and making decisions about the performance of the behavior (i.e., modeling or observational learning). Therefore, learning can occur without an observable change in behavior.
4 Reinforcement plays a role in learning but is not entirely responsible for learning.
5 The learner is not a passive recipient of information. Cognitive, environment, and behavior all mutually influence each other (i.e., reciprocal determinism).[7]

The Modeling Process

Bandura's Social Learning Theory emphasizes the importance of observing and modeling the behaviors, attitudes, and emotional reactions of others. He contends that "most human behavior is learned observationally through modeling: from observing others one forms an idea of how new behaviors are performed, and on later occasions this coded information serves as a guide for action" (Bandura, 1977b).[8] The necessary conditions for observational learning and modeling are:

1 *Attention*: In order to learn, you need to pay attention. Various factors increase or decrease the amount of attention paid. If the model is interesting or there is a novel aspect to the situation, you are far more likely to dedicate your full attention to learning. Anything that detracts your attention is going to have a negative effect on observational learning.
2 *Retention*: Remembering what you paid attention to. The ability to store information is also an important part of the learning process. Retention can be affected by a number of factors, but the ability to pull up information later and act on it is vital to observational learning.
3 *Motor Reproduction*: Once you have paid attention to the model and retained the information, it is time to actually perform the behavior you observed. This includes reproducing the mental image, physical capabilities, symbolic rehearsal, motor rehearsal, self-observation of reproduction, and accuracy of feedback. Further practice of the learned behavior leads to improvement and skill advancement.
4 *Motivation*: In order for observational learning to be successful, you have to be motivated to imitate the behavior that has been modeled. Reinforcement and punishment play an important role in motivation. External reinforcers, promised imagined incentives, and vicarious reinforcement of seeing successful models of others provide strong motive for observational learning. While experiencing these motivators can be highly effective, so can observing others experiencing some type of reinforcement or punishment.

Bandura's theory improves upon the strictly behavioral interpretation of modeling provided by Miller & Dollard (1941).[9] His Social Learning Theory is considered a bridge between behaviorist and cognitive learning theories because it encompasses attention, memory, and motivation. Therefore, Bandura's Social Learning Theory is related to Vygotsky's Sociocultural Development Theory.

Vygotsky's Social Constructivism

Lev Vygotsky's (1896–1934) emphasis on the role of social interaction and culture are the basis for his theory of social constructivism (1978). Vygotsky, a Russian teacher and psychologist, focused on the connections between people and the sociocultural context in which they act and interact in shared experiences (Crawford, 1996).[10] He believed that learning and development is a collaborative activity in which children are cognitively developed in the context of socialization and education. For learning to take place, the child first interacts with the social environment on an interpersonal level and then internalizes this experience. Concepts learned earlier and new sociocultural experiences influence the child, who then constructs new ideas.

Vygotsky's work has become the foundation for much research in cognitive development, combines the social environment and cognition, and has become known as sociocultural development theory.[11] Vygotsky believed that social interaction leads to ongoing changes in a child's thought and behavior. Four core principles are fundamental to his theory.[12]

1 Children construct their knowledge.
2 Development cannot be separated from its social context.
3 Learning can lead to development.
4 Language plays a central role in mental development.

Vygotsky examined how our social environments influence the learning process. He believed strongly that community plays a central role in the process of "making meaning."[13] He suggested that learning takes place through the interactions students have with their peers, teachers, parents, brothers, sisters, and other experts. These interactions also involve cultural artifacts, such as books or toys, as well as culturally specific practices in which a child engages in the classroom, at home, or on the playground. Children are active partners in all of these interactions, constructing knowledge, skills, and attitudes, not just mirroring the world around them. Therefore, Vygotsky (1934/1962) argued that culture is the primary determining factor for knowledge construction.[11]

Zone of Proximal Development (ZPD)[14]

For Vygotsky, the most effective learning happens when the new skills and concepts beingtaught are just on the edge of emergence—in the ZPD (Figure 5.2). When this happens, the child does not simply acquire new knowledge but actually makes progress in his/ her development.

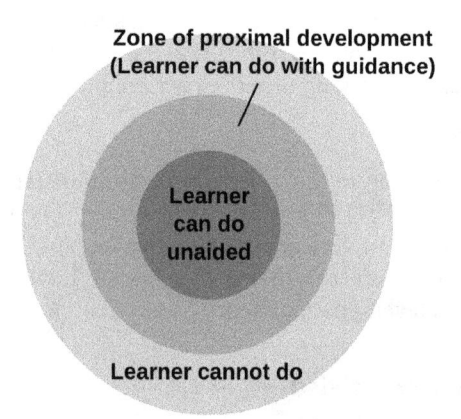

Figure 5.2 Zone of Proximal Development (ZPD).
Dcoetzee, CC0, via Wikimedia Commons.

Vygotsky (1978) defines the ZPD as "the distance between the actual developmental level as determined by independent problem solving and the level of potential development as determined through problem solving under adult guidance, or in collaboration with more capable peers."[15] Effective peer tutoring reflects this principle.

ZPD is the distance between a student's ability to perform a task under adult guidance and/or with peer collaboration and the student's ability to solve the problem independently. He suggested that teachers use cooperative learning exercises where less competent children develop with help from more skillful peers within this zone.

Scaffolding

The ZPD has become synonymous in the literature with the term *Scaffolding*. However, it is important to note that Vygotsky never used this term in his writings. Scaffolding comes from Lev Vygotsky's concept of an expert assisting a novice, or an apprentice. Wood, Bruner, and Ross's (1976) idea of scaffolding parallels the work of Vygotsky. They described scaffolding as the support given to a younger learner by an older, more experienced adult.[16] Wood (1976) further defined Scaffolding as "those elements of the task that are initially beyond the learner's capacity, thus permitting him to concentrate upon and complete only those elements that are within his range of competence."[16] Scaffolding may involve introducing children to special tools such as an alphabet chart and behaviors such as private speech or self-talk that children can use to self-assist while mastering a new skill or concept. Research confirmed that no one approach was best in helping learner progress.[17] Scaffolding is most effective when the support is matched to the needs of the learner. Wood et al. (1976) named certain processes that aid in effective scaffolding[16]:

1 Gaining and maintaining the learner's interest in the task.
2 Making the task simple.
3 Emphasizing certain aspects that will help with the solution.
4 Control the child's level of frustration.
5 Demonstrate the task.

Cognitive Development: Vygotsky versus Piaget

Both Piaget and Vygotsky appreciated the essence of building constructs and internalizing the knowledge given, rather than accepting the information as presented through rote-memory.[18] Constructivist learning environments promote the learner to gather, filter, analyze, and reflect on the information provided and to comment on this knowledge so that it will result in individualized comprehension and private learning.

Piaget's theory is guided by assumptions of how learners interact with their environment and how they integrate new knowledge and information into existing knowledge. He proposed that a child acts on his own environment, going through universal stages of development for learning. As part of their cognitive development, children develop schemes, which are mental representations of people, objects, or principles. These schemes can be changed or altered through what Piaget called assimilation and accommodation.

Vygotsky's theory concentrated on the role of social interactions and culture. He proposed that a child interacts with his environment for learning—s/he socially interacts and communicates with others to learn the cultural values of our society. Through these social interactions, s/he moves toward more individualized thinking. This co-constructed process involves people interacting during shared activities and leads to internalization, which in turn leads one to independent thinking (Woolfolk, 2004).[19] Vygotsky also emphasized the importance of cultural tools in cognition such as language, the media, television, computers, and books available for problem-solving or learning.

While Piaget advocated for discovery learning with little teacher intervention, Vygotsky promoted guided learning within the ZPD as children and their partners co-construct knowledge in the classroom. Piaget maintained that cognitive development stems largely from independent explorations in which children construct knowledge of their own. Vygotsky's guided learning involves the teacher offering intriguing questions to students and having them discover the answers through testing hypotheses (Woolfolk, 2004). In guided learning, the students are engaged in the discovery process; however, they are still receiving assistance from a more knowledgeable source.

Vygotsky placed more emphasis on the role of language in cognitive development than Piaget. While Piaget believed that language depends on thought for its development, Vygotsky viewed cognitive development to result from an internalization of language. He considered language to have a critical role in cognitive development through the transmission of information from adult to child and as a powerful tool of intellectual adaptation (Vygotsky, 1934/1962).[11]

Self-Efficacy

The Theory of Self-Efficacy is at the core of Bandura's social cognitive theory, which emphasizes the role of observational learning and social experience in the development of personality.[20] The main concept in social cognitive theory is that an individual's actions and reactions, including social behaviors and cognitive processes, in almost every situation are influenced by the actions that individual has observed in others.[21]

Self-efficacy is the extent or strength of one's belief in one's own ability to complete tasks and reach goals.[20] Self-efficacy affects every area of human endeavor. By determining the beliefs, a person holds regarding his or her power to affect situations, it strongly influences both the power a person actually has to face challenges competently and the choices a person is most likely to make. These effects are particularly apparent, and compelling, with regard to behaviors affecting health.[22]

Albert Bandura (1977) defined self-efficacy as one's belief in one's ability to succeed in specific situations.[23] As self-efficacy is developed from external experiences and self-perception and is influential in determining the outcome of many events, it is an important aspect of social cognitive theory. Self-efficacy represents the personal perception of external social factors.[21] One's sense of self-efficacy can play a major role in how one approaches goals, tasks, and challenges.[22]

Self-Efficacy in Teaching and Learning

Bandura has argued that beliefs of personal competence constitute the key factor of the person's ability to act intentionally and exercise a measure of control over his/her environment and social structures.[24] As children strive to exercise control over their world, their first interactions are overseen by adults who can empower them with self-assurance or diminish their self-beliefs. As young children are not adept at making accurate self-appraisals, they naturally rely on the judgments of others to create their own judgments of their capabilities. Teachers who provide children with challenging tasks and meaningful activities that can be mastered, and who manage these efforts with support and encouragement, help ensure the development of a robust sense of efficacy. Effective teachers know their students' capabilities.[25] They also know that trying very hard and continually failing can have a devastating effect on one's confidence. For this reason, they are careful to assign work that will indeed be challenging but that they are sure can be accomplished with proper effort.

Self-Regulation

In 1980, Albert Bandura received the Award for Distinguished Scientific Contributions from the American Psychological Association for pioneering the research in the field of self-regulated learning.[26] In his publication, *Social Foundations of Thought and Action: A Social Cognitive Theory*, Bandura reconceptualized individuals as self-organizing, proactive, self-reflecting, and self-regulating.[27] Bandura's emphasis on the capacity of agents to self-organize and self-regulate would eventually give rise to his later work on self-efficacy.

"*Self-Regulation* refers to the self-directive process through which learners transform their mental abilities into task related skills" (Zimmerman, 2001).[28] This is the method or procedure that learners use to manage and organize their thoughts and convert them into skills used for learning. Self-regulation is the process of continuously monitoring progress toward a goal, checking outcomes, and redirecting unsuccessful efforts (Berk, 2003a).[29] In order for students to be self-regulated, they need to be aware of their own thought processes, and be motivated to actively participate in their own learning process (Zimmerman, 2001).[28]

Successful learners use self-regulation to effectively and efficiently accomplish a task. They will regulate different strategies and monitor the effectiveness of that strategies while evaluating and determining the next course of action. When successful learners read a passage and realize that they do not understand what they have read, they will go back and reread, and question or summarize what it is that they need to understand. When a student with learning disabilities reads a passage and realizes that they do not understand what they have read, they tend to shut down, or just continue to read because they do not recognize the goal of reading the passage.

Students with learning disabilities often do not evaluate and monitor their own learning. In order to compensate, they allow others to regulate their learning or rely on the assistance of others to successfully complete a task. According to Zimmerman (2001), these students lack these essential *Executive Control Functions* that are necessary to complete complex academic tasks independently. Therefore, instruction in the use of self-regulation techniques should be directed toward students who are not successful in such educational settings. Zimmerman (2001) outlines the *Components of Executive Control Process*[28] that guide the learner in self-regulation of learning.

1 *Coordinating metacognitive*[30] *knowledge*: Understanding one's own cognitive, knowledge, and thought process.
2 *Planning*: Using a deliberate and organized approach to tackle a task.
3 *Monitoring*: Assessing comprehension while progressing through a task, and checking for effectiveness, testing, evaluating, and revising strategies.
4 *Failure detection*: While progressing through a task, detect when there is a misunderstanding or when an error is made.
5 *Failure correction*: When an error is detected, go back and correct any mistakes.

The Role of Self-Regulation in Self-Efficacy

According to Bandura, self-regulation strongly depends on self-efficacy theory and self-efficacy beliefs. "Perceived self-efficacy influences the level of goal challenge people set for themselves, the amount of effort they mobilize, and their persistence in the face of difficulties. Perceived self-efficacy is theorized to impact performance accomplishments both directly and indirectly through its influences on self-set goals" (Zimmerman, Bandura, & Martinez-Pons, 1992, p. 665).[31] In addition, "self-regulated learners exhibit a high sense of efficacy in their capabilities, which influences the knowledge and skill goals they set for themselves and their commitment to fulfill these challenges. This conception of self-directed learning not only encompasses the cognitive skills emphasized by metacognitive theorists, but also extends beyond to include the self-regulation of motivation, the learning environment, and social supports for self-directedness" (Zimmerman et al., 1992, p. 665).[31]

Social Learning Theory in the Music Classroom

Teachers and students benefit from applying theories of social learning in the music classroom. When teachers develop a better understanding of their students' thinking, they can better align their teaching strategies with their students' cognitive level. The music teacher's goal should be to help the individual student construct knowledge. By implementing methods of modeling, ZPD, guided practice, and strategic social interaction among students within the classroom, the music teacher creates an engaging environment that fosters students' thinking about how they make meaning.

Students need time to try out various strategies, so they can develop answers or responses. At the same time, teacher questioning techniques should guide the social interactions implicitly or explicitly. Think-alouds, an instructional strategy that allows students to talk through new steps of an endeavor aloud, help teachers determine why and how students are experiencing difficulty in the exercise. In addition, students can analyze their own thinking about their efforts. When an administrator walks into a music teacher's classroom using Vygotsky's theory to guide his/her instruction, s/he should see students engaged in scaffolding, small groups, cooperative learning, group problem-solving, cross-age tutoring, assisted learning, and/or alternative assessment.

Application of Vygotsky's theory necessitates meaningful and productive collaborative activities that need to be engaged in by both students and teachers. This approach runs contrary to the teacher-centered model in which learning is centered on the information possessed by the teacher, which flows one way, from teacher to student. In Vygotsky's view, learning can occur through play, formal instruction, or work between a learner and a more experienced learner. Music teachers must actively assist and promote the growth of their students, so the students can develop the skills they need to fully participate in our society.

In today's music classrooms, teachers need to design lessons that empower students to "make meaning through mindful manipulation of input" (Fogarty, 1999, p. 78).[32] By successfully incorporating theories of Piaget, Bandura, and Vygotsky into the classroom, the music teacher can positively impact student achievement. "When our students have the cognitive foundation to learn how to learn, they can discover what else is 'out there' in our world..." (Garner, 2008, p. 38).[33]

Applications of Piaget and Vygotsky

According to Piaget's theory, four- and five-year-old students in the music classroom will be operating at a preoperational stage of development. In the preoperational stage, the concentration is on experiences that the children are able to repeat and therefore learn at their own pace with guidance. In the music classroom, students should be moving to music, singing musical melodies, marching to musical rhythm, and experiencing music through listening activities that acknowledge this level of cognitive development. Piaget thought children needed to participate in experiences in order to learn. He claimed, "...the individual learner is a little scientist constantly constructing and reconstructing theories about the world and how it works" (Dimitriadis & Kamberelis, 2006, p. 174).[34]

While Piaget believed cognition can develop before language, Vygotsky emphasized that spoken language is necessary before the child is ready to learn more complex material. According to Piaget, children at the preoperational stage tend to use intuition to problem-solve and move toward a more logical problem-solving system as they develop. This stage is similar to Vygotsky's repertoire of play as children try to communicate with others "in the development of word meanings that then form the structure of consciousness" (Palmer, 2001, p. 36).[35] It is this consciousness that enables the child to move through the next stages of development. Young students could participate in a round of learning centers that are based on social skills such as musical language, role-playing, turn-taking, and musical play activities. The music teacher and aide would rotate throughout the centers, which allow them to play and talk with the children. At the end of the day, there would be a group review and time to gather materials to go home.

As children move to the intermediate level, emphasis would be placed on music reading and fundamentals of music theory construction. Six- and seven-year-old students would participate in note and rhythm reading exercises, basic solfeggio hand sign and singing, and musical concepts that apply reading and math into classroom activity. The music teacher may introduce simple time signatures and describe the meaning of these symbolic fractions in reading and counting musical rhythm. The music classroom at this level may have an orientation period followed by direct instruction, with activity centers to follow. It is very important that children have an opportunity to practice what is taught during the direct instruction period under the guidance of the teacher. During this time, Vygotsky's ZPD can be utilized to a greater extent than in the earlier years. In the ZPD, the adult will control "those elements of the task that were initially beyond the learner's capacity, thus allowing the learner to complete those that were within existing capabilities" (Daniels, 2001, p. 107).[36]

The most important thing teachers can do is to help their students acquire "strategic knowledge, a knowledge of the procedures people use to learn, to think, to read, and to write" (Wilhelm, 2001, p. 7).[37] Therefore, reading and writing should be the main emphasis of music instruction. Creating musical games and exercises allows young children to practice and strengthen newly acquired representational schemes (Berk, 2003b).[38] Cognitive skills such as attention, memory, logical reasoning, language and literacy, imagination, creativity, reflecting, and taking on experiences are increased by make-believe play, physical activities, and musical games. Small and large group musical activities are helpful in cooperatively solving musical problems and questions.

While similar class structure is central, the music teacher should emphasize math, science, and social contexts with eight-, nine-, and ten-year-old students. It is in these classes that Vygotsky's theory plays a larger role in teaching strategies; however, Piaget's theories continue. According to Palmer (2001), "Piaget was explicit in recommending group learning as a standard means of classroom learning" (p. 41).[35] Vygotsky's theory of scaffolding becomes an important technique in these classes in which the music teacher implements peer tutoring, independent work, small and large group activities and discussion, large group musical demonstration, music technology, and guided learning. Assessment should take place in the shape of a portfolio in which the music teacher collects evidence on each child as the demonstrate accomplishment of Music Standards of Learning. Supplemental evaluation may occur through select traditional pencil and paper assessments to demonstrate student proficiency in today's environment of standardized testing.

Observing and Imitating Others

Much of learning is a function of observing and modeling the behaviors, attitudes, and emotional reactions of others (Bandura & Walters, 1963).[39] By modeling a new behavior such as how to correctly hold an instrument, the student can quickly imitate and learn the appropriate behavior from the teacher and/or other students. The music teacher can use students as models of proper posture, appropriate behavior, characteristic tone production, and suitable musical technique in the music classroom. The teacher has other resources such as audio recordings, visual photographs, pictures, and drawings, technology through computer software, strobe tuners, Dr. Beat metronomes, and other media that can provide models in the classroom. Additionally, iPad and Smartphone Apps have been created that serve similar function by providing musical examples and models that students can imitate in the music classroom.

Bandura considered vicarious reinforcement to be one of the most powerful influencing factors on student behavior.[40] When a child observes someone else being rewarded for a particular behavior, the child is affected in the same way as if s/he had produced the behavior him/herself and been rewarded for it. Similarly, vicarious punishment is possible when the child observes a model being punished for a behavior and is less likely to produce the behavior due to this observation.

Therefore, the music teacher can elicit or cease certain behaviors from the class ensemble by directly rewarding or punishing a student model. The orchestra director can elicit similar technique in others by complimenting the musical performance of the orchestra viola section by enthusiastically saying "Fabulous job violas!! Everyone…look at the precise left hand fingering technique the viola section is using in this movement of the Brandenburg Concerto No. 3. The precision and coordination are exquisite!! Everyone needs to emulate this meticulous finger movement in the same manner on their own fingerboard." In direct contrast, the choral director suspending a "star" soprano soloist from performing with the high school chamber chorale for having alcohol on a chorus trip is a strong deterrent for other chorus students having alcohol on future choral trips. Further, suspension of the student from school for such behavior sends a strong message to all high school students regarding the possession of alcohol while participating in school functions and activities.

Self-Efficacy in Music Teaching

Effective teachers know their students' capabilities.[25] Music teachers need to know the ability level of their students. If the teacher selects music that is too difficult for his/her students who have not previously attempted such literature, the students will become frustrated in their attempts and give up easily. Students with a low level of self-efficacy who encounter challenging music can easily believe that they will never be able to perform the piece. Therefore, the music teacher must select musical exercises and experiences that are appropriately demanding to the students' performance level in order to develop student understanding, musical technique, and self-efficacy toward musical mastery. Musical tasks that are challenging and mentally stimulating provide children with demanding tasks and meaningful musical activities that can be mastered. The music teacher must manage these efforts with support and encouragement, in order to help ensure the development of a robust sense of efficacy.[25]

As students have success through meaningful musical activities, they may progress toward more demanding literature. By using a sequence of instruction combined with much support, encouragement, and positive reinforcement, the music director not only builds on students' musical ability to learn more difficult music but also increases their self-efficacy to accept the challenge of attempting more difficult musical literature in the future. As a result, students with a high level of self-efficacy will attempt more arduous literature because they have previous success and understanding that in time anything is possible. Their belief in their own musical ability—in that they can learn the music—will contribute to their eventual mastery of the music work.

Self-Regulation in the Music Classroom

Self-regulation is not an isolated skill. Children must translate what they experience into information they can use to regulate thoughts, emotions, and behaviors (Blair & Diamond, 2008).[41] It is important that adults hold developmentally appropriate expectations for children's behavior as children develop self-regulation skills gradually. Vygotsky called the choice of developmentally appropriate expectations the ZPD (John-Steiner & Mahn, 1996).[42] The ZPD is the "growing edge of competence" (Bronson, 2000, p. 20)[43] and represents those skills a child is ready to learn. Effective teachers use a variety of strategies to bridge the developmental space between what children already know and can do, and more complex skills and knowledge. According to Florez, "three teaching strategies are critical for scaffolding children's development of self-regulation: modeling, using hints and cues, and gradually withdrawing adult support" (Florez, 2011, p. 46).[44]

The music teacher needs to identify each child's ZPD in order to develop and plan the kinds of modeling and cues the child needs to continue his/her development. The teacher may verbally read the letter names of the notes in a musical exercise to model for a student the appropriate way to identify the note names and rhythms in the exercise. By demonstrating the appropriate behavior in the social context of the class, the music teacher shows the child how to accomplish a task. The music teacher then asks the student a question about his/her activity, waits for the child's response, before responding positively, and uses the self-regulation needed to complete the undertaking.

When teachers use simple directions, gestures, and touch, they provide young children with valuable cues about how and when to regulate their emotions, attention, and behavior (Florez, 2011, p. 50).[44] The music teacher can help children regulate attention by pointing to a picture of Wolfgang Mozart as s/he describes life events that impacted composer's decision to compose music. The teacher can give a certain student a glare to regulate attention or gently touch another child's back to cue the child to relax, however, realize that a touch may increase tension for many children.

At the heart of scaffolding is teachers' careful attention to timing the withdrawal of their support (Florez, 2011, p. 50).[44] According to Salonen, Vauras, and Efklides, teachers must pay careful attention to "the learner's moment-by-moment changing independent functioning" (2005, p. 2).[45] As children increasingly direct their attention, become more engaged, and endure in demanding musical exercises during general music class, they increase and use language to engage other students, and they increase their ability to perform individually. As students demonstrate independence in the music classroom, the teacher can then transfer regulating responsibilities to their control. While monitoring student progress, the music teacher can then intervene, when necessary, to provide appropriate support.

Self-Determination Theory

Self-Determination is an important concept that refers to each person's ability to make choices and manage their own life. Self-Determination Theory (SDT) is a broad theory of human personality and motivation concerned with how the individual interacts with and depends on the social environment. It defines intrinsic and several types of extrinsic motivation and outlines how these motivations influence situational responses in different domains, as well as social and cognitive development and personality.[46]

SDT is centered on the basic psychological needs of autonomy, competence, and relatedness and their necessary role in self-determined motivation, well-being, and growth. The need for autonomy refers to learners' need to be the initiator of their actions and to a sense of psychological freedom when engaging in a learning activity. The need for competence refers to learners' feelings of effectiveness and to their need to experience confidence in achieving desired outcomes. The need for relatedness refers to learners' experiences of positive and mutually satisfying relationships, characterized by a sense of closeness and trust. Many factors can contribute to the satisfaction of these three needs, but among the most important is the teachers' style of engaging with the students.

Self-Determination in Music Education

Research on SDT has been focused on the role of social, cognitive, and emotional factors, and more broadly on the kinds of behaviors humans exhibit when they interact with social environments.[47] Researchers in music education have turned to SDT as a relatively comprehensive theory of motivation. Research in SDT began with investigations of the relationship between doing something because it is inherently interesting or pleasurable (intrinsic motivation) and doing something for some reason other than the task itself (extrinsic motivation) (Deci & Ryan, 1985).[48] Motivation is central to understanding adolescents' success or lack of success in school because it refers to the energy they bring to the tasks, beliefs, values, and goals that determine which activities they devote themselves to, their persistence in achieving them, and the standards they set to determine when a task is completed (Wentzel & Wigfield, 2009).[49]

Many decades of research on achievement in schools have shown that motivation is a key ingredient for student success. As with other school subjects, music students can be motivated and engaged, or they can be unmotivated and disengaged. Such reactions reflect more than just individual differences between students, as they are also reactions to the social environment and classroom climate in which music education takes place. There are many ways in which music directors conceive of and try to affect the motivation of their students as they strive to instill a sense of commitment, high levels of musical participation, and personal growth through learning an instrument. Music teachers can better prepare students for meaningful, lifelong engagement with music by focusing on more student-centered approaches that provide support for their psychological needs and intrinsic motivation.[50]

Self-Determination in the Music Classroom

The social context of the classroom or music rehearsal can vitalize and nurture students' inner motivational resources, resulting in enthusiastic engagement, or it can neglect and frustrate students' inner motivational resources, resulting in alienation and disaffection. Music teachers can play an important role in fostering intrinsic motivation and feelings of competence in their students by providing support for autonomy in their classes. For example, every time teachers encourage students to think critically, evaluate, and then make decisions, they are providing support for autonomy.[51]

Music teachers can maximize opportunities for autonomy by emphasizing the informing nature of their feedback. For example, verbal praise, sticker charts, grading, and other performance reports can be informative if they focus on student progress and improvement, rather than the controlling nature of comparisons that transplant focus from the process of making music to some extra-musical focus. Additionally, teachers can explain the benefits of competition to students, including listening to their peers, performing for new audiences, and having an opportunity to get feedback that will help them improve their musical skills.[52]

Music teachers can create learning environments that are musically satisfying and supportive of student motivation. It is important to shape students' perceptions of musical experiences that are autonomous while fostering competence, interest, and enjoyment. Research shows that students value prominent social interactions with their peers and a sense of belonging while participating in team-building activities that integrate a combination of "business and fun." These outcomes suggest that helping students achieve such a balance could help in maximizing interest, enjoyment, and satisfaction of psychological needs while decreasing amounts of pressure and tension.[53]

It is important for teachers to emphasize the benefits of music for all students, not just those who are planning music careers. Some students join or continue in music for extra-musical reasons, like trips, scholarships, and other extra-musical benefits. Students' long-term music participation could benefit from having access to resources that allow them to pursue music outside of the school music class. Teachers could promote summer music camps, help students arrange private lessons, encourage partnerships with local university programs, help students explore studies on additional instruments, and assist students in making connections with local community music groups.[54] Private lesson participation and out-of-school music participation are important to promoting students' attitudes about the level of future engagement with music in their lives.

Questions

1 What are the fundamental differences between Classical Conditioning, Operant Conditioning, and Bandura's Social Learning Theory?
2 Describe the main principles of Social Learning Theory.
3 What are the necessary conditions for observational learning and modeling?
4 Describe Vygotsky's Theory of Social Constructivism. Include the four core principles of his theory.
5 Create a Lesson Plan Design that illustrates Vygotsky's ZPD. You should describe the class setting, teaching objective, class activity, and expected student behavior in this lesson. Also include ways that scaffolding may support this lesson.
6 Compare the similarities and differences in theories of Piaget and Vygotsky.
7 Create an imagined instructional design that illustrates the way a music teacher may cultivate student self-efficacy in the music classroom. Describe relationships between self-regulation and self-efficacy in this setting.
8 Outline the executive control functions that guide successful learners in the self-regulation of learning. Describe a classroom setting in which a music teacher may guide the student(s) through the self-regulation process in the music classroom.

9 Create an imagined classroom (i.e., elementary-, middle-, or high-school level), and describe methods and/or strategies you would use in teaching a musical concept or idea at the given cognitive stage of development of your students. Your objective is to promote the growth of your students to develop skills they need to fully participate in the classroom community.

10 Create an imagined classroom (i.e., elementary-, middle-, or high-school level), and describe ways you may incorporate observation, imitation, modeling, scaffolding, and the ZPD into your instruction on a musical concept. Also, include strategies you may use in the development of student self-regulation and self-efficacy in this setting.

Notes

1 Bandura, A. (1971). *Social learning theory*. General Learning Corporation. Retrieved June 30, 2014, from http://www.jku.at/org/content/e54521/e54528/e54529/e178059/Bandura_SocialLearningTheory_ger.pdf

2 Bandura, A. (1973). *Aggression: A social learning analysis*. Englewood Cliffs, NJ: Prentice-Hall.
  Bandura, A. (1977a). Self-efficacy: Toward a unifying theory of behavioral change. *Psychological Review, 84*(2), 191–215.

3 Bandura, A. (1963). *Social learning and personality development*. New York, NY: Holt, Rinehart, and Winston Publishing.

4 Psyche Games. (2020). PICTURE. Albert Bandura. Retrieved June 22, 2020, from https://www.psychegames.com/albert-bandura.htm

5 Bandura, A. (1972). Park, R. D. (Ed.), *Recent trends in social learning theory*. New York, NY: Academic Press, Inc.

6 Bandura, A. (1977b). *Social learning theory*. Oxford, England: Prentice Hall.

7 Grusec, J. (1992). Social learning theory and developmental psychology: The legacies of Robert Sears and Albert Bandura. *Developmental Psychology, 28*(5).

8 Bandura, A. (1977b). *Social learning theory* (p. 22). Oxford, England: Prentice Hall.

9 Miller, N. E., & Dollard, J. (1941). *Social learning and imitation*. New Haven, CT: Yale University Press.

10 Crawford, K. (1996). Vygotskian approaches to human development in the information era. *Educational Studies in Mathematics, 31*, 43–62.

11 Vygotsky, L. S. (1962). *Thought and language*. Cambridge, MA: MIT Press. (Original work published 1934).

12 Berk, L. E. (1994). *Child development* (3rd ed., pp. 50, 156–57, 254, 352), Boston, MA: Allyn and Bacon.

13 Vygotsky, L. S. (1978). *Mind in society: The development of higher psychological processes*. Cambridge, MA: Harvard University Press.

14 International Literacy Association. (2020). Literacy now: The digitally enhanced zone of proximal development by Paul Marsink (September 20, 2013). Retrieved June 22, 2020, from https://www.literacyworldwide.org/blog/literacy-now/2013/09/20/tile-sig-feature-the-digitally-enhanced-zone-of-proximal-development

15 Vygotsky, L. S. (1978). *Mind in society: The development of higher psychological processes* (p. 86). Cambridge, MA: Harvard University Press.
  McLeod, S. A. (2010). *Zone of proximal development*. Retrieved July 8, 2014, from http://www.simplypsychology.org/Zone-of-Proximal-Development.html

16 Wood, D. J., Bruner, J. S., & Ross, G. (1976). The role of tutoring in problem solving. *Journal of Child Psychiatry and Psychology, 17*(2), 89–100.

17 Wood, D., & Middleton, D. (1975). A study of assisted problem-solving. *British Journal of Psychology, 66*(2), 181–191.

18 Ozer, O. (2014). Constructivism in Piaget and Vygotsky. The Fountain Magazine. Retrieved July 8, 2014, from http://www.fountainmagazine.com/Issue/detail/CONSTRUCTIVISM-in-Piaget-and-Vygotsky

19 Woolfolk, A. (2004). *Educational psychology* (9th ed.), Boston, MA: Allyn and Bacon.

20 Ormrod, J. E. (2006). *Educational psychology: Developing learners* (5th ed.), Upper Saddle River, NJ: Pearson/Merrill Prentice Hall.

21 Miller, N. E., & Dollard, J. (1941). *Social learning and imitation*. New Haven, CT: Yale University Press.

Bandura, A. (1988). *Organizational application of social cognitive theory. Australian Journal of Management, 13*(2), 275–302.

Mischel, W., & Shoda, Y. (1995). A cognitive-affective system theory of personality: Reconceptualizing situations, dispositions, dynamics, and invariance in personality structure. *Psychological Review, 102*, 246–268.

22 Luszczynska, A., & Schwarzer, R. (2005). *Social cognitive theory*. In M. Conner & P. Norman (Eds.), *Predicting health behaviour* (2nd ed. rev., pp. 127–169). Buckingham, England: Open University Press.

23 Bandura, A. (1977a). Self-efficacy: Toward a unifying theory of behavioral change. *Psychological Review, 84*(2), 191–215. Retrieved from http://psycnet.apa.org/journals/rev/84/2/191/

24 Bandura, A. (1997). *Self-efficacy: The exercise of control*. New York: W. H. Freeman.

Pajares, F. (1997). *Current directions in self-efficacy research*. In M. Maehr & P. R. Pintrich (Eds.), *Advances in motivation and achievement* (Vol. 10, pp. 1–49). Greenwich, CT: JAI Press.

25 Pajares, F. (2009). *Self-efficacy theory*. Education.com, Inc. Retrieved July 9, 2014, from, http://www.education.com/reference/article/self-efficacy-theory/#D

26 Zimmerman, B. J. (1986). Dedication: Albert Bandura. *Contemporary Educational Psychology, 11*(4), 306.

27 Bandura, A. (1986). *Social foundations of thought and action: A social cognitive theory*. Englewood Cliffs, NJ: Prentice-Hall.

28 Zimmerman, B.J. (2001). Theories of self-regulated learning and academic achievement: An overview and analysis. In B. J. Zimmerman, & D. H. Schunk (Eds.), *Self-regulated learning and academic achievement: Theoretical perspectives* (pp. 1–65). Mahwah, NJ: Lawrence Erlbaum Associates, Publishers.

29 Berk, L. E. (2003a). *Child development*. Boston, MA: Allyn and Bacon.

30 Metacognition basically means "thinking about one's thinking." Metacognitive knowledge is one's awareness of one's own mental abilities, mental states, understanding of thinking, ability to direct one's efforts to evaluate one's cognitive activities, and strategies to remember and learn.

31 Zimmerman, B. J., Bandura, A., & Martinez-Pons, M. (1992). Self-motivation for academic attainment: The role of self-efficacy beliefs and personal goal setting. *American Educational Research Journal, 29*(3), 663–676.

32 Fogarty, R. (1999). Architects of the intellect. *Educational Leadership, 57*(3), 76–78.

33 Garner, B. K. (2008). When students seem stalled: The missing link for too many kids who don't "get it?" cognitive structures. *Educational Leadership, 65*(6), 32–38.

34 Dimitriadis, G., & Kamberelis, G. (2006). *Theory for education*. London, England: Routledge Publishing.

35 Palmer, J. A. (2001). *Fifty modern thinkers of education*. New York: Routledge.

36 Daniels, H. (2001). *Vygotsky and pedagogy*. New York: Routledge Falmer.

37 Wilhelm, J. D. (2001). *Strategic reading*. Portsmouth, NH: Boynton Cook Publishers, Inc.

38 Berk, L. E. (2003b). *Development through the lifespan*. Boston, MA: Pearson Education, Inc.

39 Bandura, A., & Walters, R. (1963). *Social learning and personality development*. New York: Holt, Rinehart, and Winston.

Bandura, A. (1977b). *Social learning theory*. New York: General Learning Press.

40 Bandura, A., Ross, D., & Ross, S. A. (1963). Vicarious reinforcement and imitative learning. *Journal of Abnormal and Social Psychology, 67*, 601–607.

41 Blair, C., & Diamond, A. (2008). Biological processes in prevention and intervention: The promotion of self-regulation as a means of preventing school failure. *Development and Psychopathology, 20*, 899–911.

42 John-Steiner, V., & Mahn, H. (1996). Sociocultural approaches to learning and development: A Vygotskian framework. *Educational Psychologist, 31*, 191–206.

43 Bronson, M. B. (2000). *Self-regulation in early childhood: Nature and nurture*. New York: Guilford.

44 Florez, I. R. (2011). Young children's self-regulation through everyday experiences. *Next for Young Children, 66*(4), 46–51. Retrieved July 13, 2014, from http://www.naeyc.org/files/yc/file/201107/Self-Regulation_Florez_OnlineJuly2011.pdf

45 Salonen, P., Vauras, M., & Efklides, A. (2005). Social interaction—What can it tell us about metacognition and coregulation in learning? *European Psychologist, 10*, 199–208.

46 Legault, L. (2017). Self-determination theory. In V. Zeigler-Hill & T. Shackelford (Eds.), *Encyclopedia of personality and individual differences* (pp. 1–9). Springer, Cham. Doi: 10.1007/978-3-319-28099-8_1162-1.

47 Evans, P. (2015). Self-determination theory: An approach to motivation in music education. *Musicae Scientiae, 19*(1), 65–83.

48 Deci, E., & Ryan, R. M. (1985). *Intrinsic motivation and self-determination in human behaviour.* New York: Plenum Press.

49 Wentzel, K. R., & Wigfield, A. (2009). Introduction. In K. R. Wentzel, & A. Wigfield (Eds.), *Handbook of motivation at school* (pp. 1–8). New York: Routledge.

50 Legutki, A. (2010). *Self-determined music participation: The role of psychological needs satisfaction, intrinsic motivation, and self-regulation in the high school band experience.* Doctoral Dissertation, University of Illinois at Urbana-Champaign.

51 Legutki, A. (2010). *Self-determined music participation: The role of psychological needs satisfaction, intrinsic motivation, and self-regulation in the high school band experience* (p. 181). Doctoral Dissertation, University of Illinois at Urbana-Champaign.

52 Legutki, A. (2010). *Self-determined music participation: The role of psychological needs satisfaction, intrinsic motivation, and self-regulation in the high school band experience* (p. 186). Doctoral Dissertation, University of Illinois at Urbana-Champaign.

53 Legutki, A. (2010). *Self-determined music participation: The role of psychological needs satisfaction, intrinsic motivation, and self-regulation in the high school band experience* (pp. 186–187). Doctoral Dissertation, University of Illinois at Urbana-Champaign.

54 Legutki, A. (2010). *Self-determined music participation: The role of psychological needs satisfaction, intrinsic motivation, and self-regulation in the high school band experience* (p. 188). Doctoral Dissertation, University of Illinois at Urbana-Champaign.

Chapter 6

Humanism

Learning Theory and Applications to Teaching

Humanistic psychology is a psychological perspective that rose to prominence in the mid-20th century in response to B. F. Skinner's behaviorism. This psychological perspective views the individual as a "whole person" greater than the sum of our parts and encourages self-exploration rather than the study of behavior in people. Psychologists Carl Rogers and Abraham Maslow introduced a positive, humanistic psychology in response to B. F. Skinner's behaviorism and Sigmund Freud's psychoanalytic theory in the early 1960s. Abraham Maslow's developmental theory emphasizes a hierarchy of needs and motivations. Carl Rogers' theory centers on the individual's capacity for self-direction and understanding of his/her own development. The humanistic approach emphasizes an individual's inherent drive toward self-actualization, the process of realizing and expressing one's own capabilities and creativity.

Learning Objectives

1　What is Humanism and Humanistic Learning Theory?
2　What are the ideals of Maslow's Hierarchy of Needs?
3　What is Rogers' Learner-Centered Approach?
4　What are the precepts of Self-Concept in teaching and learning?

Music teachers employing humanistic applications in the classroom emphasize student well-being, including the importance of human values, the development of individual potential, and the acknowledgment of human dignity.[1]

> During their study of Afro-Cuban music, the music theory teacher places students in groups of three to listen to jazz recordings of *Manteca* by the Dizzie Gillespie Orchestra,[2] Arturo Sandoval's recording of *Manteca*,[3] and *Manteca* by Maraca and his Latin Jazz All Stars.[4] The teacher requests that students replicate particular clave-based rhythms that exist in each recording, as they listen. After studying all samples, students are to compare particular rhythms in each recording that are unique to Afro-Cuban music. Through discussion and collaboration, each group is to then locate and examine three different recordings that exemplify the rhythms heard in the original recordings. The teacher directs students that each group will present their new findings in the next music theory class.

DOI: 10.4324/9781003038474-8

Humanism

Humanism, a model that emerged in the 1960s, focuses on the human freedom, dignity, and potential. A central assumption of humanism is that people act with intentionality and values (Huitt, 2001).[5] This is in contrast to the behaviorist view that all behavior is the result of the application of consequences and the cognitivist belief that discovering knowledge or constructing meaning is central to learning. Humanists deem that it is necessary to study the person as a whole, especially as an individual grows and develops over the lifespan.

Humanistic Psychology

Humanistic psychology has its roots in the existential philosophy of Jean-Paul Satre, Martin Buber, and Karl Jaspers (Lefrancois, 1999, p. 239).[6] These philosophers were profoundly concerned about what it means to be human and how humanity grows and expresses itself in each individual. Humanism is based on the fundamental observation that, although we might resemble each other in many important ways, each of us is quite different from every other. Our uniqueness is our "self," and "self" is the most central concept in humanistic psychology.

Humanistic psychologists believe that an individual's behavior is connected to his/her inner feelings and self-image. Humanistic psychologists study how people are influenced by their self-perceptions and the personal meanings attached to their experiences. Humanistic psychologists are not primarily concerned with instinctual drives, responses to external stimuli, or past experiences. Rather, they consider conscious choices, responses to internal needs, and current circumstances to be important in shaping human behavior.

Humanism in Learning

Abraham Maslow (1908–1970) and Carl Rogers (1902–1987) are among the most notable individuals in humanist psychology.[1] They center on the learner as an individual and consider that learning is not just about the intellect, but also about educating the "whole person," taking a person's interests, goals, and enthusiasm into account, so that full potential can be achieved.[7] Maria Montessori's (1870–1952) belief that a child's "true normal nature" should guide instruction is an approach to education that remains in use in schools around the globe (Standing, 1998).[8]

Abraham Maslow

In 1943, Abraham Maslow published a paper called *A Theory of Human Motivation*,[9] in which he posited that people have a hierarchy of human needs based on two groupings: deficiency needs and growth needs. Within the deficiency needs, each lower need must be met before moving to the next higher level. Once each of these needs has been satisfied, if at some future time a deficiency is detected, the individual will act to remove the deficiency.

Maslow's initial conceptualization included only one growth need—self-actualization. Self-actualization needs are the highest level in Maslow's hierarchy and refer to the realization of a person's potential, self-fulfillment, seeking personal growth, and peak experiences. Maslow (1943) defines this level as the desire to accomplish everything that one can, to become the most that one can be.[10] He describes peak experiences as "rare, exciting, deeply moving, exhilarating, elevating experiences that generate an advanced form of perceiving reality, and are even mystic and magical in their effect"[11] ... it is not necessarily about what the activity is, but the ecstatic, blissful feeling that is being experienced during it.[12]

Maslow continued to refine his theory based on the concept of a hierarchy of needs over several decades (Maslow, 1943, 1962, 1987).[13] These changes expanded his five-stage model (1943, 1954)[14] to include cognitive and aesthetic growth needs (Maslow, 1970a)[15] and later transcendence needs (Maslow, 1970b).[16] Maslow's Hierarchy of Needs (Figure 6.1) include[17]

Transcendence: To connect to something beyond one's self, service to others; to help others find self-fulfillment and realize their potential.

Self-Actualization: Realizing personal potential, self-fulfillment, personal growth, and peak experience.

Aesthetic: Appreciation and search for beauty, balance, form, and order.

Cognitive: knowledge, understanding, exploration, curiosity, meaning, predictability.

Esteem: Dignity, achievement, independence, respect from others, reputation, recognition.

Belongingness and Love: Acceptance, trust, friendship, affiliation with others, belonging.

Safety: Security, social welfare, safety against injury, health, and well-being.

Physiological: Survival such as air, food, drink, shelter, clothing, warmth, and sleep.

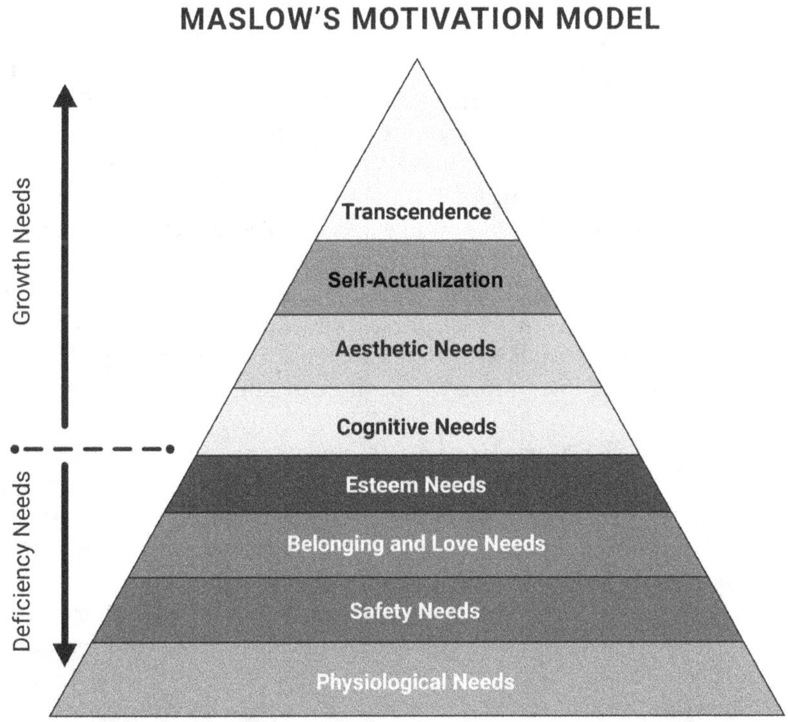

Figure 6.1 Maslow's Hierarchy of Needs.

December 29, 2020. Mcleod, Saul Dr., Public Domain, via Wikimedia Commons.

Maslow adopted a holistic approach to education and learning. His hierarchy of needs considers the complete physical, emotional, social, and intellectual qualities of an individual and how they impact on learning in the education of a child. Before a student's cognitive needs can be met, they must first fulfill their basic physiological needs. For example, a tired and hungry student will find it difficult to focus on learning. Students need to feel emotionally and physically safe and accepted within the classroom to progress and reach their full potential.[10]

The music teacher will benefit from developing a comprehensive holistic approach to teaching and learning. With a holistic perspective, the educator is concerned with the development of every person's intellectual, emotional, social, physical, creative, and artistic potentials. The humanistic music teacher seeks to engage students in the learning process and encourages the personal and collective responsibility of each learner.

Maslow's hierarchy provides a source for developing a holistic method of teaching and learning music. Here are some examples which illustrate the humanistic perspective.

Physiological: The music program often has rehearsals after the regular school day. Students coming to rehearsal hungry after a long day of school may not be in the best state to study music. To address this, the music director can implement an "Afterschool Snack Time" with refreshments and drinks to nourish students before rehearsal.

In similar manner, the director, who schedules a Saturday morning rehearsal before departure for the ensemble's performance at a music assessment festival, can program a break for brunch for students to get sustenance before their departure. Many times, parent music boosters will support the program by organizing and providing such nourishment.

Safety: In preparation for travel of the student performing ensemble to the music assessment festival, the director will secure current medical records of each student to ensure medications necessary for students traveling with the musical ensemble. The director will schedule appropriate transportation, parent chaperones, rest stop breaks, and other needs of safety and security for all members traveling to/from the assessment festival. Likewise, the music teacher works along with other faculty and administration in the school to provide a safe, secure, and orderly environment for students throughout the regular school day.

Belongingness: Student membership in music ensembles and classes often gives them a sense of belonging and ownership in the music program. The organization of music programs often provides structure, identity, a sense of place, and belonging. Acknowledging the inclusion of students from different backgrounds in the class, the study of musical literature from a diverse multitude of composers, musical styles, and genres, and embodying a culturally responsive disposition by the director develops a sense of belonging that is essential to students.

Unlike other subjects such as math or science, students are members of music classes for several years, providing opportunities to develop long-term relationships with the teacher and other students. Participating in a variety of musical, academic, and social experiences during the school day and outside of school provides the student with many ways to feel a sense of belongingness and love in the music program.

Esteem: The structure of learning in music ensembles provides opportunities for students to develop new knowledge based on related information so as to help ensure success. Student learning in music provides occasions for independent learning in conjunction with group education, study, and training that leads to achievement, accomplishment, and recognition. Student participation in music for several years provides opportunities for scaffolding of knowledge, ability, and talents among older and younger members. Through dignity and respect, members develop a sense of respect among peers.

Cognitive: The music teacher consistently plans lessons that are intellectually engaging to develop student knowledge and understanding. The music director may have students compare particular musical interpretations necessary in performing a select musical work. The instructor may ask questions to probe discussion regarding the relationships of musical elements that elicit expressive qualities in the music. Efficiency, predictability, and consistency on the part of the teacher facilitate meaningful instruction.

Aesthetic: The music teacher organizes the classroom seating, equipment, and materials in a neat and appealing way that welcomes students into the classroom. Displaying student instructional posters and interesting and colorful wall hangings in a clean classroom encourages students to enter and participate in a positive manner.

A primary objective of music education is to elevate the appreciation of diverse musical genres, styles, and the contributions of all students within the classroom. During instruction, the teacher engages students in the examination and exploration of musical form, balance, and beauty. In the instruction and rehearsal of music, the director facilitates student musical understanding and technique in striving toward artistic musical performance and aesthetic beauty.

Self-Actualization/Transcendence: As the teacher engages the individual student along with the collective ensemble in the music classroom, students should be encouraged to realize their personal growth, fulfillment, and potential. As students connect with others in the music ensemble, they should realize that they are in service to others and a part of something more than just themselves. Within this learning community, the music director encourages students to do their best in achieving personal goals and peak musical experiences in rehearsal and performance. In fostering a supportive learning environment, individual students and teacher should contribute to the group dynamic while achieving self-fulfillment.

Carl Rogers

Carl Rogers agreed with the main assumptions of Abraham Maslow; however, Rogers contended that for a person to "grow," s/he needs an environment that provides him/her with genuine openness and self-disclosure, being accepted with unconditional positive regard, and being listened to and understood. Without these, relationships and healthy personalities will not develop as they should.[18]

Carl Rogers (1959) believed that humans have one basic motive, the tendency to self-actualize; to fulfill one's potential and achieve the highest level of "human-beingness."[19] Rogers believed that every person could achieve their goals, wishes, and desires in life in order to achieve individual self-actualization.

Rogers characterized an individual who is actualizing as a fully functioning person. They are open to experiences as they occur in life, able to live in the present, trust their own feelings and instincts, take risks and think creatively, and look for new challenges in life. For Rogers, fully functioning people are well-adjusted, well-balanced, and interesting to know. Often such people are high achievers in society.

Learner-Centered Teaching

Carl Rogers' research demonstrated that more effective teachers were empathetic and caring for their students, learner-centered, and a facilitator of student learning in their classroom.[20] Rogers (1951) maintained that a person can only facilitate another's learning. As what the student does is more important than what the teacher does, the background and experiences of the learner are essential to how and what is learned. Consequently, each student processes what s/he learns differently depending on what s/he brings to the classroom.

Setting a tone of support helps to encourage students to have confidence to explore concepts and beliefs that vary from those they bring to the classroom. An open, friendly environment in which trust is developed is essential in the classroom. Fear of retribution for not agreeing with a concept should be eliminated. As new information may threaten the student's concept of him- or herself, the less vulnerable the student feels, the more likely s/he will be able to open up to the learning process.

In learner-centered teaching, the educator's acceptance of being a mentor who guides rather than the expert who tells is instrumental to student-centered, non-threatening, and unforced learning. The teacher is open to learning from the students and also working to connect the students to the subject matter. Frequent interaction between instructor and students will help achieve this goal.

Self-Concept

Carl Rogers and Abraham Maslow had major influence in popularizing the idea of self-concept. Carl Rogers used the term "self-actualization" to describe something distinct from the concept developed by Maslow: the actualization of the individual's sense of "self."[21] According to Rogers, self-actualization is the ongoing process of maintaining and enhancing the individual's self-concept through reflection, reinterpretation of experience, allowing the individual to recover, develop, change, and grow. Self-concept is "the organized, consistent set of perceptions and beliefs about oneself."[19]

The self is the humanistic term for who we really are as a person. The self is influenced by the experiences a person has in his/her life and outward interpretations of those experiences. According to Rogers (1959), we want to feel, experience, and behave in ways that are consistent with our self-image and which reflect what we would like to be like, our ideal-self.[19] The closer our self-image and ideal-self are to each other, the more consistent or congruent we are and the higher our sense of self-worth.

The humanistic approach states that the self is composed of concepts unique to ourselves. Self-concept has three components:

Self-image is the view one has of oneself. Self-image affects how a person thinks, feels, and behaves in the world.

Self-worth (or self-esteem) is how much value one places on oneself. Rogers believed feelings of self-worth develop in early childhood and is formed from the interactions of the child with the mother, father, and significant others.

Ideal-self is the person one would like to be. It consists of one's goals and ambitions in life which are forever changing. The ideal-self is different from childhood to adolescence to adulthood.[22]

Rogers believed that we need to be regarded positively by others. We need to feel valued, respected, treated with affection and loved. Positive regard is to do with how other people evaluate and judge us in social interactions. Rogers made a distinction between unconditional positive regard and conditional positive regard[23] from others.

Rogers also suggested that psychologically healthy people actively move away from roles created by others' expectations, and instead look within themselves for validation.[24] According to Rogers, everyone strives to reach an "ideal self."

Self-Concept in Music Education

Some research suggests that academic self-concept begins developing from ages three to five due to influence from parents and early educators.[25] By age 10 or 11, children assess their academic abilities by comparing themselves to their peers.[26] Researchers suggest that to raise academic self-concept, parents and teachers need to provide children with specific feedback that focuses on their particular skills or abilities.[27]

Music teachers can structure classes to foster the belief that music ability can be developed through effort. At the secondary level, entry level non-auditioned music classes in a variety of musical styles provide opportunities for student development of musical ability in the ensemble setting. Small ensemble activities can be organized so that students perceive the task positively and feel empowered to meet appropriate music challenges.[28] Such actions will impact individual students' self-concepts of music ability.

Humanistic Approaches to Teaching Music

While the acquisition of musical knowledge and competency are valued, the major emphases of humanistic approaches are greater attention to thinking and feeling, the development of self, communication, the clarification of values, openness, honesty, and self-determination. In the music classroom, the teacher must create a supportive environment to show students that they are valued and respected. Students with a low self-esteem will not progress academically at an optimum rate until their self-esteem is strengthened.[29] Group process and cooperative approaches are most compatible with these emphases.

Cooperative learning involves small-group techniques structured so that learners are rewarded for the group's results but are nevertheless individually accountable. It is characterized by face-to-face interaction, individual responsibility, and the use of interpersonal skills. In these learning endeavors, students may work in group sectionals, chamber ensembles, and small gatherings so that each child has a specific role while all work together to solve musical problems. The music teacher supervises students to facilitate learning that involves student interaction and responsibility.

Student-centered learning takes place when the music teacher becomes a facilitator, taking the focus from him-/herself as the bearer of knowledge. The student takes on an important role in this type of classroom. As the music teacher designs lessons originating from the interests of students, instruction can focus on the development of individual musical ability and understanding that impact the overall musicianship and comprehension of the entire class or ensemble. Such planning may also open opportunities for student's musical self-expression and creativity that increase self-esteem and a willingness to learn.

In discovery education, the music teacher introduces a concept and gives the student freedom to discover his/her own path to learning more about the concept. This strategy supports the concept of multiple intelligences and intellectual diversity. The music director may present fundamental principles of music composition and improvisation in a common Binary and 16-bar jazz form. After introducing such concepts, the teacher requests students to use the "Band-in-a-Box"[30] music accompaniment software program in the class media lab to research and create their own musical compositions and improvisations in a Binary 16-bar form. Students may seek texts and online sources outside of class to research this concept.

A humanistic classroom is inclusive of everyone. This type of class seeks to support both individuality and diversity by finding the similarities among students. The music teacher embraces the different backgrounds of students in the classroom and designs instruction that engages diversity of musical styles and genres of composers from all ethnic, cultural, and historical contexts. The music educator designs instruction to meet the needs of individual students as they contribute to the class or ensemble as a whole. Diversified lessons give each learner a chance to succeed and receive positive reinforcement. The teacher realizes that learning styles are individual preferences and strengths as they relate to the best conditions for learning. Therefore, the music instructor attempts to match curriculum and instruction to each learner's personal learning style (e.g., aural, visual, kinesthetic).

Music Class Scenarios

Each of the following scenarios presents the reader with humanistic applications in the music classroom.

Diversity

In the music class setting, acknowledging and treating all students as individuals with deserved respect is important in the classroom. The humanistic choral director is especially *sensitive to the diversity* in his/her classroom. Having a mixture of Black, Caucasian, and Hispanic students in his/her class, the director has deep understanding and empathy for the students of each ethnicity. The humanistic director in this setting takes great care to understand the family background, home setting from which students come, the cultural uniqueness of each ethnicity, and attempts to relate to each student. In this context, the choral director will attempt to enhance instruction with historical and cultural perspectives that are unique to the class.

Emotional Growth

Being *concerned with the emotional growth* of each student, the general music teacher is often interested and concerned with how his/her students *feel* in various learning situations. S/He believes *communication* is important and communicates in various settings his/her expectations and feelings that his/her students are valued and respected. As students interact with their environment and develop notions of who and what they are (their self-concept), the teacher dedicates attention so that each student feels that s/he *belongs to* and is *a part of the music class*. Through positive feedback such *you're really talented Johnny*, the teacher fosters *strong self-esteem* in each student. S/He attempts to integrate the cognitive and affective aspects of teaching and learning to make possible personal growth through positive learning experiences.

Learning Styles

The humanistic band director is sensitive to the *learning styles* of his students. In teaching a piece such as the Bukvich Symphony No. 1,[31] the director may use audio recordings, drawings and pictures, and video recordings to illustrate a variety of concepts (e.g., notation or historical relevance). The director may even use tactile activities to convey various textures that are created in the piece. In certain learning situations, the students may have *extrinsic learning experiences*. These practices may involve learning how to finger notes in a passage that is in the key of D. Understanding and being able to communicate that D major has an F# and C# in its key signature would be important to this process. In other circumstances such as the Bukvich Symphony, *intrinsic experiences* are important in learning. These *intrinsic experiences* are unique from individual to individual and may involve the director using audio examples or other media to convey meanings that cannot be put into words. With instruction, rehearsal, aural and visual imagery experiences, it is the goal of the director for his students to have *peak musical experiences*. These *peak experiences* are intrinsic, profoundly moving, life-changing experiences that come close to defining what is meant by *self-actualization*. At the height of an individual's growth needs, *self-actualization* is a continuous process of growth and fulfillment of one's self.

Cooperative Learning

The humanistic orchestra director uses *cooperative learning* activities to facilitate learning. S/He may set up small chamber ensembles, in which each student is responsible for an individual part. The students work independently within their group and at their own pace, with coaching from the director. They work cooperatively ensuring that all members master the assigned material in the chamber work. While the students are rewarded for the group's results, each individual is held accountable for learning his/her part and helping other members of the ensemble to learn the musical work in its entirety.

Questions

1 Describe the fundamental principles of humanism.
2 Describe Maslow's Theory of Human Motivation. Compare the differences between the deficiency and growth needs in this model.
3 Describe and provide examples of each Growth Need in Maslow's Hierarchy of Needs.
4 Describe Self-Actualization. Compare how Maslow and Rogers define Self-Actualization.
5 Describe the three components of Self-Concept. What are the differences between Self-Concept and Self-Esteem?
6 Describe the fundamental Humanistic approaches to teaching music.
7 Describe the elements of Carl Rogers' Learner-Centered Teaching. Illustrate ways Student-Centered learning is implemented in the music classroom.
8 Provide examples of ways you would develop Self-Esteem and Self-Concept in your students. Define the difference between Self-Esteem and Self-Concept in each example.
9 Provide examples of Cooperative learning in the music classroom. Your example can be in your main concentration (e.g., band, chorus, orchestra, general music) or other areas (e.g., music theory, music appreciation, fine arts survey).
10 Provide examples of ways you embrace diversity and inclusion in your classroom. Your examples should represent a variety of music classrooms (e.g., band, chorus, orchestra, general music, music theory, music appreciation, fine arts survey).

Notes

1 Sharp, A. (2012). Humanistic approaches to learning. In N. M. Seel (Ed.), *Encyclopedia of the sciences of learning*. Boston, MA: Springer. Retrieved June 28, 2020, from https://link.springer.com/referenceworkentry/10.1007%2F978-1-4419-1428-6_530
2 YouTube. (2020). Manteca, Dizzie Gillespie Orchestra. Retrieved June 28, 2020, from https://youtu.be/9xkq2EIY0N8

3   YouTube. (2020). Arturo Sandival. Manteca. Retrieved June 28, 2020, from https://youtu.be/lfiGI6-kmmg

4   YouTube. (2020). Maraca and his Latin Jazz All-Stars: Manteca. Retrieved June 28, 2020, from https://youtu.be/mGoHz1VzRiE

5   Huitt, W. (2001). Humanism and open education. *Educational psychology interactive.* Valdosta, GA: Valdosta State University. Retrieved June 28, 2020, from http://chiron.valdosta.edu/whuitt/col/affsys/humed.html

6   Lefrancois, G. (1999). *Psychology for teaching* (10th ed., p. 239), Wadsworth Publishing.

7   Isbell, D. (2011). Learning theories: Insights for music educators. *General Music Today, 25*(2), 19–23.

8   Standing, E. M. (1998). *Maria Montessori: Her life and work.* London, England: Plume.

9   Maslow, A. H. (1943). A theory of human motivation. *Psychological Review, 50,* 370–396.

10 Simply Psychology. (2020). *Maslow's hierarchy of needs.* Retrieved July 1, 2020, from https://www.simplypsychology.org/maslow.html

11 Corsini, R. J. (1998). *Encyclopedia of psychology.* NJ: John Wiley & Sons. Retrieved July 9, 2020, from https://en.wikipedia.org/wiki/Peak_experience
    Maslow, A. H. (1964). *Religions, values, and peak experiences.* London, England: Penguin Books Limited.

12 Maslow, A. H. (1962). *Toward a psychology of being.* Princeton, NJ: Van Nostrand-Reinhold.

13 Maslow, A. H. (1943). A theory of human motivation. *Psychological Review, 50,* 370–396.
    Maslow, A. H. (1962). *Toward a psychology of being.* Princeton, NJ: D. Van Nostrand Company.
    Maslow, A. H. (1987). *Motivation and personality* (3rd ed.), Delhi, India: Pearson Education.

14 Maslow, A. H. (1943). A theory of human motivation. *Psychological Review, 50,* 370–396.
    Maslow, A. H. (1954). *Motivation and personality.* New York: Harper and Row.

15 Maslow, A. H. (1970a). *Motivation and personality.* New York: Harper & Row.

16 Maslow, A. H. (1970b). *Religions, values, and peak experiences.* New York: Penguin. (Original work published 1966).

17 FreeXenen. (2020). PICTURE. Maslow's hierarchy of needs (MHoN) and the biopsychosocial model in psychology (BPS). Retrieved July 3, 2020, from https://www.freexenon.com/2019/01/04/mhon-bps/

18 Simply Psychology. (2020). Carl Rogers. Retrieved July 2, 2020, from https://www.simplypsychology.org/carl-rogers.html

19 Rogers, C. (1959). A theory of therapy, personality and interpersonal relationships as developed in the client-centered framework. In S. Koch (Ed.), *Psychology: A study of a science. Vol. 3: Formulations of the person and the social context.* New York: McGraw Hill.

20 Rogers, C. (1969). *Freedom to learn.* Columbus, OH: Charles E. Merrill.

21 Rogers, C. (2015). *Client-centred therapy* (p. 489). London: Robinson. (Original work published 1951)Retrieved July 6, 2020, from https://en.wikipedia.org/wiki/Self-actualization

22 Rogers, C. (1959). A theory of therapy, personality and interpersonal relationships as developed in the client-centered framework. In S. Koch (Ed.), *Psychology: A study of a science. Vol. 3: Formulations of the person and the social context.* New York: McGraw Hill.
    McLeod, S. A. (2008). *Self-concept.* Retrieved from www.simplypsychology.org/selfconcept.html

23 McLeod, S. A. (2014). *Carl Rogers. Simply psychology.* Retrieved from https://www.simplypsychology.org/carl-rogers.html

24 Aronson, E., Wilson, T., & Akert, R. (2007). *Social psychology* (p. 113). New York: Pearson Prentice Hall

25 Freund, P. A., & Kasten, N. (1 January 2012). How smart do you think you are? A meta-analysis on the validity of self-estimates of cognitive ability. *Psychological Bulletin, 138*(2), 296–321. Doi: 10.1037/a0026556.

26 Rubie-Davies, C. M. (May 2006). Teacher expectations and student self-perceptions: Exploring relationships. *Psychology in the schools, 43*(5), 537–552. Doi: 10.1002/pits.20169.

27 Craven, R. G., & Marsh, H. W. (1991). Effects of internally focused feedback and attributional feedback on enhancement of academic self-concept. *Journal of Educational Psychology, 83*(1), 17–27. Doi: 10.1037/0022-0663.83.1.17.

28 Reynolds, J. W. (2020). *Music education and student self-concept: A review of literature.* Retrieved July 6, 2020, from http://music.arts.usf.edu/rpme/rpmereyn.htm

29 Zhou, M., & Brown, D. (2015). *Educational learning theories* (2nd ed., p. 1), *Education open textbooks.* Retrieved from https://oer.galileo.usg.edu/education-textbooks/1

30 PGmusic.com. (2020). *Band-in-a-box.* Retrieved July 7, 2020, from https://www.pgmusic.com/bbwin.htm

31 J.W. Pepper, Inc. (2020). Symphony No. 1, Daniel Bukvich. Retrieved July 7, 2020, from https://www.jwpepper.com/Symphony-No.-1/2260198.item#/
     YouTube. (2020). Symphony No. 1 (In Memoriam Dresden, 1945). Retrieved July 7, 2020, from https://youtu.be/eb-efaaygH4

Chapter 7

Brain-Based Learning Theory and Applications to Teaching

Brain-based learning (BBL) theory is built on the structure and function of the brain.[1] BBL is a comprehensive approach to instruction using current research from neuroscience. For many years, there have been primal models of how our brains work. In the 1970s, brain theory began to examine right- and left-brain comparisons. Later, the brain was referred to in terms of a "triune brain," or a brain in three parts. The lower brain is responsible for survival learning, while the middle and the upper brain are responsible for higher-level thinking.[2] Presently, brain theory focuses more on a holistic view of the brain. The theory emphasizes a more systems-based approach wherein the whole is greater than the sum of its parts.

Learning Objectives

1 What are the parts and their primary functions of the brain?
2 What are the key principles of BBL?
3 What are effective strategies for Brain-Based Teaching and Learning?
4 What are the benefits of music education on the brain?

Music teachers employing BBL strategies in the classroom create a learning environment where all students can thrive. They design practical lessons that reflect challenges students may face in real life.

> The instrumental music teacher instructs students' social and team-building skills while preparing students for an end of the year public performance. They guide students through important steps of moving from warm-up area to stage to be seated for performance. The director models proper etiquette, behavior, and placement of sections such as percussion in preparation for performance on the concert stage. In dress rehearsal, the music teacher leads the students through the musical performance of the concert program in the exact same manner and sequence as will be executed in the public concert performance. During the process, the director uses activities that engage students in real life experiences for them to solve problems, think critically, and master the technical, musical, emotional, and social endeavors necessary to effectively collaborate with others in a musical experience.

The Brain

The human brain is the central organ of the human nervous system, and with the spinal cord makes up the central nervous system. The brain consists of the cerebrum, the

DOI: 10.4324/9781003038474-9

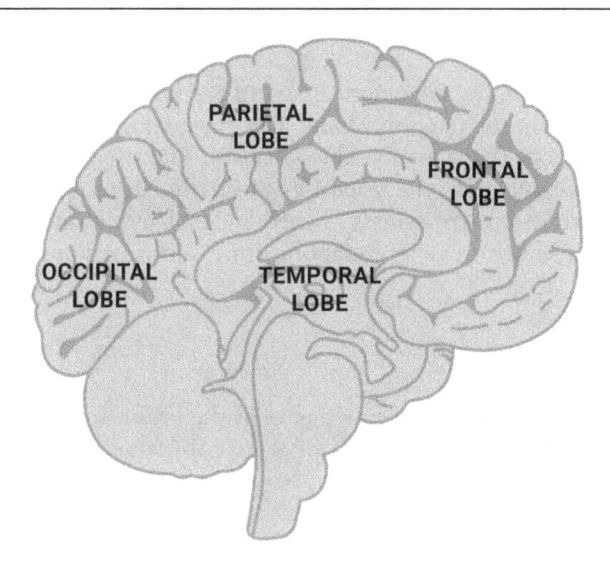

Figure 7.1 The Brain Lobes.

April 12, 2014. Camazine, CC BY 3.0 <https://creativecommons.org/licenses/by/3.0>, via Wikimedia Commons.

brainstem, and the cerebellum. It controls most of the activities of the body, processing, integrating, and coordinating the information it receives from the sense organs, and making decisions as to the instructions sent to the rest of the body.[3]

The human brain is roughly the size of two clenched fists and weighs about 1.5 kilograms. From the outside, it looks a bit like a large walnut, with folds and crevices. Brain tissue is made up of about 100 billion nerve cells (neurons) and 1 trillion supporting cells that stabilize the tissue.[4]

The cerebral cortex is the largest part of the brain. It is divided into four different lobes (Figure 7.1): the parietal lobe, temporal lobe, occipital lobe, and the frontal lobe. Each of the four lobes is responsible for different functions.

Parietal lobe:

- Spatial processing
- Sensory functioning

Temporal lobe:

- Formation of memory
- Processing sound and language

Occipital lobe:

- Visual perceptions

Frontal lobe:

- Reasoning
- Executive function
- Motor skills
- Expressive language

The Amygdala

The amygdala is referred to as the reactive part of the brain. It is part of the limbic system and is located within the temporal lobe. The amygdala is responsible for processing emotions and motivations that are related to survival. The amygdala responds to dangers by creating a fight, flight, or fright response. Overstimulation of the amygdala can be caused by fear, anxiety, embarrassment, boredom, or frustration. When the amygdala is over-stimulated, it enters a hypermetabolic state. Information cannot then be fully processed.

The Prefrontal Cortex

The prefrontal cortex houses the reflective part of the brain. It is responsible for several processes including executive functioning. Executive functioning allows for:

- Problem solving
- Organizing
- Self-monitoring
- Self-correcting
- Making connections
- Prioritizing
- Focusing
- Predicting
- Abstract thinking[5]

Plasticity

The human brain develops from infancy through adulthood through a process known as neuroplasticity.[6] Neural plasticity means that brain structures can be modified under certain conditions, most specifically as a result of injury or through learning experiences (Gottesman & Hanson, 2005).[7] A common axiom in neuroscience is that neurons that wire together fire together and, correspondingly, neurons that fire apart wire apart (Doidge, 2007).[8] This means that learning experiences cause the brain to rewire itself into neural networks. Musicians are good models for plasticity, as the brains of adults who have received significant musical training are different from those who have not (Münte, Altenmüller, & Jäncke, 2002).[9]

Pruning

Genetic instructions and learning experiences work together to sculpt a child's brain into its eventual adult configuration in a process called neural pruning.[10] Pruning, a phase in the development of the nervous system, is the process of synapse elimination that occurs between early childhood and the onset of puberty in humans.[11] Synapses are essential to the transmission of electrical or chemical impulses from one neuron or nerve cell to another throughout the nervous system. Pruning starts near the time of birth and continues into the mid-20s.[12]

A child is constantly engaged in learning, initially in daily living and later through more formal schooling. Synapses that are involved in these learning experiences grow stronger through repetition, and those that are not used gradually wither and are pruned away

(Gopnik, Meltznoff, & Kuhl, 2001).[13] As the child continues to learn, the brain imposes restrictions on itself so that what is learned influences what can be learned (Quartz, 2003).[14] The more a child learns about his/her own culture's language, music, and other perceptual inputs, the less sensitive s/he becomes to other cultures' expressions (Pons, Lewkowicz, Soto-Faraco, & Sebastián-Gallés, 2009).[15]

Neural Networks

The brain has many neural pathways that can replicate another's function in processing sensory and motor signals in parallel. Neural networks represent groups of neurons that act as collectives.[16] The brain is continually making more connections based on how the individual interacts with the environment (Jensen, 1995).[15] Environmental events, such as experiences and the actions that you take, lead to changes in your brain (Jensen, 1995).[17]

Many of the properties and processes of the brain, such as perception, attention, and memory, are best understood through the concept of neural networks (Rolls, 1989).[18] At a more global level, language and music represent neural networks or, perhaps more accurately, multiple neural networks.[16] Information storage is distributed so that any particular item is represented throughout a network rather than in a specific place; moreover, processing proceeds in parallel rather than in serial fashion (Matlin, 2004).[19] Another important detail about networks is that they learn and self-organize.

How well the structures of the brain cooperate and compete is defined as the integration of the brain. Cooperation is defined as the way that the different areas of the brain work together to store and prioritize information and complete tasks. Competition occurs when areas of the brain compete for storage space for the behaviors and resources for which they are responsible.[17] Research indicates that the human brain performs many different functions simultaneously. Consequently, learning is enhanced by a rich environment with a variety of stimuli.

The sophistication or complexity of the brain (shown in Figure 7.2) is never more evident than when the process by which learning occurs. Input comes in from outside stimuli and is routed to the thalamus for processing. Meanwhile, the information is routed simultaneously to appropriate cortical structures (occipital and temporal lobes) and the subcortical areas (the amygdale).[20] Although an intensive and complex process, the initial process takes place with lightning speed, but the subsequent process can take hours, days, or even weeks to complete (Jensen, 1995).[17]

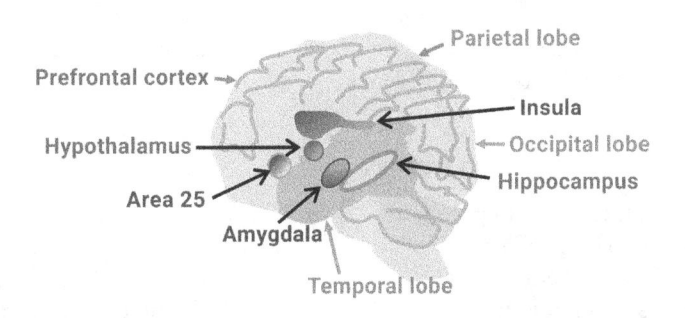

Figure 7.2 Areas of the Brain.

August 24, 2014. Brews ohare, CC BY-SA 3.0 <https://creativecommons.org/licenses/by-sa/3.0>, via Wikimedia Commons.

The Theory of Multiple Intelligences

Howard Gardner's groundbreaking book *Frames of Mind: The Theory of Multiple Intelligences* (1983) taught educators around the globe to understand the actual connections that the brain has with learning. In the late 1980s and early 1990s, thousands of American teachers became intensely interested in learning about brain-based multiple intelligences and finding multiple ways to reach their increasing numbers of diverse learners.[21]

The special significance of Howard Gardner's (1983) theory of multiple intelligences is his claim that all seven of his original intelligences, as well as his eighth, have physiological locations in the brain. His theory proposes the differentiation of human intelligence (or intellectual capacity) into specific "modalities of intelligence," rather than defining intelligence as a single, general ability or cognitive ability.[22] These intellectual capacities encompass linguistic, musical, naturalistic, spatial-visual, logical-mathematical, Interpersonal, Intrapersonal, and bodily-kinesthetic. Drawing upon research in neuropsychology, Gardner (1983) described how different functions of the brain can be related to those distinctive abilities or computations that lie at the core of a human intelligence.[23] He noted that some intelligences are "relatively independent of one another" and that "they can be fashioned and combined in a multiplicity of adaptive ways by individuals and cultures" (pp. 8–9).[24]

The enormous interest in the brain-based multiple intelligences helped to bring about the new field of BBL. Current research in the field of BBL is gleaned from the combined work of neurologists, biologists, psychologists, educators, and physicians to apply this information to teaching and learning.[25] Such investigation provides a theoretical foundation for helping students learn and for helping teachers reach diverse learners in the classroom.

Brain-Based Learning

BBL refers to teaching methods, lesson designs, and school programs that are based on the latest scientific research about how the brain learns, including such factors as cognitive development—how students learn differently as they age, grow, and mature socially, emotionally, and cognitively.[26] BBL draws upon the functioning of the brain and takes into consideration the rules of the brain for meaningful learning.[27] Jensen (1995/2000) defines BBL as "learning in accordance with the way the brain is naturally designed to learn" (p. 6).[28] BBL distinguishes between surface and meaningful knowledge. According to this approach, although memorization can be very important, meaningful knowledge is critical for being successful. Making connections among knowledge, including previous experiences, is essential in meaningful learning.

Principles of Brain-Based Learning

Since the 1990s, educators and psychologists such as Armstrong (2009); Caine, Caine, & Crowell (1999) and Caine, Caine, McClintic, & Klimek (2009); Goleman (1994); Jensen (1995/2000, 2005); and Sousa (2006) have been forerunners in the BBL movement.[29] Table 7.1 presents Geoffrey and Renate Caine's (1994; Caine et al., 1999; Caine et al., 2009) principles of BBL.[30] These principles can be used in pre-kindergarten through secondary classrooms and also in college courses. They enable and encourage teachers to teach successfully to the diversity of learners found in American classrooms.[31]

Table 7.1 Principles of Brain-Based Learning

1. *The brain is a parallel processor:* The brain performs several activities at once. Thoughts, emotions, imagination, and predispositions operate simultaneously and interact with social and cultural knowledge.
2. *Learning engages the entire physiology:* The brain and the body are engaged in learning. Everything that affects our physiological functioning affects our capacity to learn.
3. *The search for meaning is innate:* "The brain's/mind's search for meaning is very personal. The greater the extent to which what we learn is tied to personal, meaningful experiences, the greater and deeper our learning will be" (Caine & Caine, 1994, p. 96).
4. *The search for meaning occurs through patterning:* "The brain is designed to perceive and generate patterns and it resists having meaningless patterns imposed on it" (Caine & Caine, 1994, p. 88).
5. *Emotions are critical to patterning:* What we learn is influenced and organized by emotions. Our emotions are brain based; they play an important role in making decisions. In the groundbreaking The Emotional Brain, Joseph LeDoux (1996) clearly explains how the emotional neural passageways (which originate in our amygdala) influence the neural passageways needed for academic and scholarly work.
6. *The brain processes parts and wholes simultaneously:* The left and the right hemisphere have different functions, but they are designed to work together.
7. *Learning involves both focused attention and peripheral perception:* The brain absorbs information of which it is directly aware, but it also incorporates the one that lie beyond the field of attention. People hold general perceptions of the environment and pay selective attention to various parts of it.
8. *Learning always involves conscious and unconscious processes:* There is interplay between our conscious and our unconscious. Signals that are peripherally perceived enter the brain without the learners' awareness and interact at unconscious levels.
   "One primary task of educators is to help students take charge of their conscious and unconscious processing" (Caine & Caine, 1994, p. 157).
9. *We have at least two different types of memory: spatial and rote:* The rote or taxon memory systems consist of "facts and skills that are stored by practice and rehearsal" (Caine & Caine, 1994, p. 169). Spatial, or autobiographical, memory "builds relationships among facts, events, and experiences" (Caine & Caine, 1994, p. 170). The spatial memory system does not need rehearsal and allows for instant memory of experiences. The counterpart of the spatial memory system is the rote memory system, designed for storing relatively unrelated information.
10. *Learning is developmental:* We understand and remember best when facts and skills are embedded in natural spatial memory. Spatial memory is generally best invoked through experiential learning. Children, and their brains, benefit from enriched home and school environments.
11. *Learning is enhanced by challenge and inhibited by threat:* The brain downshifts under perceived threat and learns optimally when appropriately challenged. Ideally, students benefit when their assignments are challenging and the classroom environment feels safe and supportive.
12. *Each brain is uniquely organized:* We all have the same set of systems, but they are integrated differently in every brain. When teaching, we need to consider how each student learns most effectively; each student has his/her own unique set of brain strengths and weaknesses.

Source: From Connell, J. D. (2009b). The Global Aspects of Brain-Based Learning-ERIC, page 30. https://files.eric.ed.gov/fulltext/EJ868336.pdf

Note: This table provides a synopsis of Geoffrey and Renate Caine's (1994); Caine, Caine, and Crowell's (1999); Caine et al.'s (2009) Principles of Brain-Based Learning.

Teaching Strategies for Brain-Based Teaching and Learning

Brain-Based Learning: Teaching the Way Students Really Learn is among a variety of books investigating the student brain, cognitive functioning, and BBL.[32] In his book, *Top 10 Brain-Based Teaching Strategies*, Eric Jensen (2010) focuses on practical primary strategies connecting brain research to student achievement.[33] These approaches provide a plan for improving cognitive functioning, decreasing discipline issues, and fostering effective learning.

Physical Movement Supports Learning. Jensen confirms that physical movement supports learning and is critical to education.[34] Gross motor activity such as walking, games, running, dance, aerobics, team sports, and swimming wires up the brain to make more efficient connections supporting academic learning. Students need 30–60 minutes per day to lower stress response, boost neurogenesis and boost learning.

Social Conditions Influence Our Brain. School behaviors are highly social experiences, which become encoded through our sense of reward, acceptance, pain, pleasure, coherence, affinity, and stress. Teachers should use targeted, planned, diverse social grouping with mentoring, teams, and buddy systems. Teacher-to-student relationships matter, as do student-to-student relationships.[35]

The Brain Changes. The ability of the brain to rewire and remap itself via neuroplasticity is profound. In fact, every child's brain is changing every day as they attend school. Schools can influence this process through skill building, reading, meditation, building thinking skills the achieve student success, and through the arts.[36] Teachers should devote time three to five times per week to teaching attention skills, memory skills, and processing skills. Progress requires focus, buy-in, and time each day to develop these student skill sets.[37]

Stress is a Real Issue. Recent studies suggest 30–50% of all students feel moderately or greatly stressed every day.[37] While some stress is good, chronic or acute stress affects attendance, memory, social skills, and cognition. Therefore, students should be taught better coping skills, increase their perception of choice, physical activity and mentoring, and engagement with the arts. These pursuits increase the student's sense of control over one's life, which lowers stress.[38]

Use Differentiation with Learners. Brain research shows that typical students are all unique, show variations in maturation rates, and have differences in the way they learn. Differentiation is a strategy to deal with the differences in learners. Therefore, make differences the rule, not the exception in your classroom. Never expect all students to be on the same place in the same book on the same day. Allow kids to celebrate diversity, unique abilities, talents, and interests. Give them the skill sets, relationships, and hope to succeed.[38]

Teach Content in Smaller Chunks. New research suggests that students can better hold only three to seven chunks of information in their working memory before overload and new incoming data are missed (Linden et al., 2003).[39] The human brain needs time for the information to store in long-term memory. This time allows for it to retreat to the long-term memory storage.[17] Learning and memory consume physical resources such as glucose and our brain uses this quickly with more intense learning. This is why students get overloaded quickly with content. Hence, teachers should teach in small chunks, process the learning, and then rest the brain. Too much content taught in too short of time means the brain cannot process it, so students simply don't learn it. Breaks, recess, and downtime make more sense than content, content, and more content.[40]

The Arts are Essential. Recent research shows that certain arts boost attention, working memory, and visual special skills. Other arts such as dance and theatre boost social skills, empathy, timing, patience, verbal memory, and other transferable life skills.[41] The Arts should be made mandatory. Students should be given the choice of several Arts classes with Master teachers and time to excel in each discipline. Evidence suggests that students get the most value from 30 to 60 minutes a day for three to five days a week. The Arts support the development of the brain's academic operating systems in ways that provide many transferable life skills.[42]

Learning Encompasses the Emotions. While it is important to read and manage the emotional states of students in the classroom, appropriate conditions of order such as honor, patience, forgiveness, and empathy must be taught as life skills to students. Whereas most students are not getting these taught at home, the teacher should offer quick, daily skill-building with blended-in-daily practice. Just as students learn well and behave better while in good emotional states, teachers must build social skills in every lesson. They should use social structures that advocate in cooperative learning, trust, and humility every day. For students who learn patience, attention, empathy, and cooperation will be better students.

Accommodate Exceptional Learners. There are a variety of effective strategies that accommodate students with brain-based disorders including Asperger's, learning delays, dyslexia, and autism.[43] It is essential that teachers learn the latest methods and strategies to facilitate learning of exceptional learners in today's classroom. As inclusive education promotes that all students are full and accepted members of the school community in which the educational setting is the same for exceptional and nondisabled students, it is essential for teachers to create a learning environment where all students can thrive. Most students can be integrated into the classroom, but not with inclusion-only strategies. It is the responsibility of the teacher to collaborate with school specialists and programs to discover methods, procedures, and resources available to accommodate student learning in the classroom.

Review Strengthens Learning. Researchers have discovered that repetition strengthens connections in the brain. The synapses are not static. They are constantly adapting in response to activity. By following a pattern of presenting information to students, the probability that the students will not only retain the information but also be able to access or activate the information and/or skills learned faster and more accurately in the future is increased (Jensen, 1995).[44]

Accordingly, we understand and remember best when facts and skills are embedded in natural spatial memory. Every time we retrieve a memory, it goes into a volatile, flex state in which it is temporarily easily reorganized. Yet, without review, we are less likely to recall our learning. This suggests that teachers use several strategies to continually strengthen memory over time instead of assuming that once learned, the memory is preserved. Therefore, teachers should review the content halfway between the original learning and the test. Additionally, teachers should mediate the review process with students through structured reviews such as quizzes or group work that ensures quality control. Otherwise, the material is more likely to get confused and learning is lost.

Music Education and the Brain

Neuroscientists have worked for over four decades to understand how the brain processes music, affects emotions, and changes brain development. Much of the research reveals a large number of benefits from music education including improvements in memory, language acquisition, executive function, and brain plasticity. These findings offer the beginnings of an evidence-based argument in favor of music education for every child.[45] While not all these findings have direct applications to the daily practice of music education, collectively they have much to offer the profession. Notable conclusions from neuromusical studies are summarized in these concepts.

- *The human brain has the ability to respond to and participate in music.* Much of the literature that supports this assertion comes from anthropologists who tell us that "all people in all times and places have engaged in musical behaviors."[46]

- *The musical brain operates at birth and persists throughout life.* The fact that babies respond to music at birth and individuals continue to engage in musical experiences into the other end of the life spectrum gives strong evidence for the existence of neural mechanisms that seem ideally suited for processing musical information.[47]
- *Early and ongoing musical training affects the organization of the musical brain.* There are growing indications that those who study music, particularly beginning at an early age, show neurological differences compared to those who have not had such training. For example, musically trained subjects had stronger and faster brain responses to musical tasks than untrained subjects.[48]
- *The musical brain consists of extensive neural systems involving widely distributed, but locally specialized regions of the brain.* A review of neuromusical research literature leads to the conclusion that music is represented all over the brain.[49]

  - *Cognitive components.* Studies have indicated that music processing involves functionally independent modules. For instance, neural mechanisms for melodic, harmonic, and rhythmic error detection were found to be independent from each other.[49]
  - *Affective components.* Although emotional response to music is perhaps one of the most important topics of research, it is also among the most difficult to study.
  - *Motor components.* The connection between music and movement is fundamental to both expressive and receptive modes. Music making (expressive mode) is clearly a bodily kinesthetic experience.

- *The musical brain is highly resilient.* Music persists in people who are blind, deaf, emotionally disturbed, profoundly retarded, or affected by disabilities or diseases. Regardless of the degree of disability or illness, it is possible for the individual to have a meaningful musical experience.[50]

Hodges (2000) attests that there is one more idea that has profound implications for the music education profession. Neuromusical research supports the notion that music is a unique mode of knowing. The literature clearly supports the view that music is dissociated from linguistic or other types of cognitive processes. Hence, it provides a unique means of processing and understanding a particular kind of nonverbal information. By studying the effects of music, neuroscientists are able to discover things about the brain that they cannot know through other cognitive processes.[51]

Questions

1 Describe the anatomy of the brain. Discuss the functions of each lobe and part of the brain.
2 Describe plasticity, pruning, and the brain's neural networks in human development and human learning.
3 Describe Caine, Renate, and Geoffrey Caine's (1994) twelve principles of BBL.
4 Discuss how the principles of BBL can be used in the music classroom.
5 Describe the strategies for BBL.
6 Discuss how BBL approaches can improve cognitive functioning and foster effective learning.
7 Outline prominent strategies of brain-based teaching and learning that provide a plan for improving cognitive functioning, decreasing discipline issues, and fostering effective learning in the school program.

8 Describe benefits of music education on the brain.
9 Discuss the ways that cognitive, affective, and motor components are evident in the musical brain.
10 Discuss the relationships among participation in music, musical training, and music as a unique way of knowing associated with the musical brain.

Notes

1 Ramakrishnan, J. (2013). Brain based learning strategies. *International Journal of Innovative Research & Studies, 2*(5), 236–242.
2 Bonomo, V. (2017). Brain-based learning theory. *Journal of Education and Human Development, 6*(1), 27–43. ISSN: 2334-296X.
3 *The human brain.* Retrieved February 19, 2021, from, https://en.wikipedia.org/wiki/Human_brain
4 *How does the brain work?* Cologne, Germany: Institute for Quality and Efficiency in Health Care (IQWiG). Retrieved February 18, 2021, from https://www.ncbi.nlm.nih.gov/books/NBK279302/
5 *Brain-based learning—The cerebral cortex.* Retrieved February 19, 2021, from, http://etec.ctlt.ubc.ca/510wiki/Brain-based_Learning
6 Hodges, D. A., & Sebald, D. C. (2011). *Music in the human experience: An introduction to music psychology* (p. 377). New York: Taylor & Francis.
7 Gottesman, I., & Hanson, D. (2005). Human development: Biological and genetic processes. *Annual Review of Psychology, 56,* 263–286.
8 Doidge, N. (2007). *The brain that changes itself.* New York: Penguin.
9 Münte, T., Altenmüller, E., & Jäncke, L. (2002). The musician's brain as a model of neuroplasticity. *Nature Neuroscience, 3,* 473–378.
10 Hodges, D. A., & Sebald, D. C. *Music in the human experience: An introduction to music psychology* (p. 376). Taylor & Francis.
11 Chechik, G., Meilijson, I., & Ruppin, E. (1998). Synaptic pruning in development: A computational account. *Neural Computation, 10*(7), 1759–1777.
12 Brain's synaptic pruning continues into your 20s. New Scientist. Retrieved March 2, 2021, from https://www.newscientist.com/article/dn20803-brains-synaptic-pruning-continues-into-your-20s/
13 Gopnik, A., Meltznoff, A., & Kuhl, P. (2001). *The scientist in the crib.* New York: Perennial.
14 Quartz, S. (2003). Learning and brain development: A neural constructivist perspective. In P. Quinlan (Ed.), *Connectionist models of development* (pp. 279–309). New York: Psychology Press.
   Hodges, D. A., & Sebald, D. C. (2011). *Music in the human experience: An introduction to music psychology* (p. 409). New York: Taylor & Francis.
15 Pons, F., Lewkowicz, D., Soto-Faraco, S., & Sebastián-Gallés, N. (2009). Narrowing of intersensory speech perception in infancy. *Proceedings of the National Academy of Sciences, 106*(26), 10598–10602.
16 Hodges, D. A., & Sebald, D. C. (2011). *Music in the human experience: An introduction to music psychology* (p. 160). New York: Taylor & Francis.
17 Jensen, E. (1995). *Brain-based learning.* Del Mar, CA: Turning Point Publishing (388 pages).
18 Rolls, E. (1989). The representation and storage of information in neuronal networks in the primate cerebral cortex and hippocampus. In R. Durbin, C. Miall, & G. Mitchison (Eds.), *The computing neuron* (pp. 125–159). New York: Addison-Wesley.
19 Matlin, M. (2004). *Cognition* (6th ed.), New York: John Wiley & Sons.
20 Jensen, E. (1995). *Brain-based learning* (p. 28). Del Mar, CA: Turning Point Publishing.
21 Connell, J. D. (2009a). Global aspects of brain-based learning. *Educational Horizons, 88*(1), 28–39.
22 Gardner, H. (1983). *Frames of mind: The theory of multiple intelligences.* New York: Basic Books.
23 Gardner, H. (1983). *Frames of mind: The theory of multiple intelligences* (p. 63). New York: Basic Books.
24 Gardner, H. (1983). *Frames of mind: The theory of multiple intelligences* (pp. 8–9). New York: Basic Books.

25 Connell, J. D. (2009a). Global aspects of brain-based learning. *Educational Horizons, 88*(1), 28.

26 The glossary of education reform. *Brain-based learning.* Retrieved March 6, 2021, from https://www.edglossary.org/brain-based-learning/

27 Husain, Nd. Brain based learning: Pedagogical implications. In K. Yadav, H. K. Khandai, & A. Mathur (Eds.), *Innovations in Indian education system* (1st ed.), Delhi, India: Shipra Publications.

28 Jensen, E. (2000). Brain-based learning. *The new science of teaching and training* (Rev. ed.), Thousand Oaks, CA: Corwin Press. (Original work published 1995).

29 Armstrong, T. (2009). *Multiple intelligences in the classroom* (3rd ed.), Alexandria, VA: Association for Supervision and Curriculum Development.
   Caine, R., Caine, G., & Crowell, S. (1999). *Mindshifts: A brain-compatible process for professional development and the renewal of education.* Tucson, AZ: Zephyr Press.
   Caine, R., Caine, G., McClintic, C., & Klimek, K. (2009). *12 Brain/mind learning principles in action: Developing executive functions of the human brain.* Thousand Oaks, CA: Corwin Press.
   Goleman, D. (1994). *Emotional intelligence: Why it can matter more than IQ.* New York: Bantam Books.
   Jensen, E. (2000). *Brain-based learning: The new science of teaching and training.* Thousand Oaks, CA: Corwin Press. (Original work published 1995).
   Jenson, E. (2005). *Teaching with the brain in mind* (2nd ed.), Alexandria, VA: Association for Supervision and Curriculum Development.
   Sousa, D. (2006). *How the brain learns* (3rd ed.), Thousand Oaks, CA: Corwin Press.

30 Caine, R., & Caine, G. (1994). *Making connections: Teaching and the human brain* (Rev. ed.), Menlo Park, CA: Addison-Wesley.
   Caine, R., Caine, G., & Crowell, S. (1999). *Mindshifts: A brain-compatible process for professional development and the renewal of education.* Tucson, AZ: Zephyr Press.
   Caine, R., Caine, G., McClintic, C., & Klimek, K. (2009). *12 Brain/mind learning principles in action: Developing executive functions of the human brain.* Thousand Oaks, CA: Corwin Press.

31 Connell, J. D. (2009b). *The global aspects of brain-based learning-ERIC.* Retrieved March 6, 2021, from https://files.eric.ed.gov/fulltext/EJ868336.pdf

32 Jensen, E., & McConchie, L. (2020). *Brain-based learning: Teaching the way students really learn* (3rd ed.), Thousand Oaks, CA: Corwin Press.

33 Jensen, E. (2010). *10 Most effective tips for using brain based teaching & learning.* Maunaloa, HI: Eric Jensen Publishing.

34 Jensen, E. (2010). *10 Most effective tips for using brain based teaching & learning* (p. 3). Maunaloa, HI: Eric Jensen Publishing.

35 Jensen, E. (2010). *10 Most effective tips for using brain based teaching & learning* (p. 4). Maunaloa, HI: Eric Jensen Publishing.

36 Jensen, E. (2010). *10 Most effective tips for using brain based teaching & learning* (p. 5). Maunaloa, HI: Eric Jensen Publishing.

37 Johnston-Brooks, C. H., Lewis, M. A., Evans, G. W., & Whalen, C. K. (1998, September–October). Chronic stress and illness in children: The role of allostatic load. *Psychosomatic Medicine, 60*(5), 597–603.
   Koomen, H. M., & Hoeksma, J. B. (2003, Dec). Regulation of emotional security by children after entry to special and regular kindergarten classes. *Psychological Reports, 93*(3), 1319–1334.

38 Jensen, E. (2010). *10 Most effective tips for using brain based teaching & learning* (p. 6). Maunaloa, HI: Eric Jensen Publishing.

39 Linden, D. E., Bittner, R. A., Muckli, L., Waltz, J. A., Kriegeskorte, N., Goebel, R., & Munk, M. H. (2003). Cortical capacity constraints for visual working memory: Dissociation of FMRI load effects in a frontoparietal network. *Neuroimaging, 20*(3), 1518–1530.

40 Jensen, E. (2010). *10 Most effective tips for using brain based teaching & learning* (p. 7). Maunaloa, HI: Eric Jensen Publishing.

41 Posner, M., Rothbart, M. K., Sheese, B. K., & Kieras, J. (2008). How arts training influences cognition. In C. Asbury, & B. Rich (Eds.), *Learning, arts, and the brain: The Dana consortium report on arts and cognition* (pp. 1–10). Organized by M. Gazzaniga. New York/Washington, D.C.: Dana Press. Retrieved from www.dana.org

Jonides, J. (2008). Musical skill and cognition. In C. Asbury & B. Rich (Eds.), *How arts training influences cognition in learning, arts, and the brain: The Dana consortium report on arts and cognition* (pp. 11–16). Organized by M. Gazzaniga. New York/Washington, D.C.: Dana Press. Retrieved from www.dana.org

Spelke, E. (2008). Effects of music instruction on developing cognitive systems at the foundations of mathematics and science. In C. Asbury & B. Rich (Eds.), *How arts training influences cognition in learning, arts, and the brain: The Dana consortium report on arts and cognition* (pp. 17–50). Organized by M. Gazzaniga. New York/Washington, D.C.: Dana Press. Retrieved from www.dana.org

42 Jensen, E. (2010). *10 Most effective tips for using brain based teaching & learning* (p. 8). Maunaloa, HI: Eric Jensen Publishing.

43 Jensen, E. (2010). *10 Most effective tips for using brain based teaching & learning* (p. 9). Maunaloa, HI: Eric Jensen Publishing.

44 Jensen, E. (2010). *10 Most effective tips for using brain based teaching & learning* (p. 28). Maunaloa, HI: Eric Jensen Publishing.

45 Collins, A. (2014). Music education and the brain: What does it take to make a change? *Update, 32*(2), 4–10.

46 Donald H., & Haack, P. (1996). The influence of music on human behavior. In D. Hodges (Ed.), *Handbook of music psychology* (2nd ed.). University of Texas at San Antonio, San Antonio: IMR Press.

47 Jeane-Pierre, L. (1996). Prenatal auditory experience. In I. Deliege & J. Sloboda (Eds.), *Musical beginnings: Origins and development of music competence* (pp. 3–34). Oxford, England: Oxford University Press.

Papoušek, H. (2012). Musicality in infancy research: Biological and cultural origins of early musicality. In I. Deliège & J. Sloboda (Eds.), *Musical Beginnings: Origins and Development of Musical Competence* (pp. 37–55). Oxford, England: Oxford Academic. Retrieved February 23, 2023, from https://doi.org/10.1093/acprof:oso/9780198523321.003.0002

48 Faita, F., & Besson, M. (1994). Electrophysiological index of musical expectancy: Is there a repetition effect on the event-related potentials associated with musical incongruities? In I. Deliege (Ed.), *Proceedings of the 3rd International Conference for Music Perception and Cognition* (pp. 433–435), University of Liege, Belgium.

49 Parsons, L., Fox, P. & Hodges D. (1998, November). "Neural Basis of the Comprehension of Musical Melody, Harmony, and Rhythm," paper presented at a meeting of the Society for Neuroscience, Los Angeles.

50 Hodges, D. (2000). Implications of music and brain research. *Music Educators Journal, 87*(2), 18–21.

51 Hodges, D. (2000). Implications of music and brain research. *Music Educators Journal, 87*(2), 21.

Part II

Theory Applied to Practice

Cognitive Approaches in Teaching and Learning

Cognitive approaches to learning are concerned with how information is processed by learners. When teachers apply a cognitive approach to learning and teaching, they focus on the understanding of information and concepts. If students are able to understand, the connections between concepts, break down information, and rebuild with logical connections, then their retention of material and understanding will increase.

Learning Objectives

1 What are the implications of Bruner's Cognitive Development Theories?
2 What are the influences of Gardner's Multiple Intelligence Theory on learning?
3 What are the principles of Bloom's Cognitive, Affective, and Psychomotor Domains?
4 What are the relationships of curriculum, instruction, and assessment in Duke's principles of Intelligent Music Teaching?

As cognitive learning focuses on helping students make effective use of the brain, cognitive theories view students as active in "an internal learning process that involves memory, thinking, reflection, abstraction, motivation, and meta-cognition" (Ally, 2008).[1] Common cognitive learning strategies include encouraging discussion about what is being taught, helping students explore and understand how ideas are connected, asking students to justify and explain their thinking, and using visualizations to improve students' understanding and recall.[2] The following cognitive approaches contribute to effective instruction in the music classroom.

Implications of Bruner's Theories

For cognitive psychologist Jerome Bruner (1961), the purpose of education is not to impart knowledge, but instead to facilitate a child's thinking and problem-solving skills that can then be transferred to a range of situations.[3] Bruner (1966) proposed a course of cognitive development in which effective learners of all ages follow a progression from *enactive* (action-based) to *iconic* (image-based) to *symbolic* (language-based) representation when faced with new material.[4]

The concept of *discovery learning* implies that students construct their own knowledge for themselves. The teacher will design lessons that give students the information they need, but without organizing them. S/He helps students discover the relationship between bits of information to facilitate the learning process. *Spiral curriculum*, a concept widely

DOI: 10.4324/9781003038474-11

attributed to Jerome Bruner (1960), refers to a curriculum design in which key concepts are presented repeatedly throughout the curriculum, but with deepening layers of complexity, or in different applications.[5] Bruner, like Vygotsky, emphasized the social nature of learning, citing that other people should help a child develop skills through the process of scaffolding.[6] As teaching in this manner should lead to children being able to solve problems by themselves, the use of the spiral curriculum can aid the process of discovery learning.[6]

Gardner's Multiple Intelligences

Gardner's Multiple Intelligence (MI) theory (1983)[7] addresses cognitive development in the arts and human development. Gardner (2006) has had a profound impact on education, especially in the United States, by introducing the MI theory as a metacognitive approach to learning.[8] Metacognition is a way of monitoring what one knows and the factors that influence thinking (Martinez, 2006).[9] Gardner focused his studies on challenging the premise that the ability to make accurate judgments is a single entity measured by intelligence.

Gardner believed that cognition develops from an interaction between intrinsic abilities and experiences that help children learn how to develop effective learning strategies.[10] Gardner's MI theory stresses that the character of education is influenced by how well classroom instruction and curriculum are coordinated. The arts can promote and maintain an engaging, exciting, and innovative academic setting. Further, the power of thought can be organized and mastered through learning activities that include descriptions and patterns from the arts, the surrounding environment, real-world knowledge, and society that integrates self-reflection.[11]

Gardner (1991) noted that an open discussion about how old and new experiences become part of education considerably improves learning.[12] The MI theory includes exploring and introducing alternative sources to process information, relating how learning skills are developed. Gardner's MI theory corroborates diverse instructional sequences, curriculum assessments, and pedagogical practices experienced by educators each day.[13] Stimulating the varied learning styles of students promotes how they become skilled at organizing, developing, and managing their environments and life issues (Kornhaber, Fierros, & Veenema, 2004).[14] Metacognitive instructional strategies work with the MI theory and offer an advantage over traditional learning techniques that apply to rote memorization and rehearsed approaches (Kornell & Metcalfe, 2006).[15] Adolescent children particularly benefit greatly from the MI, metacognitive, and memorization strategies, and as children mature, the strategies increase options for solving problems and making decisions.[16]

Bloom's Taxonomy

Bloom's Taxonomy of Educational Objectives (1956) was developed to provide a common language for teachers to discuss and exchange assessment methods and construct learning objectives.[17] Specific learning objectives or outcomes can be derived from the taxonomy, though it is most commonly used to assess learning on a variety of levels.[18] This framework has been applied by generations of K–12 teachers, college and university instructors, and professors in their teaching.

Bloom's taxonomy is a set of three hierarchical models used to classify educational learning objectives into levels of complexity and specificity. The three lists cover the learning objectives in cognitive, affective, and sensory domains.[19] The models were named after Benjamin Bloom (1956), who chaired the committee of educators that devised the taxonomy. He also edited the first volume of the standard text, *Taxonomy of Educational Objectives: The Classification of Educational Goals*.[17]

Knowing how students learn and how their knowledge progresses is an essential element of creating learning experiences. It is not enough to plan for the lower-level thinking, where learners memorize or recite facts. Higher thinking skills must also be addressed, so students can think for themselves, assess situations, and use the facts they memorized to be good and educated humans. Bloom's taxonomy gives the structure on how to write and create materials that address the learning path correctly. This, in turn, allows student learning experiences to be logical, natural, and most beneficial for the learner.[20]

The *cognitive domain* involves knowledge and the development of intellectual skills. This includes the recall or recognition of specific facts, procedural patterns, and concepts that serve in the development of intellectual abilities and skills. In the original version of the taxonomy (1956), the cognitive domain is broken into the six levels of objectives.[21] In the revised edition of Bloom's taxonomy (2001) shown in Figure 8.1, the levels have slightly different names and the order is revised: Remember, Understand, Apply, Analyze, Evaluate, and Create, rather than Synthesize.[22]

Krathwohl's (1964) *affective domain* (Figure 8.2) is perhaps the best known of any of the affective taxonomies.[23] The affective domain includes the manner in which we deal with things emotionally, such as feelings, values, appreciation, enthusiasms, motivations, and attitudes. Affective objectives typically target the awareness and growth in attitudes, emotions, and feelings. There are five levels in the affective domain moving through the lowest-order processes to the highest. The guiding principle for movement through this hierarchy is internalization. Internalization is the process whereby your effect toward something goes from a general awareness level to a point where the effect is internalized and consistently guides or controls one's behavior.[24]

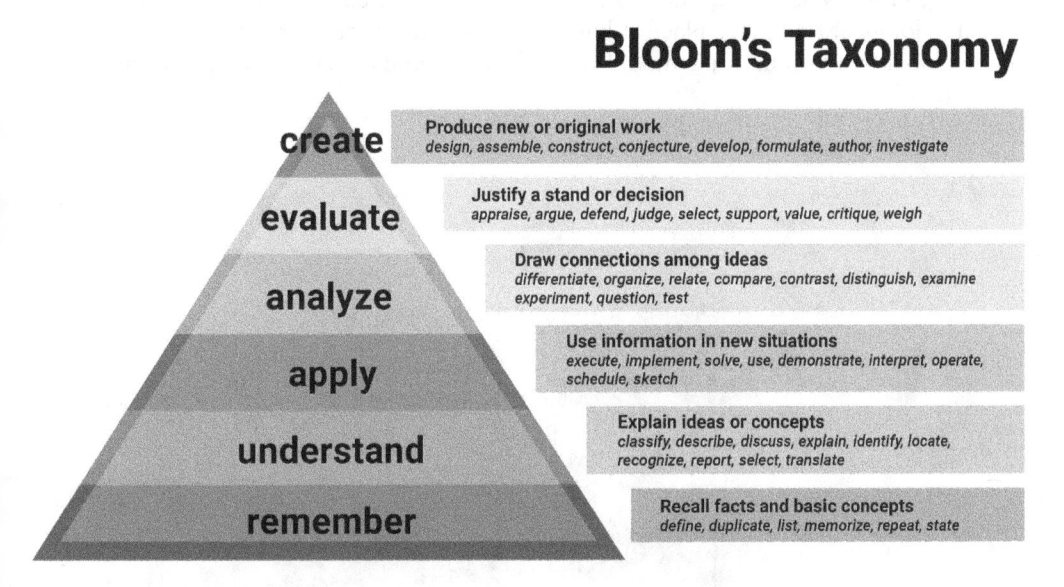

Figure 8.1 Bloom's Revised Taxonomy.

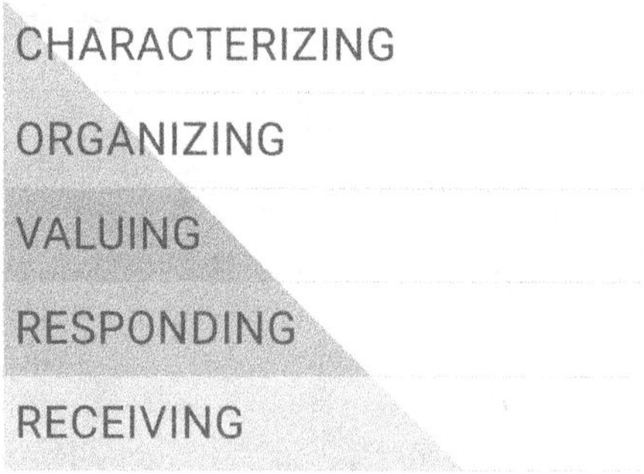

CHARACTERIZING

ORGANIZING

VALUING

RESPONDING

RECEIVING

Figure 8.2 Krathwohl's Affective Domain.

April 11, 2021. Corydave, CC0, via Wikimedia Commons.

Simpson's (1972) *psychomotor domain* (Figure 8.3) is probably the most commonly referenced and used psychomotor domain interpretation. His seven levels of motor skills represent different degrees of competence in performing a skill.[25] The psychomotor domain includes physical movement, coordination, and use of the motor-skill areas. Development of these skills requires practice and is measured in terms of speed, precision, distance, procedures, or techniques in execution. It captures the levels of competence in the stages of learning from initial exposure to final mastery.

Bloom's taxonomy serves as the backbone of many teaching philosophies, in particular, those that lean more toward skills rather than content.[26] Bloom's taxonomy provides a great foundation for developing objectives and establishing benchmarks. Bloom's taxonomy can be used as a teaching tool to help balance evaluative and assessment-based questions in assignments, texts, and in-class engagements to ensure that all orders of thinking, skill development, and affect valuing are exercised in students' learning.[27] The skill development that takes place at higher orders of thinking interacts well with a developing global focus on multiple modalities in learning and the emerging field of integrated disciplines.[28]

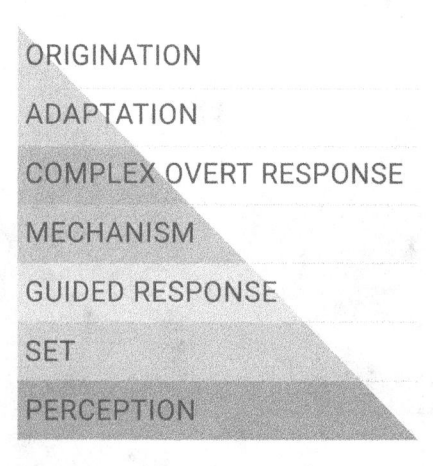

ORIGINATION

ADAPTATION

COMPLEX OVERT RESPONSE

MECHANISM

GUIDED RESPONSE

SET

PERCEPTION

Figure 8.3 Simpson's Psychomotor Domain.

April 11, 2021. Corydave, CC0, via Wikimedia Commons.

Objectives are used for instructional planning tend to emphasize one of the three domains. Separating different kinds of learning in this way facilitates analysis, study, and lesson planning. Cognitive objectives emphasize thinking and other mental processes such as recognition and recall of music elements, vocabulary, forms, and style. Affective objectives are concerned with the internalization of feelings, attitudes, emotions, and appreciation embraced in musical experience, musical preference, and emotive responses to musical performance. Psychomotor objectives emphasize physical skill and technique development applied in reading notation, singing, and playing instruments.

Bloom's Taxonomy: Implications for Music Education

The Bloom's new taxonomy (Anderson & Krathwohl, 2001) is a practical tool to translate music education outcomes into objective criteria to assess student achievement.[29] Many of the complex cognitive aspects of music learning are addressed in the new taxonomy and are inherently related to affective and psychomotor learning domains of knowledge.

The new taxonomy is a framework for aligning learning objectives, curriculum, and assessment that match the complexity of learning while addressing important aspects of subject matter-specific instruction.[30] This section shows how the cognitive framework can be applied to music education by analyzing select objectives of the original nine national standards in music education (MENC, 1995).[31] These examples of standards 1, 2, and 7 are taken from *Music Educators National Conference, Performance Standards for Music: Strategies and Benchmarks for Assessing Progress Toward the National Standards, Grades PreK–12* in the five through eighth grade-level section of that document (MENC, 1996).[32]

National standard 1. Singing, alone and with others, a varied repertoire of music.

Achievement standard: 1a. Students sing accurately and with good breath control throughout their singing ranges, alone and in small and large ensembles.

In this example, the main objectives are to "sing accurately" in the "full range of the voice" and with "breath control." Alone and in a group and a varied repertoire are further requirements of the standard. Singing is the verb that indicates the cognitive process involved. Referring to Table 8.1, singing is a type of cognitive process related to the "Apply" category because it is the "carrying out of an action." It also can be classified further in the subcategory executing because it is "applying a procedure to a familiar task." The nouns, "breath control," "range," and "accuracy," indicate knowledge of correct "Procedures," and pertain specifically to "subject specific skills, techniques, and methods," in this case, singing. Therefore, national standard 1a is placed in the "Apply" and "Procedural" cell of the taxonomy grid.[33]

National standard 2. Performing on instruments, alone and with others, a varied repertoire of music.

Achievement standard: 2d. Students play by ear simple melodies on a melodic instrument and simple accompaniments on a harmonic instrument.

In this example, the main objective is to "play by ear." "Performing on a melodic and a harmonic instrument" are further requirements pertaining to the objectives. The verb play indicates the cognitive process involved. Referring to Table 8.1, playing is a type of cognitive process related to the category "Apply" because it is the "carrying out of an action." It can also be further classified in the subcategory executing because it is "applying a procedure to a familiar task." The noun in the objective "by ear" indicates Metacognitive knowledge because it uses "knowledge of cognition in general as well as awareness and knowledge of one's own cognition." In this case, the specific types of

Table 8.1 The New Bloom's Taxonomy Applied to Select National Standards for Music Education

Type of Knowledge	Remember Recognize Recall	Understand Interpret Exemplify Summarize Infer Compare Explain	Apply Execute Implement	Analyze Differentiate Organize Attribute	Evaluate Check Critique	Create Generate Plan Produce
Factual						
Terminology						
Basic Elements						
Procedural			1a			
Skills			Singing			
Techniques and methods						
Performance criteria						
Metacognitive			2d		7a	
Knowledge of self and our own personal cognition of music			Playing by ear		Evaluating music performances	
Strategic knowledge						
Knowledge of cognitive demands for different tasks						
Self-knowledge						

Source: Copyright (c) 2022 Edward McClellan.

Metacognitive knowledge used are "strategic knowledge" because it involves "outlining as a means of capturing the structure," and "cognitive task knowledge" because the task demands "knowledge of the cognitive demands of different tasks." For that reason, national standard 2d is placed in the "Apply" and "Metacognitive" cell of the taxonomy grid.[34]

National standard 7. Evaluating music and music performances.

Achievement standard: 7a. Students develop criteria for evaluating the quality and effectiveness of music performances and compositions and apply the criteria in their personal listening and performing.

In this example, the main objective is to "develop criteria." Applying the criteria to compositions and performances are further requirements pertaining to the objective. The verbs "develop" and "apply" criteria indicate the cognitive process involved. Referring to Table 8.1, "develop criteria" is a type of cognitive process related to the category "Evaluate" because it is the ability to "make judgments based on criteria and standards." It can also be further classified into the subcategories checking because it is "detecting inconsistencies and effectiveness within a process or product," and critiquing because it is "detecting inconsistencies and between a product and external criteria to determine its external consistency." Personal listening and performing indicate the Metacognitive knowledge area. In this case, the specific type of Metacognitive knowledge used is strategic knowledge because it involves "outlining as a means of capturing the structure," specifically applying criteria to a performance of music that has personal meaning and cognitive task knowledge because the task demands "knowledge of the cognitive demands of different tasks," such as being able to evaluate a performance by using an evaluation form. As a result, national standard 7a is placed in the "Evaluate" and "Metacognitive" cell of the taxonomy grid.[35]

As shown in Table 8.1, the national standards for music education represent a wide range of complex cognitive abilities and knowledge domains. This is good news for music educators because the authors of the revised taxonomy encourage educators to enhance their pedagogical approaches by addressing the more complex cognitive and knowledge areas. It is gratifying to know music education is already doing this quite well and can participate in standardized assessment by using this widely shared educational language.[36]

Designing Learning Goals

Learning goals are most effective when they are coordinated across all levels of learning, from curriculum to course to assignment and even to lessons. Bloom's is a powerful tool to help develop learning objectives because it explains the process of learning. By using this framework, students can build on their learning and progress through the levels throughout the term.

Most recommendations for articulating student learning goals emphasize three main issues. Learning goals should (1) be student-centered, (2) emphasize the appropriate cognitive task using codified verbs, and (3) name the applicable course content. Some also recommend (4) clarifying any constraints, such as time, approved reference material, etc., and (5) listing the specific instruction that prepares students, such as a lesson, reading, module, course, etc.[37] One of the most crucial elements of a learning goal is a verb that clearly defines the intended task. These verbs both focus attention on student-doing and indicate possible methods of assessment. The most commonly referred to taxonomy of such verbs is by learning theorists Bloom and Krathwohl (1956),[38] updated by Anderson and Krathwohl (2001).[39] Figure 8.4 presents Cognitive Verbs from the six hierarchical categories of knowledge of the Cognitive Domain after Bloom and Krathwohl (1956).[38]

Table 8.2 shows examples of Music Theory goals articulated with the traditional music theory verb and the most appropriate Bloom verb in parentheses.

Table 8.2 Sample Music Theory Learning Goals with Clarifying Bloom Verbs

Student-centered	Music theory verb (Bloom verb)	Course content	Constraints as applicable	Associated instruction as applicable
Students will	diagram (analyze)	the form of a movement	after listening once	using techniques covered in the lecture on diagramming form
Students will	harmonize (select)	a short diatonic melody	in keyboard style, using appropriate progressions, inversions, and voice leading	at the end of the course
Students will	error-detect (judge)	discrepancies in pitch or rhythm between a notated and heard excerpt	after three hearings	

Source: Select Parts of This Table Were Extracted from Example 1 of: Bakker, S. (2020). *Creating Measurable Learning Objectives. Engaging Students: Essays in Music Pedagogy.* https://doi.org/10.18061/es.v7i0.7369. Copyright (c) 2020 Sara Bakker, Permission Granted. https://engagingstudentsmusic.org/article/view/7369/5691

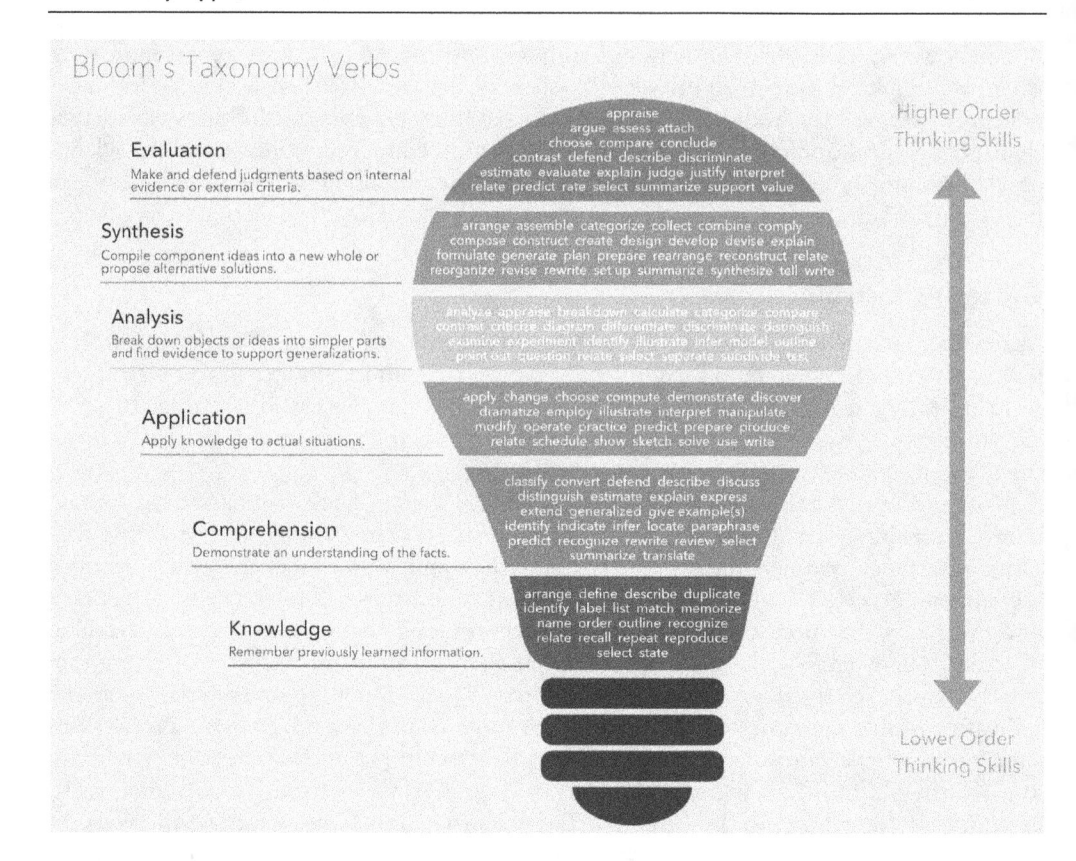

Figure 8.4 Bloom's Taxonomy Cognitive Verbs.

May 22, 2018 John Cummings. Fractus Learning, CC BY-SA 4.0 <https://creativecommons.org/licenses/by-sa/4.0>, via Wikimedia Commons.

Learning goals at this level should use carefully chosen verbs and make the learning task as explicit as possible. The models above do this by including common music theory verbs that are not on Bloom lists, as well as a representative Bloom verb, and puts that verb in the second position of the learning goal.[40]

Intelligent Music Teaching

Duke (2005) explains how teachers can meet the needs of individual students from a wide range of abilities by understanding more deeply how people learn.[41] Learning is a change in what students demonstrate in terms of knowledge, skills, or attitudes.[42] As it is more than remembering, learning "is an inherently active process that requires some doing on the part of the learner."[43] Learning requires that the students apply knowledge or skill or both in some meaningful way.

Course objectives typically include the acquisition and refinement of knowledge, skills (including intellectual and physical skills), and attitudes, all of which ultimately contribute to expert behavior in a discipline. But attitudes are most certainly a component of effective behavior in everything that we teach, although the shaping of attitudes is seldom addressed directly.[44] Unlike other disciplines, music instruction embraces the combination of cognitive, psychomotor, and affective domains in designing goals and objectives for music teaching and learning.

In order to teach well, music teachers must understand intimately and deeply the principles of our discipline and they must be able to articulate those principles clearly and precisely.[45] If teachers are unable to get much deeper into their definition of "responsible ensemble member" or "expressive singing" than to add more adjectives to their description of responsibility (e.g., dependable, prepared, punctual) or expressiveness (e.g., emotive, expansive, lyrical), then it is unlikely that teachers will be able to effectively diagnose their students' problems or to prescribe meaningful solutions.[46]

Although assessment of student learning is often considered a culminating activity, assessment is inextricably related to the goals of instruction. The time to begin thinking about assessment is in the planning stages before instruction actually begins.[47] What to teach (curriculum), how to teach (instruction), and determining whether students have learned (assessment) are not separate at all, but are inextricably interwoven.[48] Therefore, assessment is an ongoing activity, one that should be at the fore in a teacher's thinking, from the first moments of goal setting and throughout the process of planning and implementing instruction.[49]

Planning, teaching, and evaluating the effectiveness of instruction are all predicated on a clear description of what students will do to demonstrate that they've accomplished the goals set out for them.[50] As teachers move through each lesson, rehearsal, and class, they make innumerable observations about their students' knowledge, skills, and attitudes. This informal, ongoing assessment guides their decision-making moment to moment as it clarifies the extent to which their students (1) understand what they are talking about, (2) can do what they ask them, and (3) are interested enough to care.[51]

As assessment should be part of every rehearsal and every class, students should have opportunities to demonstrate what they know and are able to do independently every time they meet with the music teacher. These opportunities need not be elaborate, time-consuming, or burdensome, but they should be so frequent as to become a regular part of instruction. It is not necessary that every student respond alone every day. The teacher may select students to respond in class based on his/her perception of who can provide a good model for their classmates, who needs opportunities to practice, and whom s/he needs to learn more about. Small group demonstrations also provide students opportunities to react to one another's ideas and evaluate one another's performances.[52]

As assessment drives instruction, teachers should design activities of daily instruction that more closely resemble life beyond the classroom and design assessments that more closely resemble the activities of daily instruction. Meaningful assessment focus on what is most important about the discipline, and effective instruction includes frequent opportunities for students to actively practice what is learned.[53] Hence, the day-to-day activities of instruction should closely resemble the assessments.[54]

Learning Activities

1 For this activity, imagine that you are a teacher of a third-grade general music class. At a parent-teacher conference, a parent comes up to you and strongly opines that you should be giving the children lots of worksheets. Write a paragraph describing what you would say to the parent about how your teaching strategies are based on Bruner's philosophy, how you are applying his theory as a teacher, and why worksheets may not be the ideal learning strategy for third graders.[55]

2 Music educators use the Bloom's taxonomy to precisely focus curricula throughout the year, ensuring that students demonstrate the proper cognitive, affective, and psychomotor abilities in each course lesson, activity, and assignment. In your peer group, discuss a particular curricular goal that you may create for a music course (e.g., band, chorus, general music, orchestra, music theory, fine arts survey, other) at a certain level (e.g., elementary, middle, high school). Per your discussion, design one curricular course goal using Bloom's Taxonomy for a semester course.

3 In your peer group, discuss a particular class goal that you may create for a music course (e.g., band, chorus, general music, orchestra, music theory, fine arts survey, other) at the elementary, middle, or high school level. Referencing Table 8.1 in this chapter, design one class lesson cognitive objective using Bloom's Taxonomy. Describe the relationships of your objective to the affective and psychomotor domains of learning.

4 In your peer group, discuss the relationships between curriculum, instruction, and assessment outlined by Duke's Intelligent Music Teaching, for a common music course (e.g., band, chorus, general music, orchestra, music theory, fine arts survey, other) at the elementary, middle, or high school level. Per your discussion, write a short essay describing how you would design instruction and assessment of the given course during the first nine weeks of the semester.

Notes

1 Ally, M. (2008). Foundations of educational theory for online learning. In T. Anderson (Ed.), *Theory and practice of online learning* (pp. 15–43). Retrieved June 2, 2021, from http://www.aupress.ca/index.php/books/120146

2 Grade Power Learning. (2021). *The cognitive learning approach.* Retrieved June 2, 2021, from https://gradepowerlearning.com/cognitive-learning-theory/

3 Bruner, J. (1961). The act of discovery. *Harvard Educational Review*, 31, 21–32.

4 Bruner, J. (1966). *Toward a theory of instruction.* Cambridge, MA: Belkapp Press.

5 Bruner, J. (1960). *The Process of education.* Cambridge, MA: Harvard University Press.

6 Simply Psychology. (2021). *Bruner—Learning theory in education.* Retrieved June 2, 2021, from https://www.simplypsychology.org/bruner.html

7 Gardner, H. (1983). *Frames of mind.* New York, NY: Basic Books.

8 Gardner, H. (2006). *Multiple intelligences: New horizons* (2nd ed.), New York: Basic Books.

9 Martinez, M. (2006). What is metacognition? *Phi Delta Kappan, 87,* 696–699. Retrieved from http://www.kappanmagazine.org/

10 Coleman, V. (2013). National music education standards and adherence to Bloom's revised taxonomy (p. 10). Doctoral Dissertation, Walden University. Retrieved June 10, 2021, from https://scholarworks.waldenu.edu/cgi/viewcontent.cgi?article=2047&context=dissertations

11 Coleman, V. (2013). National music education standards and adherence to Bloom's revised taxonomy (p. 26). Doctoral Dissertation, Walden University. Retrieved June 10, 2021, from https://scholarworks.waldenu.edu/cgi/viewcontent.cgi?article=2047&context=dissertations

12 Gardner, H. (1991). *The unschooled mind: How children think, and how schools should teach.* New York: Basic Books.

13 Coleman, V. (2013). National music education standards and adherence to Bloom's revised taxonomy (p. 28). Doctoral Dissertation, Walden University. Retrieved June 10, 2021, from https://scholarworks.waldenu.edu/cgi/viewcontent.cgi?article=2047&context=dissertations.

14 Kornhaber, M., Fierros, E., & Veenema, S. (2004). *Multiple intelligences: Best ideas from research and practice.* Needham Heights, MA: Allyn & Bacon/Merrill.

15 Kornell, N., & Metcalfe, J. (2006). Study efficacy and the region of proximal learning framework. *Journal of Experimental Psychology/Learning, Memory & Cognition, 32,* 609–622.

16 Coleman, V. (2013). National music education standards and adherence to Bloom's revised taxonomy (p. 29). Doctoral Dissertation, Walden University. Retrieved June 10, 2021, from https://scholarworks.waldenu.edu/cgi/viewcontent.cgi?article=2047&context=dissertations.

17 Bloom, B., Engelhart, M., Furst, E., Hill, W., & Krathwohl, D. (1956). *Taxonomy of educational objectives: The classification of educational goals. Handbook I: Cognitive domain*. New York: David McKay Company..

18 Bloom's Taxonomy. (2021). Introduction. Retrieved June 3, 2021, from https://fctl.ucf.edu/teaching-resources/course-design/blooms-taxonomy/

19 Wikipedia. (2021). *Bloom's taxonomy*. Retrieved June 3, 2021, from https://en.wikipedia.org/wiki/Bloom%27s_taxonomy

20 Gosia. (2020). *Objectives taxonomies: Why use Bloom's taxonomy?* Retrieved June 3, 2021, from http://gosiapytel83.net/objectives-taxonomies-101-part-1-of-4-blooms-taxonomy-revision/

21 Hoy, A. (2007). *Educational psychology* (10th ed., pp. 530–531, 545), Boston, MA: Pearson/Allyn and Bacon.

22 Anderson, L., & Krathwohl, D. (Eds.). (2001). *A taxonomy for learning, teaching, and assessing: A revision of Bloom's taxonomy of educational objectives*. New York: Longman. Armstrong, P. (2010). *Bloom's Taxonomy*. Vanderbilt University Center for Teaching. Vanderbilt University. Retrieved June 3, 2021, from https://cft.vanderbilt.edu/guides-sub-pages/blooms-taxonomy/

23 Krathwohl, D., Bloom, B., & Masia, B. (1964). Taxonomy of educational objectives, the classification of education goals. *Handbook II: Affective domain*. New York: David McKay Co., Inc.

24 Faculty Focus. (2020). *Getting students to discuss by channeling the affective domain*. Retrieved June 3, 2021, from https://www.facultyfocus.com/articles/teaching-and-learning/getting-students-to-discuss-by-channeling-the-affective-domain/

25 Dave, R. (1970). Psychomotor levels. In R. J. Armstrong (Ed.), *Developing and writing behavioral objectives* (pp. 20-21). Tucson, AZ: Educational Innovators Press.

26 Krathwohl, D. R. (2002). A revision of Bloom's taxonomy: An overview. *Theory into Practice, Routledge, 41*(4), 212–218. Anderson, L., & Krathwohl, D. (Eds.). (2001). *A taxonomy for learning, teaching, and assessing: A revision of Bloom's taxonomy of educational objectives*. New York: Longman.

27 Jansen, B., Booth, D., & Smith, B. (2009). Using the taxonomy of cognitive learning to model online searching. *Information Processing & Management, 45*(6), 643–663.

28 Kress, G., & Selander, S. (2012). Multimodal design, learning and cultures of recognition. *Internet and Higher Education, 15*(1), 265–268.

29 Anderson, L., & Krathwohl, D. (Eds.). (2001). *A taxonomy for learning, teaching, and assessing: A revision of Bloom's taxonomy of educational objectives*. New York: Longman.

30 Hanna, W. (2007). The new bloom's taxonomy: Implications for music education. *Art Education Policy Review, 108*(4), 7–16.

31 Music Educators National Conference (MENC). (1995). *Opportunity-to-learn standards*. Reston, VA: Consortium of National Arts Education Associations.

32 MENC. (1996). *Performance standards for music, grades pre-K–12: Strategies and benchmarks for assessing progress toward the national standards*. Reston, VA: Music Educators National Conference.

33 MENC. (1996). *Performance standards for music, grades pre-K–12: Strategies and benchmarks for assessing progress toward the national standards* (p. 9). Reston, VA: Music Educators National Conference.

34 Hanna, W. (2007). The new bloom's taxonomy: Implications for music education. *Art Education Policy Review, 108*(4), 9, 12.

35 Hanna, W. (2007). The new bloom's taxonomy: Implications for music education. *Art Education Policy Review, 108*(4), 13.

36 Hanna, W. (2007). The new bloom's taxonomy: Implications for music education. *Art Education Policy Review, 108*(4), 13–14.

37 Baker, S. (2020). *Creating measurable learning objectives*. Peer Reviewed by: Abigail Shupe, Daniel Blim, Retrieved June 9, 2021, from https://engagingstudentsmusic.org/article/view/7369/5691

38 Bloom, H., & Krathwohl, D. (1956). *Taxonomy of educational objectives*. Retrieved June 9, 2021, from https://www.uky.edu/~rsand1/china2018/texts/Bloom%20et%20al%20-Taxonomy%20of%20Educational%20Objectives.pdf

39 Anderson, L., & Krathwohl, D. (2001). *A taxonomy for learning, teaching, and assessing: A revision of Bloom's taxonomy of education objectives*. Retrieved June 9, 2021, from https://www.uky.edu/~rsand1/china2018/texts/Anderson-Krathwohl%20-%20A%20taxonomy%20for%20learning%20teaching%20and%20assessing.pdf

40 Bakker, S. (2020). *Creating measurable learning objectives. Engaging students: Essays in music pedagogy* (Example 1). https://doi.org/10.18061/es.v7i0.7369 https://engagingstudentsmusic.org/article/view/7369.
41 Duke, R. (2005). *Intelligent music teaching.* Austin, TX: Learning and Behavior Resources.
42 Duke, R. (2005). *Intelligent music teaching* (p. 11). Austin, TX: Learning and Behavior Resources.
43 Duke, R. (2005). *Intelligent music teaching* (p. 12). Austin, TX: Learning and Behavior Resources.
44 Duke, R. (2005). *Intelligent music teaching* (p. 23). Austin, TX: Learning and Behavior Resources.
45 Duke, R. (2005). *Intelligent music teaching* (p. 37). Austin, TX: Learning and Behavior Resources.
46 Duke, R. (2005). *Intelligent music teaching* (p. 36). Austin, TX: Learning and Behavior Resources.
47 Duke, R. (2005). *Intelligent music teaching* (p. 49). Austin, TX: Learning and Behavior Resources.
48 Duke, R. (2005). *Intelligent music teaching* (pp. 50–51). Austin, TX: Learning and Behavior Resources.
49 Duke, R. (2005). *Intelligent music teaching* (p. 52). Austin, TX: Learning and Behavior Resources.
50 Duke, R. (2005). *Intelligent music teaching* (p. 72). Austin, TX: Learning and Behavior Resources.
51 Duke, R. (2005). *Intelligent music teaching* (p. 55). Austin, TX: Learning and Behavior Resources.
52 Duke, R. (2005). *Intelligent music teaching* (p. 61). Austin, TX: Learning and Behavior Resources.
53 Duke, R. (2005). *Intelligent music teaching* (p. 66). Austin, TX: Learning and Behavior Resources.
54 Duke, R. (2005). *Intelligent music teaching* (p. 71). Austin, TX: Learning and Behavior Resources.
55 *Jerome Bruner's theory of development: Discovery learning.* (2021). Retrieved June 2, 2021, from https://study.com/academy/lesson/jerome-bruners-theory-of-development-discovery-learning-representation.html

Chapter 9

Sociocultural Characteristics of Learning in the Music Classroom

The action of teaching and learning is a social process. The social interactions between teacher and student, students with one another, and even with others outside the classroom impact student learning. Students enter the classroom with their own senses of reality, experience, and narratives, and teachers have to acknowledge and integrate this into the classroom setting and the learning process.

Students bring cultural capital into the classroom and teachers have to strive to understand this sociological element in the process of teaching and learning music. Students' backgrounds demand that teachers comprehend how different societies interact with one another in order to maximize learning. The heterogeneous classroom is one predicated upon different modes of social interaction, and a teacher's understanding of this sociological component could be a critical stage in determining success or failure in the reciprocal process of teaching and learning.[1]

Learning Objectives

1 What sociocultural influences impact student learning?
2 What principles of communities of practice enhance student learning in music?
3 What approaches of culturally responsive teaching empower all students in learning music?
4 What principles of social justice can music teachers enact in the music classroom?

Sociological Influences in Music Education

The school continues to be one of the most powerful agents for socialization and the resultant change within a specific culture.[2] In this "powerful organizer of student experience,"[3] students gain knowledge through its specific cultural settings as well as those of its constituents, and this knowledge grows to be important for upcoming learning.[4] It is through the relations among learners, activity, reflection, and perspective that individuals change themselves, teachers change their teaching practice, and change the community of practice (Henry, 2001).[5]

There are many subcultures in schools that possess distinct values and norms held by the group within the wider school culture. The values and practices of a variety of subcultures have a strong influence on individual experiences (Froehlich, 2007).[6] Individuals are socialized by their choice of membership in cultures, their efforts to become familiar with the chosen cultural codes, values, and subculture practices, and by shaping these cultures

DOI: 10.4324/9781003038474-12

and contributing to their cultural production.[7] They identify with these groups, and these associations become part of their identity construction process.[8]

When students decide to pursue band, chorus, orchestra, or other school music courses, the collective impact of people and experiences in the school music culture powerfully affects those students' sense of social identity, identification with the school music program, and individual self-concept as a school music student.[9] Students' perceptions of themselves and how they sense others' perceive them while in music activities and experiences in the school setting have meaningful influence on their development in the overall school program. The ways in which veteran music students mentor, model, and enculturate their newer peers in the context of these music subcultures within the larger general culture of the school is central to their identity construction as a music student.[10]

Communities of Practice

For Wenger (1998, 2000), learning is defined as social participation.[11] Wenger believes that we are all part of distinct communities of practice (CoP), although the vast majority of these do not have labels, as membership is not always explicit. CoP—defined by Wenger and Wenger-Treyner (2015) as "groups of people who share a concern or passion for something they do and learn how to do it better as they interact regularly"—have hitherto been little examined in relation to musical practices.[12] Community members interact with one another due to a shared learning need, bond due to collective learning, and produce common resources as a result.[13]

Wenger (1998) describes the structure of a CoP as consisting of three interrelated elements:

> *Mutual Engagement*: Through participation in the community, members establish norms and build collaborative relationships that bind the community together as a social entity.
>
> *Joint Enterprise*: Through their interactions, members create a shared understanding of what binds them together. The joint enterprise or "domain" is (re)negotiated by its members.
>
> *Shared Repertoire*: The community produces a set of communal resources, known as their shared repertoire that is used in the pursuit of their joint enterprise.[14]

As an educator it is clear to see how a community of practice could aid learners, helping them to build their own learning and promoting social constructivism through interaction, resource creation, and testing. CoP provides participants with an environment that combines knowledge and practice and the opportunity to learn through relationships with their peers and teachers in the community. As music teacher, we can help create the circumstances where a community might be able to develop.[15] Wenger, McDermott, and Snyder (2002) identified seven strategies to allow communities to flourish. Designers of CoP need to:

1 *Design for evolution*: Ensure that the community can evolve and shift in focus to meet the interests of the participants without moving too far from the common domain of interest.
2 *Open a dialogue between inside and outside perspectives*: Allow interactions within and outside the community. Be open to take external perspectives when possible.

3 *Invite different levels of participation*: Ensure that participants can develop and recognize that different members will take on different roles within the CoP.
4 *Develop both public and private community spaces*: Communities that allow open and closed discussions and share information for the common good of the community develop better.
5 *Focus on value*: Demonstrate how participation in the community is beneficial to participants.
6 *Combine familiarity and excitement*: A combination of relatively routine/mundane issues combined with the unusual and unfamiliar engages participants.
7 *Create a rhythm for the community*: A regular and relatively predictable flow of activity helps engagement and persistence of the community.[16]

Kenny (2016) affirms CoP as a rich model for musical participation, community engagement, and transformation in music education. What is common to all musical experiences is the potential to create communities of musical practice (CoMP). Such communities are created through practices: ways of engaging, rules, membership, roles, identities, and learning that is both shared through collective musical endeavor and situated within certain sociocultural contexts[17] of music making, music listening, music analysis, and other musical activities.

The CoMP affords students to experience a sense of belonging, collaborative learning, and identity-building through shared music making and/or musical interest. Student participation in active, creative, and reflective musical experiences as a group of learners enables students to construct knowledge collaboratively, shape their values, and inform their emerging identities with a view to influencing their approach to music learning.[18] Providing spaces and time for such learning experiences to occur builds shared creative musical practices essential within the music classroom.

Culturally Responsive Teaching

Culture is central to learning. It plays a role not only in communicating and receiving information but also in shaping the thinking process of groups and individuals. A pedagogy that acknowledges, responds to, and celebrates fundamental cultures offers full, equitable access to education for students from all cultures.[19]

Culturally Responsive Teaching (CRT) is a pedagogy that recognizes the importance of including students' cultural references in all aspects of learning.[20] Some of the characteristics of CRT are:

Positive perspectives on parents and families. Whether through an informal chat as the parent brings the child to school, in phone conversation, or through newsletters sent home, teachers can begin a dialogue with family members that can result in learning about each of the families through genuine communication. To help parents become aware of how they can be effective partners in the education process, teachers should engage in dialogue with parents as early as possible about parents' hopes and aspirations for their child, their sense of what the child needs, and suggestions about ways teachers can help.[21]
Communication of high expectations. All students should receive the consistent message that they are expected to attain high standards in their school work. While teachers should understand students' behavior in light of the norms of the communities in which they have grown, they should respect all students as learners with

valuable knowledge and experience. Effective and consistent communication of high expectation provides the structure for intrinsic motivation, fosters an environment in which the student can be successful, and helps students develop a healthy self-concept.[22]

Learning within the context of culture. Children learn about themselves and the world around them within the context of culture.[23] People from different cultures learn in different ways. Their expectations for learning may be different. For example, students from some cultural groups prefer to learn in cooperation with others, while the learning style of others is to work independently. To maximize learning opportunities, teachers should gain knowledge of the cultures represented in their classrooms and adapt lessons so that they reflect ways of communicating and learning that are familiar to the students.[24]

Student-centered instruction. In our multicultural society, CRT reflects democracy at its highest level. It means doing whatever it takes to ensure that every child is achieving and ever moving toward realizing his/her potential.[25] Learning is a socially mediated process.[26] Children develop cognitively by interacting with both adults and more knowledgeable peers. Learning is cooperative, collaborative, and community-oriented. Students are encouraged to direct their own learning and to work with other students on projects and assignments that are both culturally and socially relevant to them.

Culturally mediated instruction. Instruction is culturally mediated when it incorporates and integrates diverse ways of knowing, understanding, and representing information. Instruction and learning take place in an environment that encourages multicultural viewpoints and allows for inclusion of knowledge that is relevant to the students. Learning happens in culturally appropriate social situations; that is, relationships among students and those between teachers and students that are congruent with students' cultures.[27]

Reshaping the curriculum. Schools must take a serious look at their curriculum, pedagogy, retention and tracking policies, testing, hiring practices, and all the other policies and practices that create a school climate that is either empowering or disempowering for those who work and learn there.[28] The curriculum should be integrated, interdisciplinary, meaningful, and student-centered. It should include issues and topics related to the students' background and culture. It should challenge the students to develop higher-order knowledge and skills.[29]

Teacher as facilitator. Teachers should develop a learning environment that is relevant to and reflective of their students' social, cultural, and linguistic experiences. They act as guides, mediators, consultants, instructors, and advocates for the students, helping to effectively connect their culturally- and community-based knowledge to the classroom learning experiences. Teachers should use the students' home cultural experiences as a foundation upon which to develop knowledge and skills. Content learned in this way is more significant to the students and facilitates the transfer of what is learned in school to real-life situations.[30]

Lind and McKoy's *Culturally Responsive Teaching in Music Education* (2016) presents teaching methods that are responsive to how different culturally specific knowledge bases impact learning music.[31] It is a pedagogy that recognizes the importance of including students' cultural references in all aspects of learning. According to Lind and McKoy, music is personal; it is a part of who we are, and it is a part of who our students are. We work and teach in a subject area that is integrated into the human psyche, a subject area that is a rich and vibrant reflection of our humanness, yet our classrooms do not always reflect this vibrancy.[32] Several positive impacts CRT may have on music programs, begins with the intrinsic value of music.

CRT validates learners and learning processes acknowledging diversity and by addressing discontinuities between school and home.[33] CRT is empowering because it brings students to the forefront of the learning process, and invites them not only to be academically competent but also to become agents of change. CRT can be transformative in that it challenges traditional curricula and pedagogy through acts of reflection and inquiry. Lind and McKoy's text meets the needs of music teachers who want to learn how to develop culturally responsive approaches to music instruction as they consider ways to make their music classrooms more inclusive and instruction more meaningful.

Diversity—Multicultural Education

For more than two centuries, traditional Western European music has been the foundation on which teachers have built music programs throughout the United States. As the United States and the world become more diverse, the importance for students to study a variety of musical styles, cultures, and genres grows.[34] In recent decades, shifts in demographics and growth in the respect for other cultures have motivated teachers to enhance traditional pedagogies and materials with teaching methods designed to address the growing musical needs of a diverse group of learners.[35]

Many of today's music classrooms are characterized by cultural diversity that demands an inclusive and comprehensive approach to how teachers teach, along with recognition of how children learn. Teachers with students from diverse backgrounds should select musical examples that not only reinforce the learning of a specific concept but also acknowledge the diversity of students involved in learning the concept.[36] Music education should study not only the performance of music but also the people, locations, and cultures involved in the creation of it.

The concepts of multiculturalism developed partially to create a climate that encouraged understanding the differences between cultural groups.[37] Multicultural music education reflects and celebrates cultural diversity within the classroom, allowing students to honor their uniqueness through music (Gonzo, 1993).[38] It promotes the understanding and acceptance of cultures from other parts of the world (Blair & Kondo, 2008; Damm, 2006; Fung, 1995).[39]

The greatest potential for multicultural music education remains the teacher. Regardless of methods or materials, the teacher is the factor that makes a difference in the classroom. To be effective in multicultural classrooms, music teachers must relate teaching content to the cultural backgrounds of their students. They must acknowledge the validity of another music culture, contextualization, and education that is reflective of the diversity both within the music and their class population.[40] It is a challenge to make the change from a Western-exclusive to a world-inclusive perspective. It requires a broader mindset, an openness to the new and different (Volk, 1998).[41]

Authenticity in Student Learning

Repertoire selection for the performance ensemble can be a gateway to exposure to music from other cultures. However, programming music in order to provide a multicultural experience is not the same as programming music in response to student interests and culture, pointing out the difference between "multicultural music education" and CRT (Abril, 2013).[42]

Once the repertoire has been selected, ensemble conductors must consider performance strategies in order to deliver an authentic experience for the students and the concert audience. Although the teacher may have gone through the rigorous process of selecting appropriate repertoire, they may teach the songs through a Westernized pedagogical lens. In choral singing, teachers frequently employ adaptations such as Western vocal technique and Western modes, meters, and vowels that may not be appropriate for songs that are not of European tradition (Goetze, 2000).[43]

Goetze (2000) provides us with strategies to help teachers avoid this common practice: (a) honor the culture by deferring to native musicians from the culture for pronunciations, translations, and performance recommendations; (b) review a plethora of written and media sources; (c) have students learn the music by the method employed within the culture (sometimes aurally); (d) teach students about their voices and the many sounds they can make that are outside of the Western techniques; (e) imitate visual aspects of the performance (movements and facial expressions where applicable); and (f) share information about the culture with students and audience members.[43] Many of these strategies are echoed in Lind and McKoy's book (2016).[31]

Instrumental performers may encounter difficulty in accurately performing multicultural music because of limitations including instrument availability (Abril, 2006; Goetze, 2000).[44] Teachers are advised to work around this barrier by having students imitate cultural sounds to the best of their ability as well as considering percussion pieces. Teaching multicultural music education in the general music classroom may also encounter influence of a typical Westernized music class. It is important that music content not be compromised when incorporating multicultural music education. It is the music teacher's responsibility to form a hybrid learning approach in which students are developing knowledge of musical elements in addition to a sociocultural understanding of musics from around the world.[45]

Music educators have the unique power to impact the lives of their learners. Making use of thoughtful, inclusive music instruction can have positive effects on students that last far beyond their time in the classroom. Teachers are reminded to carefully select repertoire and curricula that is truly representative of the students based on their identities, not on teachers' perceptions.[46] They must acknowledge another music culture, contextualize, and bring authenticity to teaching its music that is reflective of the diversity of the students in the ensemble.

Social Justice in the Music Classroom

Social justice is the view that all people deserve the same rights, opportunities, and advantages. A discipline in itself, social justice is more than just a topic in a day's lesson plan, but rather a frame of mind and a concept that permeates curricula in music classrooms that are committed to equity for all. Music is an ideal medium through which to teach social justice.[47]

What happens in the music classroom is fundamental to teaching for social justice. As teachers, we must acknowledge the lives our students are living and provide supports and focused strategies whenever possible.[47] For example, a new teacher of an instrumental music program that recognizes the disparity between students from different socioeconomic backgrounds becomes aware that some students may have easier access to instruments and private lessons than others do. With this knowledge, the teacher initiates strategies to remedy these disparities of access and inequity so that all students have instruments and opportunities for private study.

Social justice in education requires addressing economic disparities, issues in policy, and social rights that affect our students. Within education, social justice issues that affect our students include inadequate school funding, school closures, the achievement gap, and discrimination. Social justice issues that may affect a school music program include funding sources and distribution, lack of facilities and resources, and student and parent disfranchisement. While these issues are examples on a broad scale, music teachers should examine particular social justice issues or concerns within their own local school community so that circumstantial solutions can be achieved within one's own school music program.[48]

According to Wright (2010), one's social groups dictate how resources, education, opportunity, and knowledge are distributed.[49] In this way, geographical location and financial disparities between working-class, middle-class, and affluent families can create achievement gaps and limit participation within music programs by inadvertently denying access (Bates, 2012).[50] For example, expenses associated with school music ensembles and classes (i.e., instrument rentals, supplies, maintenance and repair, uniforms, lessons, and transportation) can create an access barrier, where students and families who want to participate in music may not be able to afford to do so (Bates, 2012).[50] Financial burdens and lack of resources may alienate students or deny some equal access to music programs even though a school district created opportunities with the intention of engaging all students. Familial support for student participation may also vary from social class to social class.[51]

Juliet Hess (2017) suggests that there are a number of ways that teachers can enact principles of social justice in the music classroom.[52] Schools, historically and currently, are often part of the system that constructs barriers that impede students of color and students who deal with systemic poverty from easily succeeding in school.[53] In looking to undo the structures that oppress young people, teachers can shape a curriculum and a pedagogy that purposefully places classroom musics alongside students' own musics, experiences, and interests. For example, a whole-school curriculum that features the achievements of white American or Western European men unintentionally limits the number of students who can see themselves reflected in the school. Music teachers can challenge that practice by consciously seeking out content such as those composed by women and composers of a variety of ethnicities. They can also engage teaching strategies that extend ideas of who participates in music.[54]

Teachers might work to enact CRT. Lind and McKoy (2016) note that students must have "opportunities to engage with music in ways that are congruent with their own lived cultural experiences with music."[55] In music class, that may mean that teachers broaden their program to include the musics deeply valued by the children they teach and that their selection of musics should change every year as they continue to meet different student populations with ever-evolving tastes and interests.[54] It may also mean that teachers draw on the rich musical practices that students enact outside of school. If their students engage in complex informal practices of music learning such as producing hip-hop tracks, playing in drum circles, or performing in mariachi bands, teachers might engage such practices in schools, as music education scholar Lucy Green suggests,[56] so that their program uses pedagogy that draws on formal and informal learning strategies, and both written notation and aural learning.[54]

Alongside a traditional ensemble practice, teachers might encourage a thriving hip-hop songwriting program. Teachers can also work to contextualize all musical material in the class, exploring the history and importance of mariachi and other musics relevant to specific student communities. In providing a rich sociohistorical context for all musics studied, teachers model ways that students can connect musical practices to lived experiences.[54]

Music teachers can be very intentional to communicate to all students that they are of value as individuals. When teachers ask about and teach musics that students care about deeply, they communicate that they value their experiences and their passions. Music teachers can provide students with meaningful opportunities to contribute and lead the class, and prioritize hearing from as many voices as possible.[54] When they engage students' own music interests and experiences in the classroom, teachers communicate powerfully to students that their perspectives (and their musics) are valued and valuable. In these ways, teachers communicate that student experiences should be present in their education experience.[57]

Learning Activities

1 Describe the CoP that exist within the band, chorus, orchestra, or general music class. Referencing the elements, characteristics, and circumstances of these CoP, outline strategies you would implement to develop, enhance, and strengthen these communities in the program.

2 Describe strategies that you would engage in teaching a particular music class that recognizes students' cultural references in all aspects of their learning. Discuss the ways you implement CRT, acknowledging the diversity and cultural heritage of students in the classroom.

3 Describe particular pieces of literature you may program for instruction of a particular music class. Discuss reasons for selecting such literature, strategies you may use to teach the sociocultural context of the music to students, multicultural methods you may use in teaching the music, and methods you would use to bring authenticity in the performance of the music.

4 Discuss particular issues of social justice in music education that impact students in the music classroom. Describe ways you may address one or more of these issues in your philosophy of teaching, curriculum development, and teaching that enact principles of social justice in your music classroom.

Notes

1 Ashley, K. (2021). *eNotes, How sociology helps education?* Retrieved June 13, 2021, from https://www.enotes.com/homework-help/how-sociology-help-education-92075

2 Aróstegui, J., & Louro, A. (2009). What we teach and what they learn: Social identities and cultural backgrounds forming the musical experience. *Bulletin of the Council for Research in Music Education, 182,* 19–29.

3 Fernández, E. M. (1997). *La escuela a examen* (p. 22). Madrid, Spain: Pirámide.

4 Holland, D., Skinner, D., Lachicotte, W., & Cain, C. (1998). *Identity and agency in cultural worlds.* Cambridge, England: Harvard University Press.

5 Henry, W. (2001). Music teacher education and the professional development school. *Journal of Music Teacher Education, 10,* 23–28.

6 Froehlich, H. (2007). *Sociology for music teachers. Perspectives for practice.* Upper Saddle River, NJ: Pearson Prentice-Hall.

7 McClellan, E. R. (2014). Undergraduate music education major identity formation in the university music department. *Action, Criticism, and Theory for Music Education, 13*(1), 281.

8 Mueller, R. (2002). Perspectives from the sociology of music. In R. Colwell & C. Richardson (Eds.), *The new handbook of research on music teaching and learning* (pp. 584–603). New York: Oxford University Press.

9 McClellan, E. R. (2014). Undergraduate music education major identity formation in the university music department. *Action, Criticism, and Theory for Music Education, 13*(1), 303.

10 McClellan, E. R. (2014). Undergraduate music education major identity formation in the university music department. *Action, Criticism, and Theory for Music Education, 13*(1), 302.

11 Wenger, E. (1998). *Communities of practice: Learning, meaning, and identity.* Cambridge, England: Cambridge University Press.

12 Wenger, E., & Wenger-Treyner, B. (2015). What is a community of practice? *Introduction to communities of practice* (p. 2). Retrieved January 24, 2020, from http://wenger-trayner.com/resources/what-is-a-community-of-practice

13 Kenny, A., & Wenger, E. (2017). Communities of musical practice. *Ethnomusicology Forum, 26*(2), 281.

14 Wenger, E. (1998). *Communities of practice: Learning, meaning, and identity* (pp. 72–73). Cambridge, England: Cambridge University Press.

15 Carley, S. (2015). Educational theories you must know. Communities of Practice. *St. Emlyn's.* Retrieved June 15, 2021, from https://www.stemlynsblog.org/better-learning/educational-theories-you-must-know-st-emlyns/educational-theories-you-must-know-communities-of-practice-st-emlyns/

16 Wenger, E., McDermott, R., & Snyder, W. (2002). *Cultivating communities of practice.* Boston, MA: Harvard Business Press.

17 Kenny, A. (2016). *Communities of musical practice.* New York: Routledge.

18 Kenny, A. (2017). Beginning a journey with music education: Voices from preservice primary teachers. *Music Education Research, 19*(2), 111–122.

19 Brown University. (2021). *Culturally responsive teaching.* Retrieved June 16, 2021, from https://www.brown.edu/academics/education-alliance/teaching-diverse-learners/strategies-0/culturally-responsive-teaching-0

20 Ladson-Billings, G. (1994). *The dreamkeepers.* San Francisco, CA: Jossey-Bass Publishing Co.

21 Nieto, S. (1996). *Affirming diversity: The sociopolitical context of multicultural education* (2nd ed.). White Plains, NY: Longman.

22 Rist, C. (1971). Student social class and teacher expectations: The self-fulfilling prophecy in ghetto education. *Challenging the myth: The schools, the blacks, and the poor.* Cambridge, MA: Harvard Educational Review.

23 Northeast and Islands Regional Educational Laboratory at Brown University (LAB). (2002). *The diversity kit: An introductory resource for social change in education.* Providence, RI: Brown University.

24 Brown University. (2021). *Learning within the context of culture.* Retrieved June 16, 2021, from https://www.brown.edu/academics/education-alliance/teaching-diverse-learners/learning-within-context-culture

25 Taylor-Gibson, J. (2019). Greater Boston practice for educational empowerment. Student-center instruction. Retrieved June 16, 2021, from https://www.brown.edu/academics/education-alliance/teaching-diverse-learners/student-centered-instruction

26 Goldstein, L. (1999). The relational zone: The role of caring relationships in the co-construction of mind. *American Educational Research Journal, 36*(3), 647–673.
   Vygotsky, L. S. (1978). *Mind in society: The development of higher psychological processes* (M. Cole, V. John-Steiner, S. Scribner, & E. Souberman, Eds. and Trans.). Cambridge, MA: Harvard University.

27 Brown University. (2021). *Culturally mediated instruction.* Retrieved June 16, 2021, from https://www.brown.edu/academics/education-alliance/teaching-diverse-learners/culturally-mediated-instruction

28 Brown University. (2021). *Reshaping the curriculum.* Retrieved June 16, 2021, from https://www.brown.edu/academics/education-alliance/teaching-diverse-learners/reshaping-curriculum

29 Villegas, A. (1991). *Culturally responsive pedagogy for the 1990's and beyond.* Washington, DC: ERIC Clearinghouse on Teacher Education.

30 Padron, Y. N., Waxman, H. C., & Rivera, H. H. (2002). *Educating Hispanic students: Effective instructional practices* (Practitioner Brief #5).

31 Lind, V., & McKoy, C. (2016). *Culturally responsive teaching in music education: From understanding to application*. New York: Routledge.

32 Lind, V., & McKoy, C. (2016). *Culturally responsive teaching in music education: From understanding to application* (p. 144). New York: Routledge.

33 Lind, V., & McKoy, C. (2016). *Culturally responsive teaching in music education: From understanding to application* (p. 31). New York: Routledge.

34 Woodwind Brasswind. (2021). *Bringing diversity to music education*. Retrieved June 17, 2021, from https://www.wwbw.com/the-music-room/diversity-in-music-education

35 Boyer, R. (2020). Celebrating diversity in the music classroom. *Southwestern Musician*, 48–53. Retrieved June 17, 2021, from https://www.tmea.org/wp-content/uploads/Southwestern_Musician/Articles/CelebratingDiversity-Nov2020.pdf

36 Boyer, R. (2020). Celebrating diversity in the music classroom. *Southwestern Musician*, 48. Retrieved June 17, 2021, from https://www.tmea.org/wp-content/uploads/Southwestern_Musician/Articles/CelebratingDiversity-Nov2020.pdf

37 Sarrazin, N. (2016). Musical multiculturalism and diversity. *Music and the child*. Geneseo, NY: Open SUNY Textbooks. Retrieved June 17, 2021, from https://milnepublishing.geneseo.edu/music-and-the-child/chapter/chapter-13/

38 Gonzo, C. (1993). Multicultural issues in music education. *Music Educators Journal, 79*(6), 49–53.

39 Blair, D. V. & Kondo, S. (2008). Bridging musical understanding through multicultural musics. *Music Educators Journal, 94*(5), 50–55.
   Damm, R. (2006). Education through collaboration: Learning the arts while celebrating culture. *Music Educators Journal, 93*(2), 54–58.
   Fung, C. V. (1995). Rationales for teaching world musics. *Music Educators Journal, 82*(1), 36–41.

40 Santiago, P. A. (2014). The influence of students' cultural music and classroom music activities on their attitudes towards their multiethnic peers. *Procedia—Social and Behavioral Sciences*, 116, 3475.

41 Volk, M. T. (1998). *Music, education, and multiculturalism*. New York: Oxford University Press.

42 Abril, C. (2013). Towards a more culturally responsive general music classroom. *General Music Today, 27*(1), 6–11.

43 Goetz, M. (2000). Challenges of performing diverse cultural music. *Music Educators Journal, 87*(1), 23–26.

44 Abril, C. (2006). Music that represents culture: Selecting music with integrity. *Music Educators Journal, 93*(1), 38–45.
   Goetz, M. (2000). Challenges of performing diverse cultural music. *Music Educators Journal, 87*(1), 23–26.

45 Dissinger, M. (2019). On the journey to becoming culturally responsive in a high school choir classroom: A white woman's autoethnography. Doctoral Dissertation. Teachers College, Columbia University. ProQuest Publishing ID 13883718. Retrieved June 17, 2021, from https://academiccommons.columbia.edu/doi/10.7916/d8-p0kg-5w40

46 Lind, V., & McKoy, C. (2016). *Culturally responsive teaching in music education: From understanding to application* (p. 18). New York: Routledge.
   Dissinger, M. (2019). On the journey to becoming culturally responsive in a high school choir classroom: A white woman's autoethnography (p. 28). Doctoral Dissertation. Teachers College, Columbia University. ProQuest Publishing ID 13883718. Retrieved June 17, 2021, from https://academiccommons.columbia.edu/doi/10.7916/d8-p0kg-5w40.

47 Berman, A. (2015). Teaching social justice in the music classroom. *Music Educators Journal, 22*(4), 38.

48 Palmer, E. (2018). Literature review of social justice in music education: Acknowledging oppression and privilege. *Update, 36*(2), 22–31.

49 Wright, R. (2010). Democracy, social exclusion and music education: Possibilities for change. In R. Wright (Ed.), *Sociology and music education* (pp. 263–281). London, England: Ashgate.

50 Bates, V. (2012). Social class and school music. *Music Educators Journal, 98*(4), 33–37.

51 Palmer, E. (2018). Literature review of social justice in music education: Acknowledging oppression and privilege. *Update, 36*(2), 24.
52 Hess, J. (2017). Equity in music education: Why equity and social justice in music education. *Music Educators Journal, 104*(1), 71–73.
53 Lareau, A. (2011). *Unequal childhoods: Class, race, and family life.* Berkeley: University of California Press.
54 Hess, J. (2017). Equity in music education: Why equity and social justice in music education. *Music Educators Journal, 104*(1), 72.
55 Lind, V., & McKoy, C. (2016). *Culturally responsive teaching in music education: From understanding to application* (p. 72). New York: Routledge.
56 Green, L. (2008). *Music, informal learning and the school: A new classroom pedagogy.* London: Ashgate.
57 Hess, J. (2017). Equity in music education: Why equity and social justice in music education. *Music Educators Journal, 104*(1), 73.

Chapter 10

School Music Curriculum Design

In education, a curriculum is broadly defined as the totality of student experiences that occur in the educational process.[1] The term often refers specifically to a planned sequence of instruction, or to a view of the student's experiences in terms of the educator's or school's instructional goals.

Curriculum may incorporate the planned interaction of pupils with instructional content, materials, resources, and processes for evaluating the attainment of educational objectives.[2] Depending on how broadly educators define or employ the term, curriculum typically refers to the knowledge, skills, and level of sensitivity students are expected to learn, which includes the learning standards or learning objectives they are expected to meet; the units and lessons that teachers teach; the assignments and projects given to students; the books, materials, videos, presentations, and readings used in a course; and the tests, assessments, and other methods used to evaluate student learning.[3]

Learning Objectives

1 What are the characteristics of the curriculum, hidden curriculum, and spiral curriculum?
2 What principles of Understanding by Design, Bloom's Taxonomy, and Vygotsky's ZPD that are used in effective course design and curriculum development in the school music program?
3 What elements of technology should be implemented in designing curricula for today's music classroom?
4 In what ways can popular music curricula enhance traditional school music programs in the 21st century?

The Music Curriculum

A music curriculum is a broad sequence of music courses providing comprehensive information about music and facilitating development of music skills in order to promote musical understanding. The terms *broad* and *comprehensive* refer to the quantity and breadth of courses. *Sequence* refers to hierarchies of subject matter and skill development. Such curriculum can refer to specific instructional methods or philosophies such as those developed by Carl Orff, Zoltan Kodaly, Shinichi Suzuki, Edwin Gordon, and others. These methods typically specify skills to be developed, theoretical knowledge to be acquired, and the order in which both should be presented, thus implying that skills and knowledge are equally important educational concerns.[4]

DOI: 10.4324/9781003038474-13

Regardless of the status given to music programs in schools, there are usually three features that these programs share.

The Hidden Curriculum encompasses all school experiences not explicitly included in the official education program. While the "formal curriculum" consists of the courses, lessons, and learning activities students participate in, as well as the knowledge and skills educators intentionally teach to students, the "hidden curriculum" consists of the unspoken or implicit academic, social, and cultural messages that are communicated to students while they are in school.[5] Learning to cope with delay, interruption, criticism, regimentation, peer pressure, and rejection are just a few of a school's hidden curriculum that is learned in much the same way the official curriculum content is learned. Some educators contend that many aspects of this hidden curriculum may have nearly as much bearing on success or failure in school as academic achievement.

The Spiral Curriculum refers to vertical and sequential aspects of curriculum. Music curriculum planners were quick to adopt Jerome Bruner's (1960) cyclic approach to curriculum development. Bruner suggests that "any idea (concept) can be represented honestly and usefully in the thought forms of children of school age."[6] These concepts or bits of information are not focused at one grade level, and then dropped. For example, music curricula in early childhood education help students grasp basic musical concepts such as tone, melody, and rhythm intuitively. At subsequent stages, the curriculum turns back upon itself at deeper levels of music learning. A music curriculum explores basic concepts at each level and revisits them in increasing complexity from preschool through high school, in a spiraling pattern.[7]

Music Content or subject matter consists of knowledge, skills, and responses. Music curriculum includes these domains as they reflect the nature of music experience and activity. Knowledge includes factual or conceptual information about elements of music, music history and theory, and musical style and interpretation. Skills include (1) those required for instrumental and vocal performance and (2) those having to do with perceiving musical sound and applying musical knowledge. Unlike performance skills, skills have to do with perception, and application of knowledge plays a crucial role in musical understanding. Response incorporates both knowledge and skills but is more implicit than explicit in curricular structure. Some kind of reaction is evoked by every musical experience and results from certain types of interaction with music. Thus, responses to music, like music knowledge and musical skills, must be primary concerns of music educators.[8]

Levels of Curriculum Development

School curricula are created at several levels. National and state curricula are the broadest and most general level. When curriculum planning takes place at the national level, it involves subject experts, scholars, and influence of professional music education organizations. National and state music curricula reflect recommendations of what organizations such as the National Association for Music Education and the National Association of Schools of Music consider to be the model music curriculum for students. When formulating recommendations for state and national levels, these professional groups consult more specialized organizations of music educators such as the American Choral Directors Association, American String Teachers Association, and American School Band Directors Association.[8] At the state level, a committee is formed consisting of supervisors of music, instructional supervisors, music teachers, and scholars. Under the State Education Department, this panel suggests what should constitute the overall educational program across the state.

At the systemwide level, music supervisors and music teachers from schools at all levels across the county, parish, or district consult national and state curricula to design a curriculum specific to school system music programs. Standards set for this program also consider distinct philosophies, goals, and factors of the school system in order to accommodate their population's needs and interests. These curriculum standards are usually published and made available for school administrators and teachers, who use school guides as the foundation for their school's music programs. Teachers prepare grade-level courses of study from which individual class curricula are designed.

At the school level, music teachers have latitude to tailor system-wide curricular standards to specific groups of students or individuals. Teachers work to formulate practical solutions to imparting knowledge, skills, and responses in an efficient manner, within the context of their school structure. While the teacher makes decisions regarding learning objectives, instructional methodology, and evaluation procedures to be used, students' musical experiences are the result of not only academic activities but also interaction with day-to-day situations.

National Music Standards

The National Association for Music Education (NAfME), formerly the Music Educators National Conference (MENC), first provided the *National Standards for Arts Education* (1994)[9] to the entire arts education profession.[10] MENC managed the process of developing the *National Voluntary Standards in the Arts* for the National Consortium of Arts Education Associations.

In 2014, NAfME released a new *National Music Standards* to replace the original standards. The new music standards were developed as a part of the *National Coalition for Core Arts Standards* work on standards for all arts. The new music standards provide voluntary and pragmatic flexible processes and strategies that can be welcomed, implemented, and assessed in every American school district.[11]

The 2014 Music Standards emphasize conceptual understanding in areas that reflect the actual processes in which musicians engage. The standards cultivate a student's ability to carry out the three *Artistic Processes of Creating, Performing,* and *Responding.*[11] The new standards provide teachers with frameworks that closely match the unique goals of their specialized classes. The standards are presented in a grade-by-grade sequence from pre-K through grade 8, and discrete strands address common high-school music classes such as Ensembles and Music Composition/Theory. The standards are provided in "strands" that represent the principal ways music instruction is delivered in the United States.[12] Further information on these new National Standards for Music may be found on the NAfME 2014 Music Standards website.[13]

Understanding by Design

Understanding by Design (UbD) is a framework for improving student achievement through standards-driven curriculum development, instructional design, assessment, and professional development.[14] Developed by Grant Wiggins and Jay McTighe (1998) and produced by the Association for Supervision and Curriculum Development (ASCD),[15] the emphasis of UbD is on "backward design," (Figure 10.1) the practice of looking at learning outcomes in order to design curriculum units, performance assessments, and classroom instruction.

According to UbD proponents, teachers traditionally start curriculum planning with activities and textbooks instead of identifying classroom learning goals and

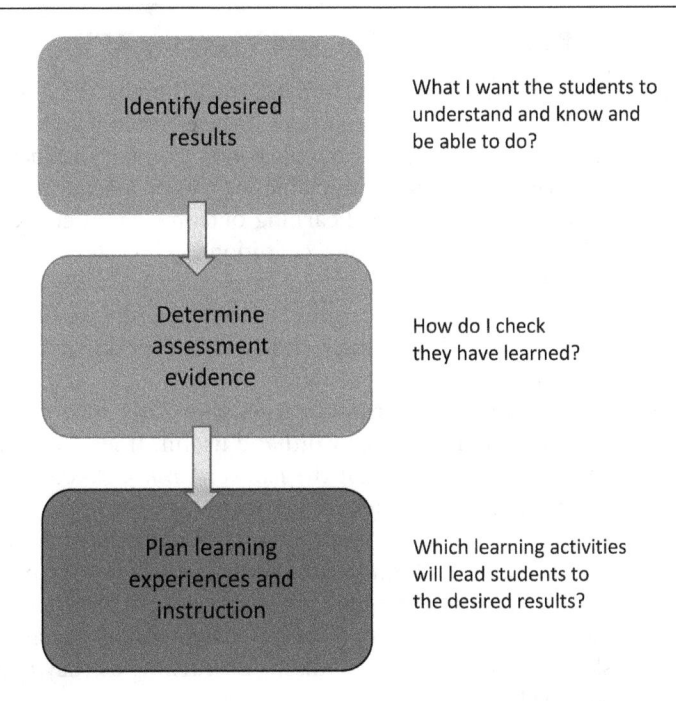

Identify desired results

What I want the students to understand and know and be able to do?

Determine assessment evidence

How do I check they have learned?

Plan learning experiences and instruction

Which learning activities will lead students to the desired results?

Figure 10.1 The Backward Design Process.

Copyright (c) 2022 Edward McClellan.

planning toward that goal. In backward design, the teacher starts with classroom learning outcomes and then plans the curriculum, choosing activities and materials that help determine student ability and foster student learning. Similar to the principles of Duke's (2005) Intelligent Music Teaching (Chapter 8), planning, teaching, and evaluating the effectiveness of instruction are all predicated on a clear description of what students will do to demonstrate that they've accomplished the goals set out for them.[16]

The Backward design approach is developed in three stages. Stage 1 starts with educators identifying the desired results of their students by establishing the overall goal of the lessons by using content standards, common core or state standards. UbD's stage 1 defines "Students will understand that…" and lists essential questions that will guide the learner to understanding. Stage 1 also focuses on identifying "what students will know" and most importantly "what students will be able to do."

Stage 2 focuses on evidence of learning by assessment. Teachers plan performance tasks and evidence of understanding. Performance tasks determine what the students will demonstrate in the unit and what evidence will prove their understanding. This can include self-reflections and self-assessments on learning. Lastly, stage 3 lists the learning activities that will lead students to the desired results.[17]

Wiggins and McTighe (2005)[18] explicitly maintain that assessment evidence should clearly be set before planning learning experiences and instruction. The process starts with the end—the desired outcomes—and then derives the curriculum from the evidence of learning (assessment). Duke (2005) also advocates that assessment is inextricably related to the goals of instruction. The time to begin thinking about assessment is in the planning stages before instruction actually begins.[19]

Bloom's Taxonomy, Backward Design, and Vygotsky ZPD

Sideeg (2016) maintains the trilogy of domains of Bloom's Taxonomy along with Wiggins and McTighe's model of backward design and Vygotsky's Zone of Proximal Development (ZPD) should be used in effective course design.[20] Bloom's taxonomy centers instruction on teaching and assessing students in systematic and predictable ways over a sequential framework of thinking, physical movement, and emotion. Learning outcome-based curricula emphasizes students' learning outcomes in terms of students' cognitions, skills, and affective attributes.

Vygotsky ZPD stresses the role of guidance in developing learner's abilities when the teacher guides the learners "towards performing actions or tasks which are just beyond their current capacity."[21] With such guidance, learners can perform beyond their own ability—within certain limits.

Writing effective learning outcomes should target this ZPD in order to make both assessment tasks and instructional activities valid and useful. If learning outcomes focus on *what the learner can do unaided* or what the *learner cannot do even with guidance*, then the whole endeavor will be meaningless.[22]

The teacher should craft learning outcomes that drive assessment tasks and instructional activities (Sideeg, 2016).[23] As Bloom's Taxonomy is a framework in progress, writing learning outcomes is a highly dynamic multi-dimensional process. In crafting learning outcomes in a particular context, one domain of Bloom's taxonomy could be more dominant. Often some tasks may span multiple domains of learning as they require affective, cognitive, and psychomotor learning.

In writing a learning outcome to describe the desired effect in each of these tasks, usually teachers choose to craft this learning outcome in terms of the dominant dimension. Levels of the cognitive domain (lower-order thinking and higher-order thinking) are interrelated and overlapping.[23] The psychomotor learning domain needs special care when it comes to isolate action verbs to write learning outcomes that involve psychomotor skills. Learning outcomes in the affective domain thrive most at the level of the program and capstone courses. Formative assessments are the best tools for assessing affective learning. Course designers should avoid the unnecessary confusion of creating two sections of "objectives" and "learning outcomes" as review of relevant literature shows the two terms used interchangeably.[24]

Music Technology Curriculum

Music teachers are increasingly using technology when developing new strategies for engaging students. Integrating technology with teaching has distinct advantages for engagement, but music educators must also be careful to take a measured approach to incorporate these tools. The best framework for including them will combine knowledge of music and education, as well as challenge teachers to stay highly focused on the knowledge and skills they want their students to develop.[25]

Public schools are designing curriculum and instruction that support the goals of 21st-century skills of creativity and innovation, critical thinking and problem-solving, and communication and collaboration. With these standards and frameworks, music educators are charged with the task of developing appropriate and successful instructional models that foster creative activities, such as music composition within a predominantly performance-based music curriculum.[26]

One of the major music education technology trends has been the increasing use of online services and mobile devices such as the smartphone or iPad alongside learning.[27]

Table 10.1 Technology Tools for Music Education

Software category	Examples
Online Music Sharing and Collaboration	SoundCloud, Google Classroom
Music Notation	Flat.io, MuseScore, Noteflight
Aural Skills Training	MusicTheory.net, Teoria
Music Production	GarageBand, Soundtrap

Source: Table Created from information in the article *How to Engage Students Utilizing Music Education Tools & Technology* (https://musiceducation.arts.ufl.edu/resources/how-to-engage-students-through-music-education/).

Online services empower teachers with the ability to create assignments using vast music libraries. Music-sharing services offer students a platform for receiving feedback on a larger scale.[25]

William Bauer's (2020) *Music Learning Today: Digital Pedagogy for Creating, Performing, and Responding to Music*[28] presents an approach to conceptualizing and utilizing technology as a tool for music learning. Designed for use by pre- and in-service music teachers, it provides the essential understandings required to become an adaptive expert with music technology, creating and implementing lessons, units, and curriculum that take advantage of technological affordances to assist students in developing their musicianship.

While this section is only an introduction to the importance of establishing technology in the music program curriculum, there are numerous other categories of technology that have helped to transform both formal music education and informal learning. The music teacher should research teaching with technology through journal articles, music technology and music education retailers, online websites, and publishers of music education and music technology resources. Here is a summary of some of the major types of music education tools and some specific examples.

Popular Music Curriculum

In the past two decades, popular music ensembles have become more common in K–12 music programs in the United States.[29] The expansion of popular music can also be seen in collegiate preservice music teacher education programs.[30] This expansion of popular music in school music education is due in part to the expansion of modern band programming. Modern band is a facet of music education that includes music technology and popular music instruments (e.g., guitar, bass, drums, keys, ukuleles, and vocals) and focuses on student-centered repertoire and songwriting (Powell & Burstein, 2017).[31] Since 2002, the nonprofit organization Little Kids Rock (LKR) has expanded the presence of modern band programming in United States public schools by offering hundreds of teacher workshops, curricular resources, and instrument donations to public school music teachers who participate in their modern band training (Powell, 2021).[32]

Byo (2018) found that the benefits and values in performance-based popular music education—music, community, identity, teacher, and classroom management—overlap considerably with the benefits and values identified by adolescents in traditional concert band, orchestra, and choir (Adderly, Kennedy, & Berz, 2003; Bartolome, 2013; Kennedy, 2002),[33] novice rock band (Green, 2008),[34] and justification-for-music-education statements (Campbell, Connell, & Beegle, 2007).[35] Modern Band is an example of meaningful, authentic, and valuable music education that is positioned between the extremes of formal and informal learning, process and product orientation, and teacher- and student-centered pedagogy.[36]

Modern bands in schools look different in various contexts. Because the music is ideally chosen by the students, or at least with student input, the repertoire played in modern band classrooms varies depending on the demographics and music preferences of the students.[37] Some modern bands look like a traditional "rock band," using instruments such as the electric guitar, bass, keyboards, drum kits, and vocals. Other modern band programs might focus more on whole-class ukulele playing, whereas others incorporate beat-making and audio production through the use of music technology (Powell, 2019).[38]

This is only an introduction to the emergence of popular music as a viable means to music education curriculum that has helped to transform both informal learning and formal music education in the 21st century. As music teachers look to engage more students in school music, the teachers themselves should seek out opportunities for professional development focused on popular music pedagogies and modern bands.[39] There are a number of available resources for music educators looking to incorporate modern band into their music programs. These resources include video play-along apps such as *4Chords* and *Ukeoke* (musopia.net), as well as collections of curricular resources from *LKR's Jam Zone* (jamone.littlekidsrock.org) and the Berklee College of Music's *PULSE* website (pulse.berklee.edu). Music educators looking to add modern band instruments such as guitars, basses, drum sets, keyboards, ukuleles, and technology can look to some nonprofit organizations such as Donors Choose, Little Kids Rock, Guitars Over Guns, and the VH1 Save the Music Foundation for assistance.[40]

Learning Activities

1 Referencing the NAfME 2014 National Music Standards, design one classroom standard for creating, performing, and responding, that could be implemented for one grade level in the band, chorus, orchestra, or general music class curriculum. Select the grade from levels K–12 and the subject area, consult the national standards, and design the curricular standards that you would implement in your school music program classroom. You may also find valuable information by researching state music standards of your choice.

2 Considering the principles of Bloom's Taxonomy, UbD, and Vygotsky's ZPD, create a framework for instruction of a course of your choice (e.g., band, chorus, orchestra, general music, or another course). In designing a primary student learning outcome, describe ways you would engage various levels of the cognitive, psychomotor, and affective domains of learning in your outcome. Also, describe ways you would integrate assessment with your goals of instruction.

3 Describe technology that you may integrate into course design and curricula for a course of your choice (e.g., band, chorus, orchestra, general music, or another course). Specify the types of software you may use and examples of software programs you may use in class instruction and student activities. Include expected outcomes of student learning for such instruction and exercise.

4 Create a popular music ensemble or popular music course for your school music program. Describe the grade level, type of popular music course, instrumentation, equipment implemented, and technology needed for your course curriculum. In your description, design an outline of the purpose of the course, overall expected learning outcomes, and activities of the course.

Notes

1 Kelly, A. V. (2009). *The curriculum: Theory and practice* (6th ed.), Thousand Oaks, CA: Sage Publications. Retrieved June 25, 2021, from https://books.google.com/books?id=qILGb7xcXFIC&pg=PA13#v=onepage&q&f=false
    Wiles, J. (2008). *Leading curriculum development* (p. 2). Thousand Oaks, CA: Corwin Press.
2 Adams, K., & Adams, D. (2003). *Urban education: A reference handbook* (pp. 31–32). Santa Barbara, CA: ABC-CLIO. Retrieved June 25, 2021, from https://archive.org/details/urbaneducationre0000adam
3 The Glossary of Education Reform. (2015). *Curriculum*. Retrieved June 25, 2021, from https://www.edglossary.org/curriculum/
4 Labuta, J., & Smith, D. (1997). *Music education: Historical contexts and perspectives* (p. 57). Upper Saddle River, NJ: Pearson Education.
5 Hidden Curriculum. (2015). Retrieved June 14, 2021, from https://www.edglossary.org/hidden-curriculum/
6 Bruner, J. (1960; 1977). *The process of education* (p. 33). Cambridge: Harvard University Press.
7 Labuta, J., & Smith, D. (1997). *Music education: Historical contexts and perspectives* (pp. 59–60). Upper Saddle River, NJ: Pearson Education.
8 Labuta, J., & Smith, D. (1997). *Music education: Historical contexts and perspectives* (p. 60). Upper Saddle River, NJ: Pearson Education.
9 National Association for Music Education. (1994). *National Standards for Arts Education*. Retrieved June 27, 2021, from https://nafme.org/my-classroom/standards/national-standards-for-arts-education/
10 Mark, M. (2000). From Tanglewood to Tallahassee in 32 years. *Music Educators Journal, 86*(5), 25–28.
11 NAfME. (2014). *New National Music Standards*. Retrieved June 27, 2021, from https://nafme.org/the-national-association-for-music-education-proudly-announces-the-new-national-core-music-standards/
12 NAfME. (2021a). *Standards*. Retrieved June 27, 2021, from https://nafme.org/my-classroom/standards/
13 NAfME. (2021b). *2014 Music standards*. Retrieved June 27, 2021, from https://nafme.org/my-classroom/standards/core-music-standards/
14 McTighe, J., & Seif, E. (2021). *A summary of underlying theory and research base for understanding by design*. Retrieved June 28, 2021, from https://www.jaymctighe.com/wp-content/uploads/2011/04/UbD-Research-Base.pdf
15 Wiggins, G., & McTighe, J. (1998). *Understanding by design*. Assn. for Supervision & Curriculum Development.
16 Duke, R. (2005). *Intelligent music teaching* (p. 72). Austin, TX: Learning and Behavior Resources.
17 Wiggins, G., & McTighe, J. (2006). *Understanding by design* (p. 24). Upper Saddle River, NJ: Merrill Prentice Hall.
18 Wiggins, G., & McTighe, J. (2005). *Understanding by design*. Upper Saddle River, NJ: Merrill-Prentice-Hall.
19 Duke, R. (2005). *Intelligent music teaching* (p. 49). Austin, TX: Learning and Behavior Resources.
20 Sideeg, A. (2016). Bloom's Taxonomy, Backward Design, and Vygotsky's Zone of Proximal Development in crafting learning outcomes. *International Journal of Linguistics, 8*(2), 182.
21 Dolya, G. (2010). *Vygotsky in action in the early years: The 'key to learning' curriculum*. Routledge: Taylor and Francis Group.
22 Sideeg, A. (2016). Bloom's Taxonomy, Backward Design, and Vygotsky's Zone of Proximal Development in crafting learning outcomes. *International Journal of Linguistics, 8*(2), 175.
23 Sideeg, A. (2016). Bloom's Taxonomy, Backward Design, and Vygotsky's Zone of Proximal Development in crafting learning outcomes. *International Journal of Linguistics, 8*(2), 182–183.
24 Sideeg, A. (2016). Bloom's Taxonomy, Backward Design, and Vygotsky's Zone of Proximal Development in crafting learning outcomes. *International Journal of Linguistics, 8*(2), 183.

25 University of Florida. (2021). *How to engage students utilizing music education tools & technology*. Retrieved June 28, 2021, from https://musiceducation.arts.ufl.edu/resources/how-to-engage-students-through-music-education/

26 Nielson, L. (2013). Developing musical creativity: Student and teacher perceptions of a high school music technology curriculum. *Update, 31*(2) 54–62.

27 Johnson, L., Levine, A., Smith, R., & Stone, S. (2010). *The 2010 horizon report*. Austin, TX: New Media Consortium.

28 Bauer, W. (2020). Music learning today (2nd ed.). New York: Oxford Publishing.

29 Powell, B., Krikun, A., & Pignato, J. M. (2015). "Something's happening here!" Popular music education in the United States. *IASPM Journal, 5*(1), 4–22.

30 Davis, V. (2018). Higher Ed Rocks: Don't fret the small stuff. *Journal of Popular Music Education, 2*(3), 283–288.
   Powell, B., Hewitt, D., Smith, G. D., Olesko, B., & Davis, V. (2020). Curricular change in collegiate programs: Toward a more inclusive music education. *Visions of Research in Music Education, 35*(1), 1–22.

31 Powell, B., & Burstein, S. (2017). Popular music and modern band principles. In G. D. Smith, Z. Moir, M. Brennan, S. Rambarran, & P. Kirkman (Eds.), The Routledge research companion to popular music education (pp. 243–254). Abingdon, England: Routledge.

32 Powell, B. (2021). Modern band: A review of literature. *Update, 39*(3), 39–46.

33 Adderly, C., Kennedy, M., & Berz, W. (2003). A home away from home: The world of the high school music classroom. *Journal of Research in Music Education, 51*, 190–205.
   Bartolome, S. J. (2013). It's like a whole bunch of me!: The perceived values and benefits of the Seattle Girls' Choir experience. *Journal of Research in Music Education, 60*, 395–418.
   Kennedy, M. C. (2002). It's cool because we like to sing: Junior high boys' experience of choral music as an elective. *Research Studies in Music Education, 18*, 26–37.

34 Green, L. (2008). *Music, informal learning and the school: A new classroom pedagogy*. Burlington, VT: Ashgate.

35 Campbell, P. S., Connell, C., & Beegle, A. (2007). Adolescents' expressed meanings of music in and out of school. *Journal of Research in Music Education, 55*, 220–236.

36 Byo, J. (2018). Modern band as school music: A case study. *International Journal of Music Education, 36*(2), 259–269.

37 Burstein, S. (2016). *Transformation of habitus and social trajectories: A retrospective study of a popular music program*. Doctoral dissertation, University of Southern California, CA. USC digital Library. Retrieved from http://digitallibrary. usc.edu/cdm/ref/collection/p15799coll40/id/320915
   Burstein, S., & Powell, B. (2019). Approximation and scaffolding in modern band. *Music Educators Journal, 106*(1), 39–47.

38 Powell, B. (2019). The integration of music technology into popular music ensembles: Perspectives of modern band teachers. *Journal of Music, Technology & Education, 12*(3), 297–310.

39 Powell, B. (2021). Modern band: A review of literature. *Update, 39*(3), 44.

40 Ruiz, M. I. (2019). *J Dilla Music Tech Grant launched by Save the Music*. Retrieved from https://pitchfork.com/news/j-dilla-music-tech-grant-launched-by-save-the-music/
   Powell, B. (2021). Modern band: A review of literature. *Update, 39*(3), 44.

Part III

Applications to the Music Classroom

Chapter 11

Effective Instructional Design

Instructional design (ID) is the design, development, and delivery of learning experiences. It constructs those experiences in such a way that learners acquire either knowledge or skills.[1] The process consists broadly of determining the state and needs of the learner, defining the end goal of instruction, and creating some intervention to assist in the transition. The outcome of this instruction may be directly observable and scientifically measured or completely hidden and assumed.[2] There are numerous ID models but many are based on the ADDIE model with the five phases: analysis, design, development, implementation, and evaluation.[3]

Learning Objectives

1 What are the prominent components of the instructional design model?
2 What are the principles of effective instruction in the music classroom?
3 What are the plans of action for student-centered instruction, experiential learning, sequential instruction, differentiated instruction, and classroom management in the music classroom?
4 What are the principles of the Music Learning Community as an Instructional Model?

As a field, ID is historically and traditionally rooted in cognitive and behavioral psychology, though recently constructivism has influenced thinking in the field.[4] One of the most influential individuals in the field is Benjamin Bloom whose highly respected taxonomy classifies learning objectives into three specific domains: cognitive; affective; and psychomotor.[2] These taxonomies still influence the design of instruction today.[5]

In 1965, Robert Gagné expanded upon this classificatory model. While his work retained the three primary classifications defined by Bloom, he also defined five learning outcomes (verbal information, intellectual skills, cognitive strategy, attitude, and motor skills), and nine events of instruction that comprise *The Conditions of Learning*. Gagné's work remains the foundational basis of ID practices.[6]

Conditions of Learning

Gagné's conditions of learning theory (1985) draw upon general concepts from various learning theories in order to define what learning is. Gagné's theory provides a description of the conditions under which learning takes place by referring to situations in ordinary life and in school where learning occurs.[7] According to Gagné, learning occurs in a series

DOI: 10.4324/9781003038474-15

of nine learning events, each of which is a condition for learning that must be accomplished before moving to the next in order. Similarly, instructional events should mirror the learning events:

- Gaining Attention
- Informing Learners of the Objective
- Stimulating Recall of Prior Learning
- Presenting the Stimulus
- Providing Learning Guidance
- Eliciting Performance
- Providing Feedback
- Assessing Performance
- Enhancing Retention and Transfer[8]

Gagné's work has had a significant influence on American education.[9] Gagné (1974) defined instruction as "the set of planned external events which influence the process of learning and thus promote learning."[10] Gagné's main focus for ID was how instruction and learning could be systematically connected to the design of instruction. He emphasized the design principles and procedures that need to take place for effective teaching and learning.[11]

The ADDIE Model

Perhaps the most common model used for creating instructional materials is the ADDIE Model.[12] Behzadaval and Vahedi (2019) claim the main elements of the ADDIE ID model can guide music teachers to form and develop their teaching plans.[13] As learning music encompasses a wide range of skills that should be mastered, the different activities that take place in each phase of ADDIE vary according to the situation and learning environment. But the five main phases are almost always present when ADDIE is used in instruction.

In the *Analysis phase*, the instructional problem is clarified, instructional goals and objectives are established and the learning environment and learner's existing knowledge and skills are identified. Instructional goals should be characterized based on the learners' background knowledge (Wang & Hsu, 2009).[14] Musical objectives not only correspond to content but also include understanding the different ways that music can be comprehended and the realm of the contexts in which it occurs (Philpott, 2004).[15] Some of the questions that are addressed during the analysis phase include:

- Who are your student learners and what are their characteristics?
- What is the learning context?
- What are the delivery options?
- What is the performance context?
- What is the timeline for completion?[16]

The *Design phase* deals with learning objectives, assessment instruments, exercises, content, subject matter analysis, lesson planning, and media selection. The design phase should be systematic and specific. Systematic means a logical, orderly method of identifying, developing, and evaluating a set of planned strategies targeted for attaining the lesson's goals. Specific means each element of the ID plan needs to be executed with attention to details. These are questions used in the design phase:

- What do you want your students to know and be able to do at the end of instruction?
- What theories and models of ID, learning strategies, and evaluation instruments will you use to shape content and according to the intended learning outcomes by domain (cognitive, affective, psychomotor)?
- What educational strategies will you need to employ to meet the goals and objectives of instruction?
- What kind of activities are required for the learners, in order to meet the goals identified in the analysis phase?
- What tasks are identified and broken down to be more manageable during instruction?[16]

The *Development phase* involves selection or preparation of instructional materials, designing the learning activities that will be implemented, production of required materials, and finalizing instructional methodology to be executed (Noroozi & Razavi, 2016).[17]

During the *Implementation phase*, the instructor tests all materials to determine if they are functional and appropriate for the learners. The music teacher ensures that the books, musical instruments, hands-on equipment, tools, and technology are in place and that the learning applications are functional.[17] The instructor and learners collaborate to prepare the learners for new learning including training them on new tools such as instruments, software, or hardware. The music teacher may implement their own training on course curriculum, learning outcomes, method of delivery, and testing procedures important to instruction. In the process, the design can be steadily evaluated for further enhancement in the implementation phase (Kurt, 2017).[18]

The *Evaluation phase* ensures the materials achieved the desired goals. It consists of two parts: formative and summative assessments.[16] Formative assessment is present in each stage of the ADDIE process. Summative assessment contains tests or evaluations created for the content being implemented. The ADDIE model (Figure 11.1) is an iterative process of

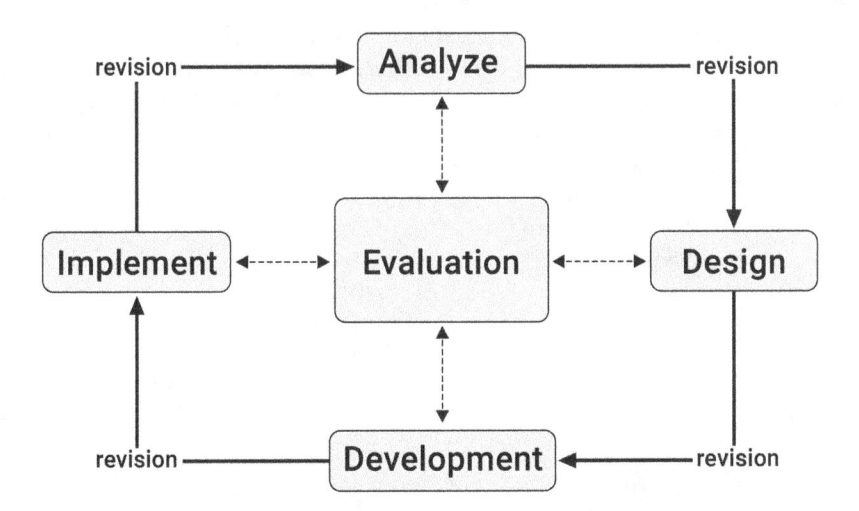

Figure 11.1 ADDIE Model: Instructional Design.

ID, which means that at each stage the music teacher can assess the instructional elements and revise them if necessary. This final phase is vital for the ID because it provides data used to alter and enhance the design. Connecting all phases of the model are external and reciprocal revision opportunities. As in the internal Evaluation phase, revisions should and can be made throughout the entire process.[19] Most of the current ID models are variations of the ADDIE model.[20] Here are questions used in the evaluation phase:

- Formative evaluation:

  - Did the students learn what they needed to?
  - What assessment tools will you use to measure learning?
  - What were the assessment outcomes?

- Summative evaluation:

  - Did the students meet the standards of the course?
  - What would you change to make it better?

Music teachers can utilize ADDIE as a leading tool to design their teaching. One significant point about ID is that music teachers should have sufficient understanding of learning theories and approaches, and music teaching methods to apply ADDIE. Learning music encompasses a wide range of skills to master musical understanding, physical-motor development, and emotional expression to accomplish aesthetic maturity (a quality of critical response to an art form external to one's self). Music teachers in the process of ID can identify non-musical goals, such as social skills, self-expression, and responsibility, to design special activities to reinforce them, and ultimately assess whether learners attain the goals. Music teachers applying ID will have a written plan that demonstrates each part of instruction like an architectural plan. Formative and summative evaluation enables music teachers to judge how a designed plan is working and enhance the disadvantages.[13]

Music Class Instruction

Music teachers are constantly making decisions about how they will teach, and many factors influence this process.[21] Often, past experiences are cited as a primary influence on novice teacher decision-making. These experiences could include interactions with high-school teachers, applied teachers, college ensemble conductors, college music education professors, the student teaching cooperating teacher, the university student teaching supervisor, and the content and activities of college courses (Bauer & Berg, 2001; Wiggins, 2001).[22] While such interactions can provide insights, effective music teachers carefully consider their approach and the students in the classroom, the subject matter to be taught, and the social environment in the classroom (Schwab, 1983).[23] Teachers who make decisions based solely on how s/he previously learned the subject matter omit consideration for the students and the learning environment in the present. Without considering all four common places, the potential for teacher decisions to affect student learning positively is diminished.[21]

Effective music teachers have to be knowledgeable about their subject matter and have a deep understanding of the qualities of music, its construction, interpretation, performance, and production. It is argued that music teachers have to be skilled musicians and have developed performance abilities to be an effective teacher. At the same time, it is important to know how to organize the contents of lessons and how to deliver the information. Good musicians can become more effective teachers when they expand and improve their skills as pedagogues attending music education studies programs that range from Bachelor to Doctorate for music teachers.[24]

Regarding teaching methods, effective instructors usually adopt a *learner-centered approach*, in which students are not passive knowledge receivers, but active protagonists in their learning process (Hattie, 2009).[25] Effective teachers are focused on students and their learning experience, providing support and offering accessible challenging tasks. In addition, effective instructors constantly pay attention to the feedback that students give them, in order to effectively adapt their teaching strategies to their pupils' needs. This teaching methodology is mainly focused on the learning process (instead of outcomes) and it aims to support students' autonomous building up of musical knowledge. Scaffolding of the music student's skills and mental representation of musical performance can be recognized as some of the most relevant constructive teaching strategies.[26]

In the learner-centered classroom, the teacher as facilitator encourages young musicians to self-reflect, peer-evaluate, and problem-solve about music making and creating. The teacher develops student music-learning outcomes, assesses cognitive, affective, and performance skills, and effectively directs the learning experiences and behavior in their music classrooms. As well, the successful ensemble director guides the quality of their students' performances and executive skills.[27] The director shifts instruction from that of a music technician delivering direct solutions for student technical performance to using a variety of instructional approaches such as modeling, aural imagery, and questioning to facilitate student mastery of musical performance.

Experiential Learning

Experiential learning refers to a belief that children learn best through direct experience rather than through abstract representations like books. Children need to touch, feel, and manipulate materials to learn about the world around them. Experiential learning activities, both inside and outside the classroom, are designed to *actively engage* students to *learn by doing*, and *then reflecting on the process and experience* and *actively creating their own understanding*.[28]

In terms of music education, this means that children need to learn "through" music making rather than "about" music making.[21] Students are engaged in authentic musical experiences—actively creating and performing music, making musical decisions, and figuring out for themselves how the piece "works."[29] The students are the center of the action, interacting with the music in ways that result in *doing that informs their thinking and, reciprocally, with thinking that informs their doing*.[30] Experiential learning in music class can take the form of simulations and role-playing, student teaching and research, group work in and out of the classroom, open-ended discussion activities, active and open-ended questioning guidance, clinical experiences, and field trips.

Sequential Instruction

Sequential instruction refers to a pedagogical approach such as a belief that learning is best facilitated through a step-by-step approach to instruction.[21] The order and organization of learning activities affect the way information is processed and retained (Glynn & DiVesta, 1977; Lorch & Lorch, 1985; Van Patten, Chao, & Reigeluth, 1986).[31] A number of theories (e.g., Bruner,[32] Reigeluth,[33] Scandura[34]) suggest a simple-to-complex sequence. According to Gagné's Conditions of Learning theory, sequence is dictated by pre-requisite skills and the level of cognitive processing involved.[7]

In the Kodály method, music learning is accomplished through a five-step sequence that begins with the *prepare phase*. In this phase, students experience a new concept primarily through listening or moving. The experience is repeated in a number of ways so students become familiar with attributes of the new content. Next, in the *make conscious phase*, students name now-familiar musical content and often associate visual symbols as well. From there, instruction moves to the *reinforcement phase* where students put this new material to work within their music-making activities that include other familiar content. In the *practice phase* students explore new content in unfamiliar materials like new songs. They also apply this content with familiar materials on other instruments such as recorder or barred percussion. In the *final phase*, students use the new content to *create* new materials through improvisation or composition.[21]

How can we clearly identify the correct sequencing of music instruction? While many possibilities exist, here are some common sequences of instruction.

The instruction moves from sound to sight. Musical ideas are first presented aurally and children are encouraged to learn them through their aural explorations before notation is introduced. In beginning band or string class, students would not simply open their method book to read notation but might begin by singing the etudes or playing them on their instruments without notation. After performing these tunes and patterns on their instruments, students would then learn to read the same from notation.

The instruction moves from simple to complex. Ideas are presented in their most simple form and then combined with other ideas and skills so that a complex understanding of the content is achieved. The music teacher may start by directing students to listen to the sound of his voice, then identifying his basic sounds, followed by a few simple notes on the recorder. The teacher then introduces solfege, a system for learning to sing notes on a musical scale. By learning the notes Do-Re-Mi-Fa-Sol-La-Ti-Do, students are able to sing a musical scale with the first and last notes being an octave apart. As student learning progresses, students become capable of singing single-voice melodies, eventually followed by two-part harmonies.

Experience before theory. Learners are engaged in music-making activities first and then theoretical understanding is brought to the activity after the learner begins to own the experience. In teaching improvisation, the teacher might start by showing the musicians in her performing ensemble five pitches they can choose from as they begin to form melodies over a given accompaniment. The students would be allowed to experiment, with teacher guidance, with these pitches in various combinations until they have demonstrated the ability to perform an improvised melody that "fits" the accompaniment. After this experience, the teacher would "uncover" the knowledge and skills demonstrated by the students and discuss the theory of how they used the pitch content over the harmonic progression of the musical selection.[35]

Instruction moves from the known to the unknown. Ideas are presented in relation to what the students already experience in their own lives and then are moved to unknown contexts. In a middle-school choral classroom, a teacher could ask students to sing the beginning of "Twinkle Twinkle Little Star." After several successful attempts of the students singing the familiar opening to this tune, the teacher could then label the opening interval as a perfect fifth and note that this is the same interval used to open the selection they are beginning rehearsal with that day. The teacher would then ask the students to look at the music and sing the perfect fifth they now have in their tonal memory, transferring the familiar sound to unfamiliar notation.[36]

Instruction moves from the concrete to the abstract. Students begin learning content through activities that allow them to touch and see materials and then move to more abstract understandings like improvisation.[37] The elementary music teacher begins by teaching students to sing and move to the melody "Old McDonald Had a Farm." As the students learn the melody and gestures to the song, the teacher introduces and identifies the "melody" through written notation on the whiteboard. After identifying this "melody" in these concrete forms, the teacher guides students to recognize this and other "melodies" the class listens to in audio and video recordings played in the class.

Differentiated Instruction

Differentiated instruction[38] is a framework for effective teaching that involves providing all students within their diverse classroom community of learners a range of different avenues for understanding new information (within the same classroom) in terms of acquiring content; processing, constructing, or making sense of ideas; and developing teaching materials and assessment measures so that all students within a classroom can learn effectively, regardless of differences in their ability.[39] Differentiated instruction is the process of "ensuring that what a student learns, how he or she learns it, and how the student demonstrates what he or she has learned is a match for that student's readiness level, interests, and preferred mode of learning."[40]

Students vary in culture, socioeconomic status, language, gender, motivation, ability/disability, learning styles, personal interests, and more. Teachers must be aware of these diversities as they plan in accordance with the curricula. By considering varied learning needs, teachers can develop personalized instruction so that all children in the classroom can learn effectively.[38] Teachers can differentiate in four ways: (1) through content, (2) process, (3) product, and (4) learning environment based on the individual learner.[41] Differentiation stems from beliefs about differences among learners, how they learn, learning preferences, and individual interests.[42]

Differentiating instruction may mean teaching the same material to all students using a variety of instructional strategies, or it may require the teacher to deliver lessons at varying levels of difficulty based on the ability of each student. Teachers who practice differentiation in the music classroom may:

- Design lessons based on students' learning styles.
- Group students by shared interest, topic, or ability for assignments.
- Assess students' learning using formative assessment.
- Manage the classroom to create a safe and supportive learning environment.
- Continually assess and adjust lesson content to meet students' needs.[43]

There is much differentiation that happens organically in the music class, but there are also differentiation strategies that teachers can employ with thought and intention. Here are some strategies to implement in your lesson plans:

Include Variety. By including activities that cover the gamut of Bloom's Taxonomy in lessons, music teachers can help address each student's ability. For example, in one lesson, the teacher could ask students what ta and ti-ti rhythms are called (which would be remembering), the teacher could have students apply their knowledge of rhythms by playing rhythm patterns on non-pitched percussion, and could also have students create using ta and ti-ti (creating).[44] This variety would not only lead to an active, engaging lesson but also would allow students opportunities to showcase their knowledge at their own ability level.

Use Scaffolding. As the teacher gives students the chance to figure out how to play "Bounce High" on barred instruments with "G" as sol, she can ask the student who figures it out sooner than others to figure it out with "C" as sol, or A as sol (if the F# bar is added). If a student struggles with figuring it out with "G" as sol, she might write in the note letters for the student or give a simpler song without la, such as "See Saw."[44] In the music classroom, the teacher scaffolds student leaning giving students the tools they need to succeed.[45]

Have Students Self-Differentiate. The teacher can give students musical tasks at different levels. For example, if one ostinato is simpler than others and one is more difficult, the teacher could have the students choose the ostinato they would like to perform. This is a great way for students to perform at their own ability level and feel comfortable. In teaching a more difficult part in an Orff arrangement, the teacher can look for students who could perform the percussion to assign parts in the ensemble. Students who are ready for the challenge will volunteer, and those who are not quite ready will likely not.[44] Students who get to exercise some kind of choice over their assignments and assessments are usually more engaged. Music teachers can get advanced students to work on more advanced music in a self-guided environment while they catch up other students on the concert repertoire. Other options include assigning advanced students more difficult sight-reading exercises or etudes to help with phrasing and articulation.[45]

Balance Group Work and Individual Work. Ensembles can balance group and individual work with group rehearsal in class and individual practice at home. However, some students learn better in groups and some learn better on their own. Some students need the opportunity to work on things we traditionally consider "home practice" such as notes, rhythms, and instrumental techniques in groups at school. Others will learn "ensemble skills" such as intonation, careful listening, and musical interpretation better on their own. Flipping these traditional roles around can be a great way to work differentiated instruction into the heart of your lesson plan. Instead of having students play scales for homework, have them play in a trio with a friend and a tuner (as a member of the ensemble). Students who need the group experience will get valuable time working on scales. Students who are out of tune because they don't know what to listen for will be able to focus on just the tuner and their partner.[45]

Classroom Management

Classroom management is commonly understood as the structures and procedures that establish and reinforce an emotionally healthy, academically productive learning environment.[46] While certain routines can help set the stage for learning, teachers must critically examine such routines and expectations to establish a classroom environment that supports learners' varying needs and backgrounds.[47] Presumably, a successfully managed classroom correlates with student engagement, of which there are three main categories: (1) behavioral engagement, which references overall attention and participation; (2) emotional or affective engagement, which captures motivation, enjoyment, and interpersonal connection with others in the classroom; and (3) cognitive engagement, which refers to students' concentration, interest, and investment in the content.[48]

Effective classroom management requires awareness, patience, good timing, boundaries, and instinct. There's nothing easy about shepherding a large group of easily distractible young people with different skills and temperaments along a meaningful learning journey. Rabadi and Ray (2017) took an informal survey on Facebook, Twitter, and Instagram to get a deeper understanding of experienced teachers' top classroom management strategies. After review of more than 700 responses, these are some of the most cited and creative responses.

Take Care of Yourself to Take Care of Your Students. To learn effectively, your students need a healthy teacher.[49] Countless studies corroborate the idea that self-care reduces stress, which can deplete your energy and impair your judgment. While self-care is more of a habit or practice for your own well-being than an actual classroom management strategy, the benefits include improved executive function, greater empathy, and increased resilience—all qualities that will empower you to make better decisions when confronted with challenging classroom situations.[50]

Focus on Building Healthy Student-Teacher Relationships is essential to a thriving classroom culture, and even sets the stage for academic success. Simple efforts like greeting students outside the classroom before the start of the day pay outsized dividends. Students appreciate it so much when the teacher just stops to listen and take interest in them. Many educators note that a teacher's ability to balance warmth and strong boundaries is key to successful relationships—and classroom management. "Be consistent but flexible. Love them unconditionally, but hold them accountable. Give them voice but be the leader."[49]

Set Rules, Boundaries, and Expectations (And Do It Early). Students don't thrive amid chaos. They need some basic structure—and consistency—to feel safe and to focus. Establish the code of conduct early in the year, and be sure that everyone—including the teacher—makes an effort to stay true to it. Predictability counts: "Follow through with rewards and consequences. If you say it, mean it. And if you mean it, say it. Be clear, be proactive, and be consistent. Broad consensus among educators confirms that modeling appropriate classroom behavior sets the tone for children. "Your attitude as the teacher really determines what the tone and environment of your classroom is like. If you want calm and productive, project that to your students."

Take a Strength-Based Approach. A strength-based lens means never forgetting to look beneath the surface of behavior, even when it's inconvenient. "Find ways to make your hardest kid your favorite kid...for when you connect with them, it makes everything smoother." All students want to be successful. If they are misbehaving, it is kind of like when a baby cries; there is something wrong in their world. If they are misbehaving for attention then find out why they need the attention and how you can give them what they need." And always continue to work to deepen the connection, being mindful of the context and using language thoughtfully. "Don't sound surprised when remarking on struggling students' successes. Instead of saying, 'Wow! That was amazing,' it's better to say, 'I'm proud of you, but not surprised. I always knew you could do it.'"

Involve Parents and Guardians. It is important that parents are involved and know what is going on so they can support and reinforce at home. "Never forget that every student is someone's child." The majority of teachers send home reports of both positive and negative behaviors—it's critical to do the former, too—and also use email and text services to communicate about upcoming events, due dates, and student progress. "Parents-guardians-caregivers want to hear that you see the good in their child. A positive connection with home can often help in the classroom." "Catch them doing good and call their parents to let them know you noticed." The benefits of parental communication find their way back to the classroom.[49]

Learning Community as Instructional Model

The learning community is a fundamental feature of the music classroom. It tends to unite people forming bonds that may not exist otherwise. It connects different cultures, promoting diversity and growth among its members. Music making encourages creative thinking, discipline, leadership, and problem-solving. It is a medium for individual and group expression.

Reflecting on principles of Wenger's (1998) Community of Practice[51] in Chapter 9, a music teacher establishes a feeling of community among students and staff. They create a sense of belonging while meeting the needs of individual members of the program. Effective teachers set the tone for rehearsal by employing clear concise expectations during purposeful class routines. They maintain energy and passion through their pacing and utilize a variety of rewards that motivate them while training their students. Teachers engage students in challenging yet enjoyable class activities to intrinsically motivate them in learning. A smile, thumbs up, verbal praise, or award may also be used as an extrinsic motivation to encourage students in accomplishing class goals. Effectual music teachers design lessons that encounter success and lead toward excellence on the part of students. Through shared musical events and activities, emotional connections among community members will undoubtedly occur in the engaging experience of making music.

With productive positive leadership of the music teacher, members of the learning community feel some sense of loyalty and belonging to the music program that drive their desire to keep working and helping others. Student leadership, collaboration, and contribution are encouraged as essential valued attributes of the music-learning community. The learning community gives students the chance to meet individual needs by expressing their own personal opinions, asking for help or specific information during the learning process, and sharing stories of events with their own personal issues such as emotional connections made during musical experience.[52]

Learning Activities

Pair up with another student to discuss and then complete each activity.

1　Applying the ADDIE model, construct instruction for a course of your choice (e.g., band, chorus, orchestra, general music, music theory, fine arts survey, or another course) for the grade of your choice (e.g., K–12). Address each phase of ADDIE as you design your instruction for an individual lesson or a unit of study (three to five lessons) for the course.

2　Write a minimum of one-page reflection on the methods and strategies you would employ to facilitate a learner-centered approach and experiential learning in a course of your choice (e.g., band, chorus, orchestra, general music, music theory, fine arts survey, or another course) for the grade of your choice (e.g., K–12).

3　Write a minimum of one-page reflection on methods and strategies you would employ to differentiate instruction in a course of your choice (e.g., band, chorus, orchestra, general music, music theory, fine arts survey, or another course) for the grade of your choice (e.g., K–12). Your reflection may address one lesson or unit of study for the course.

4　Write a minimum of one-page reflection on methods and strategies you would employ to cultivate a learning community in a course of your choice (e.g., band, chorus, orchestra, general music, music theory, fine arts survey, or another course) for the grade of your choice (e.g., K–12). Include guidelines you would engage to manage the class and/or rehearsal.

Notes

1 Merrill, M. D., Drake, L., Lacy, M. J., & Pratt, J. (1996). Reclaiming instructional design. *Educational Technology, 36*(5), 5–7.

2 Forest, Ed. (2016). Instructional design. *Teaching & learning.* Retrieved July 7, 2021, from https://web.archive.org/web/20161220091647/http://educationaltechnology.net/instructional-design/

3 Kurt, S. (2017). ADDIE Model: Instructional design. *Educational technology.* Retrieved July 7, 2021, from https://educationaltechnology.net/the-addie-model-instructional-design/

4 Mayer, R. E. (1992). Cognition and instruction: Their historic meeting within educational psychology. *Journal of Educational Psychology, 84*(4), 405–412.
    Duffy, T., & Cunningham, D. (1996). Constructivism: Implications for the design and delivery of instruction. In D. Jonassen (Ed.), *Handbook of research for educational communications and technology* (pp. 170–198). New York: Simon & Schuster Macmillan.
    Duffy, T., & Jonassen, D. (1992). Constructivism: New implications for instructional technology. In T. Duffy & D. Jonassen (Eds.), *Constructivism and the technology of instruction* (pp. 1–16). Hillsdale, NJ: Erlbaum.

5 Clark, B. (2009). *The history of instructional design and technology.* Retrieved July 7, 2021, from https://web.archive.org/web/20121203232320/http://www.slideshare.net/benton44/history-of-instructional-design-and-technology?from=embed
    Wikipedia. (2012). *Bloom's taxonomy.* Retrieved July 7, 2021, from https://en.wikipedia.org/wiki/Bloom%27s_taxonomy

6 Reiser, R., & Dempsey, J. (2012). *Trends and issues in instructional design and technology.* Boston, MA: Pearson.

7 Gagné, R. (1985). *The conditions of learning* (4th ed.). New York: Holt, Rinehart & Winston.

8 International Centre for Educators' Styles. (2021). *Gagné's conditions of learning theory.* Retrieved July 8, 2021, from https://eiclsresearch.wordpress.com/types-of-styles/learning-styles/gagne-robert/gagnes-conditions-of-learning-theory/

9 Gale Encyclopedia of Biography. (2012). *Robert Mills Gagné.* Retrieved July 8, 2021, from https://web.archive.org/web/20121122052956/http://www.answers.com/topic/robert-mills-gagn

10 Gagné, R. (1974). Educational technology and the learning process. *Educational Researcher, 3*(1), 3–8.

11 Psychological Principles in System Development-1962. (2012). Retrieved July 8, 2021, from http://www.nwlink.com/~donclark/history_isd/gagne.html

12 Morrison, G. (2010). *Designing effective instruction* (6th ed.). Hoboken, NJ: John Wiley & Sons.

13 Behzadaval, B., & Vahedi, M. (2019). The role of instructional design in music education. *International Conference on Research in Teaching and Education,* 25–37.

14 Wang, S., & Hsu, H. (2009). Using the ADDIE model to design second life activities for online learners. *TechTrends, 53*(6), 76–81.

15 Philpott, C. (2004). The body and musical literacy. In C. Philpott & C. Plummeridge (Eds.), *Issues in music teaching* (pp. 79–91). New York: Routledge.

16 Culatta, R. (2021). *ADDIE model.* Retrieved July 9, 2021, from https://www.instructionaldesign.org/models/addie/

17 Noroozi, D., & Razavi, S. (2016). *Instructional design foundation.* Tehran, Iran: Samt.

18 Kurt, S. (2017). *ADDIE model: Instructional design.* Retrieved July 9, 2021, from https://educationaltechnology.net/the-addie-model-instructional-design/

19 Wikipedia. (2021). *Instructional design: ADDIE process.* Retrieved July 9, 2021, from https://en.wikipedia.org/wiki/Instructional_design

20 Piskurich, G. (2006). *Rapid instructional design: Learning ID fast and right* (2nd ed.). Hoboken, NJ: John Wiley & Sons, Inc.

21 Raiber, M., & Teachout, D. (2013). *The journey from music student to teacher* (p. 135). New York: Taylor and Francis.

22 Bauer, W., & Berg, M. (2001). Influences on instrumental music teaching. *Bulletin of the Council for Research in Music Education, 150,* 53–66.
    Wiggins, J. (2001). *Teaching for musical understanding.* Boston, MA: McGraw-Hill.

23 Schwab, J. J. (1983). The practical 4: Something for curriculum professors to do. *Curriculum Inquiry, 13*(3), 239–265.

24 Biasutti, M., & Concina, E. (2018). The effective music teacher: The influence of personal, social, and cognitive dimensions on music teacher self-efficacy. *Musicae Scientiae, 22*(2), 264–279.

25 Hattie, J. A. C. (2009). *Visible learning: A synthesis of 800+ meta-analyses on achievement.* Oxford, England: Routledge.

26 Biasutti, M., & Concina, E. (2018). The effective music teacher: The influence of personal, social, and cognitive dimensions on music teacher self-efficacy. *Musicae Scientiae, 22*(2), 265.

27 Hansen, D., & Imse, L. (2016). Student-centered classrooms. *Music Educators Journal, 103*(2), 20–26.

28 Barton, T. (2019). *Experiential learning in and out of classrooms.* Retrieved July 12, 2021, from https://servelearn.co/blog/experiential-learning-in-and-out-of-classrooms/

29 Blair, D. (2009). Stepping aside: Teaching in a student-centered music classroom. *Music Educators Journal, 95*(3), 42–45.

30 The concept of reflection while engaged in experiential learning through the solving of problems is central to the work of John Dewey. See the following items:
    Dewey, J. (1902). *The child and the curriculum.* Chicago, IL: University of Chicago Press.
    Dewey, J. (1916). *Democracy and education.* New York: McMillan.
    Dewey, J. (1998). *Experience and education: The 60th anniversary edition.* West Lafayette, IN: Kappa Delta Pi. (Original work published 1938).

31 Glynn, S. M., & DiVesta, F. J. (1977). Outline and hierarchical organization for study and retrieval. *Journal of Educational Psychology, 69*(1), 69–95.
    Lorch, R. F., Jr., & Lorch, E. P. (1985). Topic structure representation and text recall. *Journal of Educational Psychology, 77*(2), 137–148.
    Van Patten, J., Chao, C. I., & Reigeluth, C. M. (1986). A review of strategies for sequencing and synthesizing instruction. *Review of Educational Research, 56*(4), 437–471.

32 Bruner, J. (1966). *Toward a theory of instruction.* Cambridge, MA: Harvard University Press.

33 Reigeluth, C., & Stein, F. (1983). The elaboration theory of instruction. In C. Reigeluth (Ed.), *Instructional design theories and models.* Hillsdale, NJ: Erlbaum Associates.
    English, R. E., & Reigeluth, C. M. (1996). Formative research on sequencing instruction with the elaboration theory. *Educational Technology Research & Development, 44*(1), 23–42.

34 Scandura, J. M. (1973). *Structural Learning I: Theory and Research.* London, England: Gordon & Breach.
    Scandura, J. M. (1976). *Structural Learning II: Issues and Approaches.* London, England: Gordon & Breach.

35 Raiber, M., & Teachout, D. (2013). *The journey from music student to teacher* (pp. 145–146). Taylor and Francis.

36 Raiber, M., & Teachout, D. (2013). *The journey from music student to teacher* (p. 146). Taylor and Francis.

37 Raiber, M., & Teachout, D. (2013). *The journey from music student to teacher* (pp. 138–139). Taylor and Francis.

38 Tomlinson, C. A. (1999). Mapping a route toward a differentiated instruction. *Educational Leadership, 57*(1), 12.

39 Tomlinson, C. A. (2004). *How to differentiate instruction in mixed-ability classrooms* (2nd ed.). Alexandria, VA: Association for Supervision and Curriculum Development.

40 Rock, M. L., Gregg, M., Ellis, E., & Gable, R. A. (2008-01-01). REACH: A framework for differentiating classroom instruction. Preventing School Failure: *Alternative Education for Children and Youth, 52*(2), 31–47.

41 Ministry of Education. (2007). *Differentiated instruction teacher's guide: Getting to the core of teaching and learning.* Toronto, Canada: Queen's Printer for Ontario.

42 Tomlinson, C. A. (1999). *The differentiated classroom: Responding to the needs of all learners.* Upper Saddle River, NJ: Pearson Education.

43 Weselby, C. (2021). What is differentiated instruction? Examples of how to differentiate instruction in the classroom. *Resilient educator.* Retrieved July 13, 2021, from https://resilienteducator.com/classroom-resources/examples-of-differentiated-instruction/

44 Miracle, A. (2019). *Differentiation in the music room.* Retrieved July 13, 2021, from https://mrsmiraclesmusicroom.com/2018/11/differentiation-in-music-classroom.html

45 Ryan, S. (2017). Using differentiated instruction in music lesson plans. *SmartMusic.* Retrieved July 13, 2021, from https://www.smartmusic.com/blog/using-differentiated-instruction-in-music-lesson-plans/

46 Evertson, C., & Weinstein, C. (2011). *Classroom management as a field of inquiry.* Mahwah, NJ: Lawrence Erlbaum.

47 Martin, L. (2021). Reconceptualizing classroom management in the ensemble: Considering culture, communication, and community. *Music Educators Journal, 107*(4), 21–27.

48 Fredericks, J., Blumenfeld, P., & Paris, A. (2004). School engagement: Potential of the concept, state of the evidence. *Review of Educational Research, 74*(1), 59–109.

49 Rabadi, S., & Ray, B. (2017). 5 Principles of outstanding classroom management. *George Lucas Educational Foundation.* Retrieved July 14, 2021, from https://www.edutopia.org/article/5-principles-outstanding-classroom-management

50 Center on the Developing Child. (2021). *The science of adult capabilities.* Harvard University. Retrieved July 14, 2021, from https://developingchild.harvard.edu/science/deep-dives/adult-capabilities/

51 Wenger, E. (1998). *Communities of practice: Learning, meaning, and identity.* Cambridge, England: Cambridge University Press.
Wenger, E., & Wenger-Treyner, B. (2015). What is a community of practice? *Introduction to communities of practice* (p. 2). Retrieved January 24, 2020, from http://wenger-trayner.com /resources/what-is-a-community-of-practice.

52 Bonk, C., Wisher, R., & Nigrelli, M. (2004). Learning communities, communities of practices: Principles, technologies and examples. In K. Littlton (Ed.), *Ch. 12, Learning to collaborate.* Hauppauge, NY: Nova Science Publishers.

Chapter 12

Assessment and Evaluation in the Music Classroom

Assessment or evaluation is the systematic process of documenting and using empirical data on the knowledge, skills, attitudes, and beliefs to refine programs and improve student learning.[1] Assessment data can be obtained from directly examining student work to assess the achievement of learning outcomes or can be based on data from which one can make inferences about learning.[2] Assessment can focus on the individual learner, the learning community such as a class, ensemble, or other organized group of learners, a course, an academic program, the institution, or the educational system as a whole.[3] As a continuous process, assessment establishes measurable and clear student learning outcomes for learning, provisioning a sufficient amount of learning opportunities to achieve these outcomes, implementing a systematic way of gathering, analyzing, and interpreting evidence to determine how well student learning matches expectations, and using the collected information to inform improvement in student learning.[4]

Learning Objectives

1 What are the elements of and types of assessment?
2 What are the primary tools for assessment in the music classroom and program?
3 In what ways can the music teacher design learning outcomes, teaching methods, and assessments for effective instruction in the classroom?
4 What three roles of assessment contribute to effective music instruction and student growth in music learning?
5 What principles, processes, and assessment tools of reflective practice contribute to the professional growth of the music teacher?

Types of Assessment

The term *assessment* is generally used to refer to all activities teachers use to help students learn and to gauge student progress.[5] Goolsby (1999) suggests that four types of assessment commonly used in music settings are (a) placement (auditions, chair tests, etc.); (b) diagnostic (identifying performance skills and knowledge difficulties); (c) formative (the regular monitoring of students for learning outcomes); and (d) summative (concert, festivals, etc.).[6] These conceptual definitions and goals provide the foundation for the creation and implementation of assessments.

Placement assessments are used to place students according to prior achievement or personal characteristics, at the most appropriate point in an instructional sequence, in a unique instructional strategy, or with a suitable teacher[7] conducted through placement

DOI: 10.4324/9781003038474-16

testing (i.e., the audition that music teachers use to assess performance readiness for placement in school ensembles). Placement assessment is conducted prior to instruction or intervention to establish a baseline from which individual student growth can be measured. This type of assessment is used to know what the student's skill level is about the subject (music). It helps the teacher to explain the material more efficiently. These assessments are not graded.[8]

Diagnostic assessments take place before instruction and provide information about what students already know and can do (Hale & Green, 2009)[9] for the purpose of identifying a suitable program of learning. This essential information often serves two purposes: (a) to clarify the limits of a student's zone of proximal development (ZPD) (Vygotsky, 1978),[10] and/or (b) to determine a student's musical aptitude (Gordon, 1998).[11] Knowing a student's ZPD in a certain topic area allows the teacher to provide meaningful instruction.[12] Music aptitude is defined as "a measure of the student's potential to learn music."[13]

Formative assessments occur either during or after instruction and are used to "elicit information which will be of use to the pupil and the teacher in deciding what ought to be done next in order to develop learning" (Fautley, 2010, p. 9).[14] A primary feature of formative assessment is feedback (Havnes, Smith, Dysthe, & Ludgisven, 2012).[15] Teachers conducting large ensembles often make use of informal formative assessment.[16] Formative assessment might be a teacher or peer or the learner, providing feedback on a student's work and may not necessarily be used for grading purposes. Formative assessments can take the form of diagnostic, performance quizzes, or oral questions. Formative assessments are carried out concurrently with instructions. The formative assessments aim to see if the students understand the instruction before doing a summative assessment.[8] Most often, formative assessment is conducted informally; however, formally conducted formative assessments are very useful.[17]

Summative assessments occur after instruction has been completed and are used to determine what a learner may or may not know and/or can do independently at certain points in time.[17] This type of assessment is typically graded (e.g., pass/fail, 0-100) and can take the form of unit tests, exams, midterm playing tests, final composition projects, and even concerts or musical programs.[18] Summative assessments may be used to determine whether a student has passed or failed a course.[8]

Summative and formative assessments are often referred to in a learning context as *assessment of learning* and *assessment for learning,* respectively. Assessment of learning is generally summative in nature and intended to measure learning outcomes and reports those outcomes to students, parents, and administrators. Assessment of learning generally occurs at the conclusion of a class, course, semester, or academic year. Assessment for learning is generally formative in nature and is used by teachers to consider approaches to teaching and next steps for individual learners and the class.[19]

Performance-based assessment is similar to summative assessment, as it focuses on achievement. A well-defined task is identified and students are asked to perform, create, or do something, often in settings that involve real-world application of knowledge and skills. Proficiency is demonstrated by providing an extended response. Performance formats are further differentiated into musical products and performances. The performance may result in a product, such as a musical performance, etude or exercise, musical recital, composition performance, or project.[20]

Summative assessments are most appropriately used for *program assessment.* Asmus (1999) defines program assessment as "the determination of an educational program's strengths and weaknesses through a well-conceived and well-implemented plan of data collection and analysis" (p. 21).[21] Such an assessment might allow a teacher to evaluate the effectiveness of a year-long curriculum in meeting the overall learning goals she established for her seventh-grade general music class. Program assessment may help a high-school band director evaluate a four-year curriculum in meeting the music learning needs of students who have been in the band program for their entire high-school tenure.[22]

Assessment Tools

It has become increasingly important that music educators maintain an active awareness of assessment importance and practice in the field. Outcomes of instruction (i.e., student-learning outcomes) include the students' demonstration of specific knowledge, skills, abilities, and/or dispositions gained from their learning environment. Classroom assessment processes are integrated into all the instructional processes occurring in the classroom, and teachers' educational decisions are based primarily on their inferences of student-learning outcomes.[23]

All education, and particularly music education, is concerned with student learning across three primary domains: cognitive, psychomotor, and affective (Bloom, 1956; Hanna, 2007).[24] Different types of data can be collected based on the type(s) of learning that is being facilitated during instruction. The psychomotor domain addresses learning associated with skills or the ability to do something. Learning required for a young violinist to grip her bow correctly would reside in the psychomotor domain. The cognitive domain addresses learning that is knowledge based. Understanding and being able to describe the common compositional techniques used in the Swing era would be an example of learning in the cognitive domain. Learning that connects with feelings, emotions, motivations, and attitudes is addressed in the affective domain. An example might be, as part of the rehearsal and preparation of Ticheli's *Cajun Folk Songs*, that band students are asked to consider musical traditions and how they are preserved, changed, or lost. At some point, the teacher may invite students to "share stories of music they might remember from their childhood that their own [future] children may never experience" (O'Toole, 2003, p. 276).[25] It is appropriate and necessary for music teachers to address all three learning domains in their instruction. Data addressing all three domains should be collected as part of regular assessments.[26]

Tools in the Music Classroom

Assessment can be either *formal* or *informal*. Formal assessment usually implies a written document, such as a test, quiz, paper, or music performance rubric. A formal assessment is given a numerical score or grade based on student performance, whereas an informal assessment does not contribute to a student's final course grade. An informal assessment usually occurs in a more casual manner and may include observation, inventories, checklists, rating scales, rubrics, performance and portfolio assessments, participation, peer and self-evaluation, and discussion.

As a professional music educator, you will need to determine what form of assessment is most appropriate for use in each situation in the music classroom. Each of these assessment tools varies depending upon the amount and type of information they provide both to the teacher and the student.[27]

Pencil and paper tests. The use of written exams varies depending upon the classroom setting (Russell & Austin, 2010).[28] Most ensemble classes do not engage in this type of assessment regularly. However, O'Toole (2003) notes that this is an efficient tool for assessing substantive knowledge (cognitive domain) about music. She also notes that

Percussion Hand Position Checklist

Hand Position	YES	NO
Sticks should form an upside-down "V" with the beads striking the head just off center.		
Grasp the stick between the fleshy part of the thumb and the first joint of the index finger, about 5 inches from the butt end of the stick.		
Wrap all other fingers gently around the stick. Keeping these fingers relaxed is extremely important—do not squeeze the stick.		
Play with palms facing downward and a smooth, relaxed wrist motion.		

Figure 12.1 Percussion Hand Position Checklist.

McClellan, E. R. (2021a). Example of Checklist. August 1, 2021. Copyright (c) 2022 Edward McClellan.

there are two basic ways to collect data from written exams. One is through selected response (e.g., fill-in-the-blank, multiple choice, matching) and the other through created response (e.g., short answer, essay).[25] It is also possible to collect affective data with creative response questions that are well crafted. Written exams assessing common terminology, historical elements, and music theory concepts would be appropriate in any music classroom.[29]

Checklists (Figure 12.1) are assessment tools that set out specific criteria, which educators and students may use to gauge skill development or[30] progress. Checklists set out skills, attitudes, strategies, and behaviors for evaluation to systematically collect psychomotor or performance data about a student or group of students. Checklists consist of a set of statements that correspond to specific criteria; the answer to each statement is either "Yes" or "No", or "Done" or "Not Done." A student, a group of students, or an entire class may use checklists; they may be "single use" or designed for multiples usage. By observing student performance, the evaluator checks the statement corresponding to the observed behavior. Checklists can also play a role in a student's ability to self-assess, along with a variety of other tools.[31]

Rating Scales (Figure 12.2) are observation tools that allow teachers to indicate the degree or frequency of the behaviors, performance skills, tasks, and strategies displayed by the learner. Each behavior is rated on a continuum from lowest to highest. Rating scales state the criteria and provide three or four response selections to describe the quality or frequency of student work. Teaching students to use descriptive words, such as *always, usually, sometimes,* and *never* helps them pinpoint[32] specific strengths and needs. Rating scales also give students information for setting goals and improving performance. On a rating scale, the descriptive word is more important than the related number. The more precise and descriptive the words for each scale point, the more reliable the tool. Effective rating scales use descriptors with clearly understood measures, such as frequency. Scales that rely on subjective descriptors of quality, such as fair, good, or excellent, are less effective because the single adjective does not contain enough information on what criteria are indicated at each of these points on the scale.[33]

Achievement charts are guidelines that set standards for performance or musical products posted in the music classroom. They are based on standards and contain a

Student's Name	Solo		Date		
Skill	Descriptor	Always	Mostly	Somewhat	Not Yet
Tone	Plays with a gentle beautiful tone				
Tonguing	Starts the tone with "too"				
Legato	Connects notes				
Fingerings	Use correct fingerings				
Finger positions	Covers holes completely; uses fingerpads				
Rhythms	Plays rhythms accurately				
Fluency	Plays complete example on first attempt				

Figure 12.2 Rating Scale: Recorder Solo Assessment.

McClellan, E. R. (2021b). Example of Rating Scale. August 1, 2021. Copyright (c) 2022 Edward McClellan.

series of indicators for each level of performance. They are assessment tools that document performance on the basis of clearly defined criteria. They enable music teachers to perform *in-depth assessments* and are developed by both music educators and students. Compared to checklists, they convey more *specific* data about teaching and assessment. To the extent possible, achievement charts should be *created with student participation*. To start, explain what high-quality work consists of. Once the "standard" has been set, it is easy to define satisfactory performance and unsatisfactory performance. The best achievement charts have *three to five levels* to allow for objective assessment of a musical skill or task.[31]

Rubrics. Wesolowski (2012) describes a rubric as a "form of a criteria-specific performance scale. It is a set of scoring criteria used to determine the achievement level of a student's performance on assigned tasks" (p. 37).[34] A rubric (Figure 12.3) divides each task into constituent parts including details of various performance levels for each task, often organized from lower levels to higher levels. Each performance level is described in enough detail that the observer and the learner have clear ideas of what has or has not been accomplished in the performance. By reading the descriptors in levels above what was achieved during the assessment, learners can develop understandings of what needs to be done to improve their performance. Again, this tool can also be used for peer- and self-assessment.[35]

Rubrics contain four essential features (Stevens & Levi, 2013):

1 *A task description* or *a descriptive title of the task* students are expected to produce or perform;
2 *A scale (and scoring)* that describes the level of mastery (e.g., exceeds expectation, meets expectation, doesn't meet expectation);
3 *Components/dimensions* students are to attend to in completing the assignment/tasks (e.g., types of skills, knowledge, etc.); and
4 *Description of the performance quality (performance descriptor)* of the components/dimensions at each level of mastery.[36]

A description of performance quality give students a clear idea about what must be done to demonstrate a certain level of mastery, understanding, or proficiency. As with rating scales, there are many different types of rubrics (Wesolowski, 2012).[34]

The *Portfolio* is designed to become a resource that students may continue to use, build, and share beyond the classroom.[37] Collections of evidence documenting each student's achievement in music can be organized into assessment portfolios.[38] With the help of technology, these portfolios can include written, video, audio, and multimedia

Name _____ Class _____ Date _____

Element	3	2	1	Scale/Score
Tone	Characteristic; Breath consistently supports purposeful dynamics in all ranges and melodic lines.	Uncharacteristic; Breath support is inconsistent across all ranges and melodic lines.	Often Unfocused; Distorted tone; Breath support is lacking across all ranges and melodic lines.	**Criteria** • Performance description • Level of proficiency, marginal, unacceptable
Dynamics	Full range of dynamics are used; Melodic lines are shaped across the lines of music.	Some dynamics are used; Notes have varying volumes; Melodic lines have some shape.	Little dynamics are used; Notes are at the same volume.	• Mastery, partial mastery, progression toward mastery
Articulations	Note shapes are clean, accurate, and exact.	Note shapes are clean and accurate most of the time.	Note shapes are not distinct and accurate most of the time.	

Total _____/ 9

Figure 12.3 Music Performance Rubric.

McClellan, E. R. (2021c). Example of a Music Performance Rubric. February 25, 2022. Copyright (c) 2022 Edward McClellan.

(recordings of demonstrations, interviews, presentations, etc.)[39] evidence of student learning. Portfolios require students to reflect on their work, assessing the work's quality and documenting their progress. In certain kinds of portfolios, students then formalize this knowledge through written reflections that become a guideline for reviewing the portfolio's contents.[40]

Several types of portfolios exist, but they all generally fall into two categories as either process folios or product folios (O'Toole, 2003).[25] Process folios document the learner's journey as s/he works to achieve particular skills and understandings. Artifacts in the portfolio demonstrate progress (or not) as these skills and understandings are being developed. A product folio is different in that learners are required to select representative artifacts that demonstrate their highest levels of achievement. The selection process is often coupled with student reflections concerning why they choose each artifact and how it demonstrates acquisition of certain skills or understandings.[38]

Effective portfolio assessment takes good planning and management from the music educator.[38] In their book *Measurement and Assessment in Teaching*,[41] Robert Linn and David Miller (2005) present five "key steps" for creating and using portfolios: (1) specify the purpose, (2) provide guidelines for selecting portfolio entries, (3) define the student's role in selection and self-evaluation, (4) specify evaluation criteria, and (5) use portfolios in instruction and communication. While portfolios can be used to collect rich data, other tools (i.e., checklists, rating scales, rubrics) are often used to evaluate portfolio contents. Using these tools, portfolios can be peer- and self-assessed as well.[42]

Reflective Journals are personal records of students' learning experiences. Students typically are asked by their instructors to record learning-related incidents, sometimes during the learning process but more often just after they occur. Entries in journals and learning logs can be prompted by questions about course content, assignments, exams, students' own ideas or students' thought processes about what happened in a particular class or rehearsal. Journals and learning logs are then submitted to the instructor for feedback. Both paper-based and online journals or logs can be turned in before or after each class period or at any other designated time.[43]

Journals often focus subjectively on personal experiences, reactions, and reflections while *learning logs* are more documentary records of students' work process (what they are doing), their accomplishments, ideas, or questions.[44] Music teachers use journaling (1) to encourage participants to examine their experiences of singing through reflective writing in response to prompts that call for self-assessment and focused attention on elements of music, (2) to build camaraderie through written exchanges among participants, and (3) to provide opportunities for individualized instruction when students communicate directly with them about difficulties with musical learning and performing (Cohen, 2012).[45] Some music teachers use learning logs as means of documenting practice time outside of class, which asks students to list their practice times, goals for practice, and whether or not they achieved these goals.[45] Journaling often provides learners the chance to express their feelings, attitudes, and motivations in their writings. This affords the teacher possibilities to address learning in the affective domain.[45] As with all formative assessments, it is imperative that students receive feedback on their journals in a timely fashion.[46]

Assessment Alignment with Instruction

Due to the amount of testing that takes place in today's American schools, students are often conditioned to think of testing as something that is done to them and that learning must stop so that assessment can take place.[47] However, relevant literature builds on the constructivist principle of alignment in curriculum in which learning outcomes, teaching methods used, and assessment tasks are aligned to each other and all are "tuned to learning activities addressed in the desired learning outcomes" (Biggs, 2007).[48] In constructive alignment, learning outcomes "specify the activity that students should engage ... as well as the content of the activity ... The teacher's tasks are to set up a learning environment that encourages the student to perform those learning activities, and to assess student performances against the intended learning outcomes" (Biggs & Tang, 2011, p. 97).[49]

These fundamental principles of music teaching and learning have been previously emphasized in Chapters 8 and 10. The theory of backward design goes one step beyond constructive alignment to specify the order of executing the three components aligned: (1) the teacher identifies the desired results, (2) determines the acceptable evidence (measures), and (3) plans the learning experiences and instruction.[50] In his *Intelligent Music Teaching*, Duke (2005)[51] describes assessment as an ongoing process inseparably interlaced into daily instruction and/or rehearsal. Assessment is a means of data collection to find out what students know and what they've learned to do. What is evaluated should be material that the teacher desires for the students to learn, not just a subset of the material covered in class. Therefore, student test results should not be surprising.[52]

Considering the various types of assessment and tools for assessing student learning, it is essential for the music teacher to begin with the end in mind. Recognize class objectives, curriculum standards, and what students should know, understand, and be able to do. The teacher should determine what benchmarks are acceptable along the way and consider a range of assessment methods to be implemented. In creating learning plans, the teacher should structure classes, rehearsals, and learning experiences to reach final goals of learning. Music teachers should contemplate what knowledge and skills students will need to achieve desired results. This process may be equated to using a "roadmap."[53] The teacher starts with final goals for learning, creates or plans out ongoing assessments, and finally designs instructional lesson plans.

The Roles of Assessment

Student assessment is integral to music teaching and learning. In cultivating a student-centered learning environment, it is essential for teachers to find ways to measure each student's growth in music learning. Music teachers are also responsible for providing feedback to help students extend their understanding of musical concepts and to assist all students in enhancing their musical proficiencies. With these goals, Scott (2021) examines multiple roles of assessment: (1) assessment of learning, (2) assessment for learning, and (3) assessment as learning.[54]

Assessment of learning is "the traditional function assessment plays in providing a summative profile of what students have achieved [in terms of learning outcomes] as a result of instruction" (p. 32).[55] It is based on assessment information collected and collated by the teacher. *Assessment for learning* represents a constructivist perspective in which students, as active learners, use assessment feedback to extend their current levels of understanding. Teachers use the information gained through assessment to modify instruction to meet the needs of individuals. Thus, assessment takes on a formative role through its integration with instruction.[55] *Assessment as learning* is self-reflective. It places the student in the central role as the assessor and evaluator of learning. Scott (2012) notes that "Students monitor their own learning, reflect on what they have accomplished, and use this to inform future learning as they continually strive to perform at more sophisticated levels" (p. 33).[56]

The ultimate goal of any educational endeavor is for the teacher to facilitate learning that becomes independent of the teacher, developing a self-regulated learner.[57] As Scott (2012) asserts,

> Music teachers already implement many of the strategies associated with 'assessment for' and 'assessment as' learning. As teachers and students expand their experiences with assessment as a learning tool, students will increasingly be empowered to take ownership of their own learning. Thus, assessment has the potential to facilitate our students' journeys toward lifelong music making.
>
> (p. 35)[58]

Reflective Practice as a Teacher

When music teachers engage in reflective teaching, they are dedicating time to evaluate their own teaching practice, examine their curricular choices, consider student feedback, and make revisions to improve student learning.[59] Reflective practice is a process that facilitates teaching, learning, and understanding, and it plays a central role in the teachers' professional development.

Reflective practice is an important tool in practice-based professional learning settings where teachers learn from their own professional experiences, rather than from formal learning or knowledge transfer. It is the most important source of personal professional development and improvement. It is also an important way to bring together theory and practice; through reflection, a person is able to see and label forms of thought and theory within the context of his or her work. A teacher who reflects throughout his/her practice is not just looking back on past actions and events but is taking a conscious look at emotions, experiences, actions, and responses, and using that information to add to his/her existing knowledge base and reach a higher level of understanding.[60]

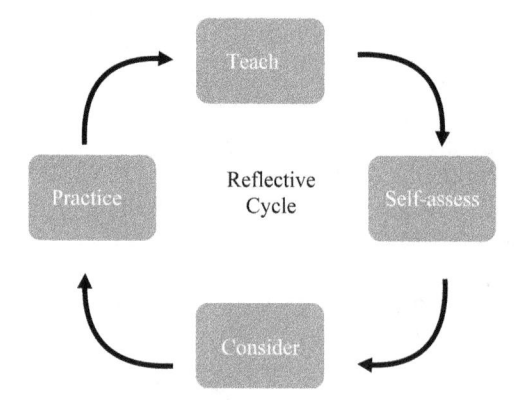

Figure 12.4 The Reflective Practice Cycle.

McClellan, E. R. (2021d). The Reflective Cycle Model. August 1, 2021. Copyright (c) 2022 Edward McClellan.

Reflective teaching involves examining one's underlying beliefs about teaching and learning and one's alignment with actual classroom practice before, during, and after a course is taught.[59] The process of reflection is a cycle that needs to be repeated.

- Teach
- Self-assess the effect your teaching has had on learning
- Consider new ways of teaching that can improve the quality of learning
- Try these ideas in practice
- Repeat the process

Reflective practice is "learning through and from experience towards gaining new insights of self and practice" (Finlay, 2008).[61] As a reflective practitioner the music teacher continuously reviews the learning process to make sure all students make maximum progress.[62] Here are a few ways to begin the process of reflection:

Maintaining a Professional Journal provides a point of entry to cultivate pedagogical improvement, and develop more effective daily practices. Keeping a daily teaching journal provides a way to make notes on what did and did not go well in the classroom. Reflective writing creates cognitive awareness in considering previous actions and builds confidence by placing value on teacher thought.[63] Journaling makes the process more disciplined and gives a place for ideas and insights to take root. The music teacher can keep notes on what went well in lessons, what could have gone better, thoughts on student learning and behavior, why they may have gotten off in learning, and a running list of ideas for what will be done next year.[64]

Peer Observation. Having a second pair of eyes often gives us valuable information we would have missed. As a music teacher, you can invite a colleague to visit your classroom and gather data about your lesson, the student engagement, and the atmosphere. After you have discussed the observation with your colleague, you can then add it to your journal and include your own insights. This entry can relate back to areas you identify for further reflection.[64]

Video-Recording Teaching Practice. Music teachers can set up a personal or school video camera to video-record their lessons informally or formally. Video recording your class lesson or rehearsal can provide evidence for your own reflection. You can also request a copy of the school observation evaluation document from your supervisor or school administrator that you may use during your review to self-assess your teaching practice, student behavior, and learning in your music classroom.[59]

Student Feedback. The music teacher can seek feedback from their students about the classroom. While these observations can provide valuable perspective and show appreciation for student insights,[60] it is crucial to assure students that their responses will be anonymous and should be constructive in contributing to the music classroom. Often, a question about a particular lesson or certain issue in rehearsal can be added to quiz, journal assignment, or online Google Form for the class.[64] As teacher, you can design a student rehearsal rubric or self-assessment for self-analysis of what is or is not happening, and what students are experiencing in your classes and rehearsals.[65] As with peer feedback, you can add this data to your journal and then give your insights with it.

We never want to become stale or complacent in our teaching. The way to become even more effective is through looking back so we can leap forward.[64] Dr. Stephen Miles, supervisor of visual and performing arts for the Washington County Public Schools in Hagerstown, Maryland, states,

> The key to reflective practice is to become fully aware of what we are doing pedagogically. Because only then can we begin to engage in a cycle of continuous pedagogical growth—revisiting, reflecting, refining. This will allow us to make decisions based on thoughtful inquiry and reflection rather than dogmatic practice.
>
> As we become more comfortable and adept at reflective practice, and as we catalyze this same type of reflective mindset in our students, we can begin to see and hear our classes and rehearsals in a whole new way.
>
> (Dr. Stephen Miles)[66]

Learning Activities

Pair up with another student to complete each activity.

1 Describe examples of a placement assessment, diagnostic assessment, formative assessment, and summative assessment that you may use in a course of your choice (e.g., band, chorus, orchestra, general music, music theory, fine arts survey, or another course) for the grade of your choice (e.g., K–12). Share these examples with your partner and collect feedback on each other's examples.

2 Design a musical task, skill, or activity you will measure and assess in a lesson you will teach the class. After describing the instructional activity and learning outcome(s), detail the ways your assessment will provide feedback in as many domains (i.e., cognitive, psychomotor, and affective) as possible to the student and teacher at the conclusion of the lesson. Analyze your assessment and instructional activity with your partner to determine the instruction that will be most effective in your lesson.

3 Beginning with the desired result, acceptable benchmarks, what the student should know, understand, and be able to do, and the assessment(s) you may use, plan the learning experiences and instruction that will meet final goals of learning for your team-taught lesson. Describe how you may structure instruction that serves as many domains (i.e., cognitive, psychomotor, and affective) as possible and implements ongoing assessment. Share your design with another pair of students, for each pair to provide feedback to the other on the design of their lesson.

4 Design a plan of reflective practice that you may implement to structure your own self-assessment as a music teacher. In your plan include ways you will begin your

reflective process, the structure of your reflective practice, and partnerships you may establish to execute this plan. Share your plan with your partner for their review, critique, and feedback.

Notes

1 Allen, M. J. (2004). *Assessing academic programs in higher education*. San Francisco, CA: Jossey-Bass.
2 Kuh, G. D., Jankowski, N., & Ikenberry, S. O. (2014). *Knowing what students know and can do: The current state of learning outcomes assessment in U.S. Colleges and Universities*. Urbana: University of Illinois and Indiana University, National Institute for Learning Outcomes Assessment.
3 Nelson, R., & Dawson, P. (2014). A contribution to the history of assessment: How a conversation simulator redeems Socratic method. *Assessment & Evaluation in Higher Education, 39*(2), 195–204.
4 Suskie, L. (2004). *Assessing student learning*. Bolton, MA: Anker.
5 Black, P., & William, D. (1998). *Inside the black box: Raising standards through classroom assessment*. Phi Beta Kappan. Retrieved July 19, 2021, from https://kappanonline.org/inside-the-black-box-raising-standards-through-classroom-assessment/
6 Goolsby, T. W. (1999). Assessment in instrumental music. *Music Educators Journal, 86*(2), 31–50.
7 Madaus, G. F., & Airasian, P. W. (1969). *Placement, formative, diagnostic, and summative evaluation of classroom learning*. Paper presented at American Education Research Association Annual Meeting, 1970, 1–24. ERIC Number: ED041829.
8 Mctighe, J., & O'Connor, K. (2005). Seven practices for effective learning. Educational Leadership, 63(3), 10–17.
9 Hale, C., & Green, S. (2009). Six key principles for music assessment. *Music Educators Journal, 95*(7), 27–31.
10 Vygotsky, L. S. (1978). *Mind in society: The development of higher mental processes*. Cambridge, MA: Harvard University Press.
11 Gordon, E. E. (1998). *Introduction to research and the psychology of music*. Chicago, IL: GIA Publications.
12 Raiber, M., & Teachout, D. (2014). *The journey from music student to teacher* (pp. 254–255). New York: Taylor and Francis
13 Gordon, E. E. (1998). *Introduction to research and the psychology of music* (p. 5). Chicago, IL: GIA Publications.
14 Fautley, M. (2010). *Assessment in music education*. Oxford, England: Oxford University Press.
15 Havnes, A., Smith, K., Dysthe, O., & Ludvigsen, K. (2012). Formative assessment and feedback: Making learning visible. *Studies in Educational Evaluation, 38*, 21–27.
16 Raiber, M., & Teachout, D. (2013). *The journey from music student to teacher* (pp. 254–255). New York: Taylor and Francis.
17 Raiber, M., & Teachout, D. (2014). *The journey from music student to teacher* (p. 255). New York: Taylor and Francis.
18 Raiber, M., & Teachout, D. (2014). *The journey from music student to teacher* (p. 257). New York: Taylor and Francis.
19 Earl, L. (2003). *Assessment as learning: Using classroom assessment to maximise student learning*. Thousand Oaks, CA, Corwin Press.
20 Reed, D. (2021). Diagnostic assessment in language teaching and learning. MSU Newsletter. Retrieved July 20, 2021, from https://web.archive.org/web/20110914175741/http://clear.msu.edu/clear/newsletter/files/fall2006.pdf
21 Asmus, E. (1999). Music assessment concepts. *Music Educators Journal, 86*(2), 19–24.
22 Raiber, M., & Teachout, D. (2014). *The journey from music student to teacher* (pp. 256–257). New York: Taylor and Francis.
23 Wesolowski, B. (2020). "Classroometrics": The validity, reliability, and fairness of classroom music assessments. *Music Educators Journal, 106*(3), 29–37.
24 Bloom, B. S. (1956). *Taxonomy of educational objectives, Handbook I: The cognitive domain*. New York: David McKay.

Hanna, W. (2007). The new Bloom's taxonomy: Implications for music education. *Arts Education Policy Review, 108*(4), 7–16.

25 O'Toole, P. (2003). *Shaping sound musicians* (p. 276). Chicago, IL: GIA Music.

26 Raiber, M., & Teachout, D. (2014). *The journey from music student to teacher* (pp. 257–260). New York: Taylor and Francis.

27 Raiber, M., & Teachout, D. (2014). *The journey from music student to teacher* (p. 260). New York: Taylor and Francis.

28 Russell, J., & Austin, J. (2010). Assessment practices of secondary music teachers. *Journal of Research in Music Education, 58*(1), 37–54.

29 Raiber, M., & Teachout, D. (2014). *The journey from music student to teacher* (p. 260). New York: Taylor and Francis.

30 McClellan, E. (2021a). PICTURE. Checklist. Percussion Hand Position. Original Document—Edward McClellan.

31 LD@school. (2014). *Checklists and achievement charts*. Retrieved July 21, 2021, from https://www.ldatschool.ca/checklists-achievement-charts/

32 McClellan, E. (2021b). PICTURE. Rating Scale. Recorder Solo Assessment. Original Document—Edward McClellan.

33 Alberta Education. (2008). *Assessment strategies and tools: Checklists, rating scales and rubrics*. Retrieved July 20, 2021, from https://www.learnalberta.ca/content/mewa/html/assessment/checklists.html

34 Wesolowski, B. (2012). Understanding and developing rubrics for music performance assessment. *Music Educators Journal, 98*(3), 36–42.

35 Raiber, M., & Teachout, D. (2014). *The journey from music student to teacher* (p. 262). New York: Taylor and Francis.

36 Stevens, D. D., & Levi, A. J. (2013). *Introduction to rubrics: An assessment tool to save grading time, convey effective feedback, and promote student learning.* Stylus Publishing, LLC.

37 Sunderland, M. (2021). ePortfolios: *Making ethics meaningful.* UC Berkeley, Engineering 125. Retrieved July 22, 2021, from https://engineeringethics.edublogs.org/e-portfolios-2/

38 Raiber, M., & Teachout, D. (2014). *The journey from music student to teacher* (p. 265). New York: Taylor and Francis.

39 Berkeley Center for Teaching & Learning. (2021). *ePortfolio.* Retrieved July 22, 2021, from https://teaching.berkeley.edu/resources/assessment-and-evaluation/design-assessment/e-portfolio

40 Mills, M. (2009). Capturing student progress via portfolios in the music classroom. *Music Educators Journal, 96*(2), 32–38.

41 Linn, R., & Miller, D. (2005). *Measurement and assessment in teaching* (9th ed., p. 283). Upper Saddle River, NJ: Prentice-Hall.

42 Raiber, M., & Teachout, D. (2013). *The journey from music student to teacher* (p. 265). New York: Taylor and Francis.

43 Berkeley Center for Teaching & Learning. (2021). *Reflective journals and learning logs.* Retrieved July 22, 2021, from https://www.niu.edu/citl/resources/guides/instructional-guide/reflective-journals-and-learning-logs.shtml

44 Equipped for the Future. (2004). *Teaching/learning toolkit. Learning logs.* Retrieved July 22, 2021, from https://lincs.ed.gov/keywords/equipped-future-eff
Berkeley Center for Teaching & Learning. (2021). *Reflective journals and learning logs.* Retrieved July 22, 2021, from https://www.niu.edu/citl/resources/guides/instructional-guide/reflective-journals-and-learning-logs.shtml

45 Cohen, M. (2012). Writing between rehearsals: A tool for assessment and building camaraderie. *Music Educators Journal, 98*(3), 43–48.
Raiber, M., & Teachout, D. (2014). *The journey from music student to teacher* (p. 267). New York: Taylor and Francis.

46 Cohen, M. (2012). Writing between rehearsals: A tool for assessment and building camaraderie. *Music Educators Journal, 98*(3), 43–48.

47 Raiber, M., & Teachout, D. (2013). *The journey from music student to teacher* (p. 267). New York: Taylor and Francis.

48 Biggs, J. (2007). *Aligning teaching for constructing learning.* Cardiff University, England: The Higher Education Academy.

49 Biggs, J., & Tang, C. (2011). *Teaching for quality learning at university.* New York: McGraw Hill.

Sideeg, A. (2016). Bloom's taxonomy, backward design, and Vygotsky's zone of proximal development in crafting learning outcomes. *International Journal of Linguistics, 8*(2), 182.

50 Sideeg, A. (2016). Bloom's taxonomy, backward design, and Vygotsky's zone of proximal development in crafting learning outcomes. *International Journal of Linguistics, 8*(2), 173.

Wiggins, G., & McTighe, J. (1998). What is backward design? *Understanding by design* (1st ed., pp. 7–19). Upper Saddle River, NJ: Merrill Prentice Hall. Retrieved July 23, 2021, from https://web.archive.org/web/20160721163755/http://www.fitnyc.edu/files/pdfs/Backward_design.pdf

51 Duke, R. (2005). *Intelligent music teaching.* Austin, TX: Learning and Behavior Resources.

52 Prewett, G. (2009). *Review on intelligent music teaching, Robert A. Duke.* Retrieved July 23, 2021, from http://www.geoffprewett.com/BookReviews/IntelligentMusicTeaching.html

Duke, R. (2005). *Intelligent music teaching* (p. 51.). Austin, TX: Learning and Behavior Resources.

53 McTighe, J., & Thomas, R. S. (2003). Backward design for forward action. *Educational Leadership, 60*(5), 52–55.

54 Scott, S. (2012). Rethinking the roles of assessment in music education. *Music Educators Journal, 98*(3), 31–35.

55 Scott, S. (2012). Rethinking the roles of assessment in music education. *Music Educators Journal, 98*(3), 32.

56 Scott, S. (2012). Rethinking the roles of assessment in music education. *Music Educators Journal, 98*(3), 33.

57 Raiber, M., & Teachout, D. (2014). *The journey from music student to teacher* (p. 271). New York: Taylor and Francis.

58 Scott, S. (2012). Rethinking the roles of assessment in music education. *Music Educators Journal, 98*(3), 35.

59 Yale Poorvu Center for Teaching and Learning. (2021). *Reflective teaching.* Retrieved July 24, 2021, from https://poorvucenter.yale.edu/ReflectiveTeaching

60 Priya, M., Prasanth, M., & Prince, J. P. (2017). Reflective practices: A means to teacher development. *Asia Pacific Journal of Contemporary Education and Communication Technology, 3*(1), 126–131. Retrieved July 24, 2021, from https://apiar.org.au/wp-content/uploads/2017/02/13_APJCECT_Feb_BRR798_EDU-126-131.pdf

61 Finlay, L. (2008). Reflecting on 'reflective practice.' Practice-based Professional Leaning Centre Paper 52, 1-27. The Open University. Retrieved July 24, 2021, from http://ncsce.net/wp-content/uploads/2016/10/Finlay-2008-Reflecting-on-reflective-practice-PBPL-paper-52.pdf

62 Cambridge Assessment. (2021). *Getting started with reflective practice.* Retrieved July 24, 2021, from https://www.cambridge-community.org.uk/professional-development/gswrp/index.html

63 Lindroth, J. (2015). Reflective journals: A review of the literature. *Update, 34*(1), 66–72.

64 Knight, S. (2018). Three reflective practices for effectiveness. *Association for Supervision and Curriculum Development.* Retrieved July 24, 2021, from https://www.ascd.org/blogs/three-reflective-practices-for-effectiveness

65 Miles, S. (2019). *Mirror, Mirror: A look at reflective practices for music teachers.* SmartMusic. Retrieved July 24, 2021, from https://www.smartmusic.com/blog/mirror-mirror-a-look-at-reflective-practice-for-music-teachers/

66 Miles, S. (2019). Supervisor of visual and performing arts, Washington County Public Schools, Hagerstown, Maryland.

Cambridge Assessment. (2021). *Getting started with reflective practice.* https://www.cambridge-community.org.uk/professional-development/gswrp/index.html

Index

Note: *Italicised* folios refers figures and **bold** tables.

accommodation 42, 43, 48; of exceptional learners 91
achievement charts 149–150
ADDIE Model 134–136, *135*
Aebersold, J. 53
aesthetic needs 75, *75*, 77
affective components, musical brain 92
affective domain 101, *102*, 107, 126, 148, 152
Afro-Cuban music 73
Agne, K. J. 15
American Choral Directors Association 123
American School Band Directors Association 123
American String Teachers Association 123
amygdala 86, **89**
analysis phase, ADDIE Model 134
Anderson, L. 105
anecdotal evidence 15–17
anecdotal knowledge 47
Aristotle 40
Armstrong, T. 88
arts 90, 100; brain changes 90; education 6, 124; fine 108
assessment as learning 153
assessment/evaluation 146–156; alignment with instruction 152; defined 146; diagnostic 147; reflective practice as teacher 153–155, *154*; roles of 153; tools in the music classroom 148–152; types of 146–148
assessment for learning 147, 153
assessment of learning 147, 153
assessment tools 148–152; achievement charts 149–150; checklists 149; pencil and paper tests 148–149; portfolio 150–151; rating scales 149, *150*; reflective journals 151–152; rubrics 150, *151*
assimilation 42, 43, 48, 61
Association for Supervision and Curriculum Development (ASCD) 124
attention 59; scaffolding 67; selective 50; in short-term memory 47
authenticity in student learning 115–116

backward design approach 124, *125*, 126, 152
Bandura, A. *58*, 58–59; on self-efficacy 62; on self-regulation 64; social cognitive theory 57, 62; *Social Foundations of Thought and Action: A Social Cognitive Theory* 63; social learning theory *58*, 58–59; vicarious reinforcement 66
Barnard, H. 16
Bauer, W.: *Music Learning Today: Digital Pedagogy for Creating, Performing, and Responding to Music* 127
behavioral learning theory 25–31
behavioral psychology 26, 133
behaviorism 5, 25–35, 73; behavioral learning theory 25–31; behavior modification 33; classroom management organization 34–35; definition of 26; learning based upon environmental control 31–32; reinforcers in the classroom 33
behavior modification 33
Behzadaval, B. 134
belief system 4, 14, 15, 17
belongingness and love needs 75, *75*, 76
Berklee College of Music's *PULSE* 128
Bloom, B. 133; *Taxonomy of Educational Objectives: The Classification of Educational Goals* 100–105, **104**, *106*, 126
brain 84–85, *85*; areas of 87; changes 90; lobes 85; and music education 91–92; as parallel processor **89**; processes **89**; social conditions influencing 90; uniquely organized **89**
Brain-Based Learning: Teaching the Way Students Really Learn (Jensen and McConchie) 89
brain-based learning (BBL) theory 84–92; amygdala 86; brain 84–85, *85*; defined 88; multiple intelligences, theory of 88; music education and brain 91–92; neural pathways 87; neural plasticity 86; neural pruning 86–87; prefrontal cortex 86; principles of 88, **89**; teaching strategies and learning 89–91

Broadbent, D. 46
Bruner, J. S. 38, 44, 45, 61, 123; cognitive development 45–46, 99; conceptual learning 48; on curriculum design 100
Buber, M. 74
Bulletin for the Council of Research on Music Education 16
Byo, J. 127

Caine, G. 88
Caine, R. 88
Cajun Folk Songs (Ticheli) 148
charts *see* achievement charts
checklists 149
Ching, C. P. 7
chunking 50, 51, 52
classical conditioning 26–28, 27, 58
classroom activities 7
classroom management 140–141; educational psychology influence on 5; organization 34–35; performance-based popular music education 127
cognition 38, 40; Gardner views on 100; oriented researchers 40–41; social environment and 60
cognitive approaches to learning and teaching 99–108; Bloom's *Taxonomy of Educational Objectives* 100–105, **104**, *106*, 126; Bruner's theories 99–100; Gardner's multiple intelligence (MI) 100; intelligent music teaching 106–107; learning activities 107–108; learning goals **105**, 105–106
cognitive components, musical brain 92
cognitive development 45–46, 61–62; six indicators (benchmarks) revealing 46; stages of 42–43
cognitive dissonance 17–18
cognitive domain 5, 101, 126, 148
cognitive learning theory 40–41
cognitive needs 75, 75, 77
cognitive task knowledge 104
cognitive theorists 41
cognitivism 5, 38–54; Bruner's constructivist theory 48; cognitive development 45–46; cognitive learning theory 40–41; cognitivist approaches in the music classroom 48–52; constructionism 44; constructionist instruction 52–54; constructivism 43–45; constructivist instruction 52–54; discovery learning 45; Gestalt learning theory 38–40; information processing theory 46–47; in music teaching 47–48; Piaget's theory 41–43
cognitivist approaches in music classroom 48–52
communication of high expectations in CRT 113–114
communities of musical practice (CoMP) 113
communities of practice (CoP) 112–113

Components of Executive Control Process 63
concrete operational stage (ages 7–11) 43
conditioned response (CR) 26
conditioned stimulus (CS) 26, 27
conditions of learning theory (Gagné) 133–134
conscious phase, music learning 138
conservation, defined 43
constructionism 44, 52
constructionist instruction 52–54
constructivism 5, 38, 43–45; social 59–61
constructivist instruction 52–54
constructivist movement 43
contiguity 26
Contributions to Music Education 16
cooperation, defined 87
cooperative learning 79; music class 81; social structures 91
Cooperative Research Act 16
coordinating metacognitive knowledge 63
Crowell, S. 88
culturally mediated instruction in CRT 114
culturally responsive teaching (CRT) 113–115, 116, 117
Culturally Responsive Teaching in Music Education (Lind and McKoy) 114–115, 116–117
curriculum 122–128; backward design 126; Bloom's Taxonomy 126; development 123–124; music 122–123; music technology 126–127, **127**; National Music Standards 124; popular music 127–128; understanding by design (UbD) 124–125; Vygotsky's zone of proximal development (ZPD) 126

declarative knowledge 47
defined concepts (Gagné) 45–46
design phase, ADDIE Model 134–135
develop criteria 104
development of curriculum 123–124; *see also* curriculum
development phase, ADDIE Model 135
Dewey, J. 18, 38, 43
diagnostic assessments 147; *see also* assessment/evaluation
differentiated instruction 139–140; *see also* instruction
differentiation: of human intelligence 88; with learners 90, 139; in music classroom 139
discovery education 79
discovery learning 45, 99
diversity 142; individuality and 79; in multicultural education 115–116; multiple intelligences and intellectual 79; music class 80
Dollard, J. 59
Duke, R. 31, 106; *Intelligent Music Teaching* 106–108, 125, 152

education *see* discovery education; music education
educational psychology 5
educational thought 5
education theory and research 5
Efklides, A. 67
The Emotional Brain (LeDoux) **89**
emotional growth, music class 80
emotions 4; critical to patterning **89**; development 14; expression 136; hierarchy of needs (Maslow) 76; in learning 90–91; social learning theory 59
empirical evidence 15–17
empiricist theories 4
enactive stage (from birth to about age 3) 45
encoding (or registration) 40, 51
ensemble skills 140
episodic knowledge 47
equilibrium 42, 49
esteem needs 75, 75, 76
evaluation phase, ADDIE Model 135
Every Child Achieves Act 6
evidence *see* anecdotal evidence
executive control functions 63
executive functioning 86, 141
expectations 141; of adults for children's behavior 67; classroom environment 140; setting clear 34; students 114
experience before theory 138
experientialism 5
experiential learning 44, 89, 137
explicit knowledge 47
explicit long-term memory 47
extinction 29

failure correction 63
failure detection 63
final phase, music learning 138
formal assessment 148
formal curriculum 123
formal learning 3, 117, 127–128, 153; *see also* learning
formal operations stage 43
formative assessments 126, 135, 147
Forsythe, J. L. 32
4Chords (app) 128
Frames of Mind: The Theory of Multiple Intelligences (Gardner) 88
frontal lobe 85

Gagné, R. 45–46, 133–134, 137
Gardner, H. 100; *Frames of Mind: The Theory of Multiple Intelligences* 88; multiple intelligence (MI) 88, 100
Gestalt learning theory 38–40
Goetze 116
Goolsby, T. W. 146
Gordon, E. 122

Green, L. 117
Greenwood G. E. 15
Greer, R. D. 31
group work and individual work, balancing of 140
growth as a reflective teacher *see* reflective teacher

Heitzman, R. 7
Hess, J. 117
hidden curriculum 123
Hodges, D. A. 108
human brain 84, 85; ability to respond to and participate in music 91; long-term memory 90; plasticity 86
humanism 73–81; approaches to teaching music 79–80; Carl Rogers 77–78; defined 74; humanistic psychology 74; in learning 74; Maslow's Hierarchy of Needs 74–77, 75; music class 80–81; Self-Concept 78–79
humanistic psychology 73, 74
Hutchings, P. 8

iconic stage (from about age 3 to about age 7) 45
ideal-self, self-concept 78
implementation phase, ADDIE Model 135
implicit knowledge 47
implicit long-term memory 47
including activities in lessons 139
informal assessment 148
information processing: in classroom 50–52; theory 46–47
inquiry-based learning 6–8
in-service teachers 7, 127
instruction: differentiated 139–140; moving from concrete to the abstract 138–139; moving from from simple to complex 138; moving from known to the unknown 138; moving from sound to sight 138
instructional design (ID) 133–142; ADDIE Model 134–136, *135*; classroom management 140–141; conditions of learning theory 133–134; differentiated instruction 139–140; experiential learning 137; learning community as instructional model 142; music class instruction 136–137; sequential instruction 137–139
instructional model, learning community as 142
Intelligent Music Teaching (Duke) 106–108, 125, 152
internalization 62, 101, 103
International Journal of Music Education 16
International Society of Music Education 16
intrinsic experiences, music class 81
intuitive thinking 48

Jaspers, K. 74
Jensen, E. 88; *Brain-Based Learning: Teaching the Way Students Really Learn* 89; *Top 10 Brain-Based Teaching Strategies* 89–91
joint enterprise 112
joint repertoire 112
Journal of Music Teacher Education 16
J. S. Bach's Suite no. 2 for Unaccompanied Cello 39

Kelly, G. 44
Kenny, A. 113
Klimek, K. 88
knowledge: cognitive task 104; coordinating metacognitive 63; defined 43; episodic 47; explicit 47; metacognitive 104; procedural 47; strategic 104; *see also* anecdotal knowledge; declarative knowledge
Kodály, Z. 122, 138
Koffka, K. 39
Koffka's Law of Prägnanz 39
Köhler, W. 39–40
Krathwohl, D. 101, *102*, 105
Kuhn, T. L. 32

Law of Closure 39
Law of Common Direction 39
Law of Effect 28
Law of Proximity 39
Law of Similarity 39
Law of Simplicity 39
learner-centered approach 137
learner-centered teaching 77–78
learners: Bruner's constructivist theory 48; cognition-oriented researchers 40; constructivism 43, 44; CRT 115; differentiation with 90; exceptional 91; learning and 5; music educators 116; Piaget's theory 61
learning: activities 107–108; based upon environmental control 31–32; community as instructional model 142; conscious and unconscious processes 89; within the context of culture in CRT 114; definition of 3, 25, 112; as developmental 89; emotions in 90–91; enhanced by challenge and inhibited by threat 89; goals **105**, 105–106; humanism in 74; inquiry-based 6–8; logs 152; physical movement supports 90; physiology 89; styles 3, 80–81; theory, conditions of 133–134
LeDoux, J.: The Emotional Brain **89**
Lehman, P. 4
Lind, V.: *Culturally Responsive Teaching in Music Education* 114–115, 116–117
Linn, R.: *Measurement and Assessment in Teaching* 151
Little Kids Rock (LKR) 127; *Jam Zone* (jamone.littlekidsrock.org) 128
long-term memory 46, 47, 50–51

Madsen, C. K. 25, 31
Mann, H. 16
Maslow, A.: hierarchy of needs 74–77, *75*; *A Theory of Human Motivation* 74
MayDay Group 16
McClintic, C. 88
McConchie, L.: *Brain-Based Learning: Teaching the Way Students Really Learn* 89
McDermott, R. 112
McKoy, C.: *Culturally Responsive Teaching in Music Education* 114–115, 116–117
McTighe, J. 124–125, 126
Measurement and Assessment in Teaching (Linn and Miller) 151
metacognitive behavior 41
metacognitive knowledge 104
Miles, S. 155
Miller, D.: *Measurement and Assessment in Teaching* 151
Miller, L. D. 15
Miller, N. E. 59
modern bands 127–128
monitoring 63, 100, 146
Montessori, M. 38, 43
motivation 59, 73; extrinsic 68, 142; human personality and 68; intrinsic 68, 114
motor components, musical brain 92
motor reproduction 59
Mozart, W. 67
Mr. Wilson's Blues Improvisation Unit Lesson 52
Mr. Wilson's Constructionist Approach 53–54
Mr. Wilson's Constructivist Approach 52–53
multicultural education, diversity in 115–116
multicultural music education 116
multiple intelligences, theory of 88, 100
musical brain 92; as resilient 92
musical training 92
music classroom 80–81; cognitivist approaches in 48–52; instruction 136–137; self-determination theory (SDT) 68–69; self-regulation in 67; social justice in 116–118; social learning theory in 64
music content 123
music curriculum 122–123; *see also* curriculum
music education: and brain 91–92; definition of 5; philosophy of 4; research 6; self-determination theory (SDT) 68; sociological influences in 111–113; undergraduate students 6
Music Educators National Conference (MENC) 124
music educators/teachers 14, 50, 108, 116, 117, 118, 140, 148, 152–153; ADDIE 136; BBL strategies 84; Bloom's taxonomy 108; employing social learning 57; experienced 15; feedback 32; fundamental impression 17; intrinsic motivation 68; learning

environments 69; middle and high school 33; opportunities for autonomy 69; reflective 18; responsibility of 14; role of 4, 8; social learning 57; teaching effectiveness of 32; technology 126; training of 6
Music Learning Today: Digital Pedagogy for Creating, Performing, and Responding to Music (Bauer) 127
Music Perception 16
music teaching: belief system 17; in cognitivism 47–48; intelligent 106–107; self-efficacy 66–67
music technology curriculum 126–127, **127**
mutual engagement 112

National Association for Music Education (NAfME) 6, 16, 123–124
National Association of Schools of Music 123
National Coalition for Core Arts Standards 124
National Consortium of Arts Education Associations 124
National Music Standards 124
National standard 1 103
National standard 2 103
National standard 7 104
National Standards for Arts Education 124
National Voluntary Standards in the Arts 124
Naturalism 4
negative reinforcement 29, 33
neural pathways 87
neural plasticity/neuroplasticity 86
neural pruning 86–87

observing and imitating others 66
occipital lobe 85
open-mindedness 18
operant conditioning theory 28
Orff, C. 122
organizing space 34
O'Toole, P. 148

Palmer, J. A. 65
Papert, S. A. 44
parents and guardians 141
parietal lobe 85
Pavlov, I. 25, 26, 27
peak musical experiences, music class 81
peer group 108
peer observation 154
pencil and paper tests 148–149
percussion hand position checklist. *149*
performance-based assessment 147
performance-based classroom 49–50
philosophy: definition of 14; of music education 4, 16

physical movement, supports learning 90
physiological needs 75, *75*, 76
Piaget, J. 41–48, *43*
Piaget's theory 41–43, 64–67
placement assessments 146–147
planning 63
plasticity/pruning/neural networks 86
playing more and talking less 34–35
popular music curriculum 127–128
portfolio 150–151
positive perspectives on parents and families in CRT 113
positive reinforcement 29
practice phase, music learning 138
prefrontal cortex 86
preoperational stage (ages 2–7) 43
prepare phase, music learning 138
preservice teachers 6, 7
Price, H. 31
Principles of Gestalt Psychology 39
procedural knowledge 47
professional journal, maintaining of 154
program assessment 148; defined 147
psychomotor domain (Simpson) 102, *102*
punishment 29, 30, 57, 59
putting theory into practice 8
Puzzle Box 28

Rabadi, S. 141
rating scales 149, *150*
rationalist theories 4
Ray, B. 141
recall long-term memory 51
reflective journals 151–152
reflective practice 8, 14, 18–19; as teacher 153–155, *154*
reflective teacher 13–19; anecdotal evidence 15–17; belief system 15; cognitive dissonance 17–18; empirical evidence 15–17; music teacher's responsibility 14; reflective practice 14, 18–19
rehearsal 50–51
Reimer, B. 4
reinforcement: phase in music learning 138; schedules of 29–31; types of 28–29
reinforcers in the classroom 33
Research and Issues in Music Education 16
Research in Music Education 16
reshaping the curriculum in CRT 114
retention 59
retrieval (or recall) 40, 51
review strengthening learning 91
Rogers, C. 73, 77–78; learner-centered teaching 77–78
Ross, G. 61
rote memory 89
rubrics 150, *151*
rules, boundaries, and expectations 141

safety needs 75, *75*, 76
Salonen, P. 67
Satre, J.-P. 74
scaffolding 61; in lessons 139
schema 42
schemata 42, 43
scholarship of teaching and learning (SOTL): definition of 3
Scott, S. 153
search for meaning is innate **89**
search for meaning through patterning **89**
selective attention 50
self-actualization needs 75, *75*, 77
self-care 141
self-concept 78; in music education 79
self-determination theory (SDT) 68–69; in music classroom 68–69; in music education 68
self-differentiate, students 140
self-efficacy, theory of 62; defined 62; in music teaching 66–67; self-regulation in 64; in teaching and learning 62–63
self-image: inner feelings and 74; self-concept 78
self-regulation 63; in the music classroom 67; in self-efficacy 64
self-worth, self-concept 78
sensorimotor stage (birth-age 2) 43
sensory register memory 46
sequence in music curriculum 122
sequential instruction 137–139
shared repertoire 112
short-term memory 47
Shulman, J. H. 7
Sideeg, A. 126
Simon, H. 44
Simpson's psychomotor domain 102, *102*
Skinner, B. F. 25, 28, 33, 58; behaviorism 73
Skinner Box 28–29
Snyder, W. 112
social conditions, influencing brain 90
social constructivism 59–61, 64–67
Social Foundations of Thought and Action: A Social Cognitive Theory (Bandura) 63
social justice in music classroom 116–118
social learning theory 5, 57–69; by Albert Bandura 58, *58*–59; cognitive development 61–62; modeling process 59; in the music classroom 64; Piaget's theory 64–67; principles of 58–59; role of self-regulation in self-efficacy 64; Self-Determination Theory (SDT) 68–69; self-efficacy in teaching and learning 62–63; self-regulation 63; theory of self-efficacy 62; Vygotsky's Social Constructivism 59–61, 64–67
Society of Music Teacher Education 16
sociocultural characteristics 111–118; Culturally Responsive Teaching (CRT)
113–115; diversity in multicultural education 115–116; social justice in the music classroom 116–118; sociological influences in music education 111–113
sociological influences in music education 111–113
Sousa, D. 88
spatial memory **89**
spiral curriculum 99–100, 123
the spiral curriculum (Bruner) 99–100, 123
stimuli 26
strategic knowledge 104
strength-based approach 141
stress 44, 90, 141
student attentiveness 32
student-centered instruction in CRT 114
student-centered learning 79
student feedback 153, 155
student learning, authenticity in 115–116
student on-/off-task behavior 32
student-teacher relationships 141
subject matter 3, 7, 32, 78, 103, 123, 136
summative assessments 135, 147
Suzuki, S. 122
symbolic stage (from about age 7) 45–46

Taxonomy of Educational Objectives: The Classification of Educational Goals (Bloom) 101
teacher as facilitator in CRT 114
teacher educators, linking theory to practice 7
teaching, definition of 3
teaching and learning, study of 3–8; cognitive approaches in 99–108; educational psychology 5; education theory and research 5; holistic approach 76; inquiry-based learning 6–8; music education 5–6; philosophy of music education 4; reflective practice 8; teaching strategies for brain-based 89–91
teaching content 90
teaching music, humanism approaches to 79–80
teaching practice, video-recording 154–155
temporal lobe 85
theories of education 5
theory, definition of 8
theory and practice 5, 8, 14, 43, 44
A Theory of Human Motivation (Maslow) 74
theory of multiple intelligence 88, 100
Thorndike, E. L. 28, 33
Thorndike's *Law of Effect* 28
Ticheli, F.: *Cajun Folk Songs* 148
tools in music classroom *see* assessment tools
Top 10 Brain-Based Teaching Strategies (Jensen) 89–91
transcendence needs 75, *75*, 77
transfer of learning 50
triune brain 84; *see also* brain

Ukeoke (musopia.net) (app) 128
unconditioned stimulus (US) 26
understanding by design (UbD) 124–125

Vahedi, M. 134
Vauras, M. 67
video-recording teaching practice 154–155
von Foerster, H. 44
von Glasersfeld, E. 44
Vygotsky, L. 44, 100
Vygotsky sociocultural theory 57
Vygotsky's social constructivism
    59–61, 64–67
Vygotsky's zone of proximal development
    (ZPD) 126

Walters, R. 58
Watson, John B. 26
Watzlawick, P. 44
Wenger, E. 112, 142
Wenger-Treyner, B. 112
Wertheimer, M. 39
Wesolowski, B. 150
Wiggins, G. 124–125, 126
Wood, D. J. 61
Wright, R. 117

Yarbrough, C. 31

zone of proximal development (ZPD) 60,
    60–61, 62, 64, 65, 67, 126, 147

Printed in the USA
CPSIA information can be obtained
at www.ICGtesting.com
LVHW081933041124
795688LV00042B/1382

9 780367 481773